Editor in Chief...Pamela Uschuk
Advisory Editors..Terry Acevedo
Carmen Caltayud
Denise Chavez
Matt Mendez
Prose Editors..Beth Alvarado
Luis Alberto Urrea
Poetry Editors..Octavio Quintanilla
Carmen Tafolla
Edward Vidaurre
Managing Editor...Andrew Allport
Assistants To The Editor...Susan Foster
Whitney Judd
Mark Lee
Howie Faerstein
Design Editor..Alexandra Cogswell

Cutthroat's Contributing Editors

Sandra Alcosser, Charles Baxter, Frank Bergon, Janet Burroway, Robert
Olen Butler, Ram Devineni, Rick DeMarinis, Joy Harjo, Richard Jackson,
Marilyn Kallet, Zelda Lockhart, Demetria Martinez, John McNally, Dennis
Sampson, Rebecca Seiferle, Luis Alberto Urrea, Lyrae van Clief-Stefanon
and Patricia Jabbeh Wesley. In memorium: Leonard "Red" Bird, Jane Mead,
and Pennelope Niven.

Send submissions, subscription payments and inquiries to:
CUTTHROAT, A JOURNAL OF THE ARTS
5401 N. Cresta Loma Dive
Tucson, Arizona 85704
ph: 970-903-7914
email: cutthroatmag@gmail.com

Our website: http://www.cutthroatmag.com//

Make checks payable to Cutthroat, A Journal of the Arts
We are self-funded so all **Donations gratefully accepted.**

CUTTHROAT THANKS

Website Design..Laura Prendergast
Pamela Uschuk
Cover Layout..Alexandra Cogswell
Pamela Uschuk
Magazine Layout..Alexandra Cogswell
Pamela Uschuk
Logo Design...Lynn McFadden Watt
Front Cover Art...Anita Endrezze
The Wall
Torn Paper Collage
Back Cover Art..Alfred Quiroz
"Milagros Border Wall Installation"
Inside Art..Octavio Quintanilla
FRONTEXTOS
ink, charcoal, watercolor on paper

AND THANK YOU TO:

The Black Earth Institute, especially Michael McDermmott, for collaborating on this project by providing financial support and by helping to promote it.

Alexandra Cogswell for her expertise in designing our cover and devotion to our journal. Andrew Allport, Susan Foster, Howie Faerstein, Mark Lee, William Pitt Root, Carmen Tafolla and Edward Vidaurre for proofreading.

Special thank you to donors Teresa Acevedo, Beth Alvarado, Frederick Aldama, James Anderson, Deidre Kateri Aragon, Wendy Barker, Cynthia Alessandro Briano, May Castro, Richard Carnero, Ann Dernier, Scott Duncan, Paul Duran, Victoria Featherstone, Amy Ferris, Ann Fisher-Wirth, Ron and Jean Fundingsland, Lisha Garcia, Michel Gasguy, GoFundMe Team, Nancy Aide Gonzalez, Reyna Grande, Dick and Gay Grossman, Dorothy Grupp, Joy Harjo, Beverly LaFontaine, Kalen R. Landow, Ezzy Languzzi, Catherine Marenghi, Michael McDermmott, Connie Mitchell, Ofelia Montelongo, Michael Moore, Juan Morales, Andrew Navarro, Lisa Padilla, Lucyna Prosko, Danny Rosen, Barbara Sherman, Pamela Stewart, Tom Stock-Hendel, Francisco Stork, Laura Gray-Street, Marilyn Kallet, Jesse Maloney, Mark Maynard, Catherine Murphy, Milo Feldt Nichols, Katherine Durham Oldmixon (Garza), Juan R. Palomo, Liana Ponce, Melissa Prichard, Martha Rivas, Cirenio Rodgriguez, William Pitt Root, Jordan Rosenfeld, Shelli Rottschafer, Rogina Ruiz, Grace Sanchez, Raul Sanchez, Kat Talley-Jones, James Tracy, Natalia Trevino, Sonya Unrein, Evelyn Urrea, Whitney Vale, Elosia Valenzuela, Richard Vargas, Alma Luz Villanueva, Pamela Uschuk, Marna Wisdom, Tessa Xuan, Richard Yañez who helped fund the publication of this collection.

We also thank our subscribers around the world.

PURO CHICANX WRITERS OF THE 21ST CENTURY

Cutthroat, A Journal Of The Arts and *The Black Earth Institute* collaborated to publish this historic collection of writings about Chicanx culture. The writings span all topics from the rasquache to the refined. In these pages is writing that goes deep into Chicanx culture and reveals heritage in new ways. This is work that challenges, that is irreverent, that is defiant and inventive. This is Puro Chicanx. The idea of Puro Chicanx is about Mexican ancestral heritage, about attitude and may overlap with other Latinx cultures. Our focus is on Chicanx culture that has been a large part of this country for hundreds of years and is still under-explored and understood only at a distance by the dominant culture.

The Editors

Table Of Contents

214 PROSE/PROSA

Hubo un momento en que nos miramos
a los ojos
y nos dimos cuenta
de que ya habíamos
comenzado a escribir
el final
de nuestra
historia

Hubo un momento/ For a moment, we looked into each other's eyes
Frontexto
Octavio Quintanilla

POESIA/POETRY

Homeland

by Bella Alvarez

The Colombian word for faggot
marica
sits too pretty between my teeth,
but slut
zurrón
slips slow and easy past my lips.
Here we drink *aguardiente,*
slice tongues free from unforgiving mouths.
One aluminum boat-tail twists us into trenches for fifty years —
guerilleras tucking bullets under breasts, ribs folding towards crystalline dust-
and my grandfather remembers mountains pulling airplanes into
wallowing cave-mouths, pupils collapsing like clean silence.
In Colombia we call pretty girls *monas* —
whities.
To make cocaine we burn fingers, shed skin, coax powder from gasoline.
My uncle died afraid of the color green: he saw shadow-men lurking in syringes,
breath heavy with copper.
Here we swallow emeralds, chew bitter leaves.
The Colombian word for son-of-a-bitch
hijueputa
curls down spines like shrapnel.

go ask yr dad

by Steven Alvarez

como
       chingas
como
       chingas
como
       como

c   h   i   n   g   a   s

badmexican

by samantha arriozola

badmexican can't speak her language fluently.
can't claim her fading heritage color.
what a tie dye mexican that forgot to soak
in salt water. she's been washing out to white.
such a colonist-seedling mexican. tu-mami-may-be-
brown-pero-tu-papi-got-conquistador-skin mexican.
hoarding the carrots and onions from the *chiles
en vinagre* mexican. you can't even call home.
and you can't even talk to your cousins.
what type of mexican got a nuclear family?
what an american mexican. what a mexican
dash american. what an american you have become.
what a kale chip eatin, cosco patronizin,
sparkling water and red cup drinkin,
american you have become. an ingrown
hair history on the edge of your tongue
that you've tried to grasp and release
with the effort of fingernails. try again.

To Be A Child Of Immigrants

by Xochitl-Julisa Bermejo

You learn the hustle young
while TGIF plays in the background.
Tanners in the kitchen, and you and your brother
on a living room floor assembly line.
Merchandise must be individually packaged.
Slip metallic decals in the shape of cowboy hats
into cellophane envelopes, fold the flap,
staple it shut. Stack multicolored bandanas
by state—Durango, Jalisco, Chihuahua, Nayarit.
Saturday morning, no time for cartoons.
Wake early. Pack the van. Saturday afternoon,
display the inventory. Saturday evening,
watch men in 501s, bandanas wagging
from back pockets, dance with one leg propelling.
Gritos bounce off Budweiser-soaked floors,
bodies move like broken, crowds build like fire.
Try your best to not be frightened,
to sell what you can. Parrot your mother,
the way she flirts with costumers, makes them laugh.
Remember your great-grandfather sold raspados
in the church square with syrups made from scratch.
Remember your grandfather constructed
a rascuache barbershop behind his Boyle Heights
home furnished with an authentic barber chair,
white porcelain and smooth. Remember your father
drove you on afternoon turnarounds to Tijuana
for new stock in a brown Volkswagen van.
Hot, beige vinyl stuck to your skin.
Across the border, cousins manning a taco shop
didn't speak your language, skinned goats
hung hooked from the kitchen ceiling, pink chicle
became payment for a day's work.

Retrofitting Bridges: Tales Of A Lost Soul In Nepantla

by Gustavo Barahona-Lopez

I came to you (my self) at a time of unmitigated confusion.
Wind and rain enveloped me like a
ghostly cloak, silencing my shrieks of pain
and reason.

I need you to love me, even when you hate me.

My skin cracks

and ruptures
into heart-shaped snowflakes.

They shatter into sand, a dust as brittle as identity.

I add love
to insult.

Stir in hate
with a dash of
consciousness
and bake to perfection.

I used to feed
you mediocrity,
now you revel at
being consumed
by a utopia that will
always remain
a potentiality.

I retrofit bridges
because my life depends on it.
My being is fused to the support beams.
As I step onto them,
sections of concrete instantaneously
combust around me,

leaving   gaping   holes.

I have lost count of the number of times I
have drowned trying to cross.

I am in a perennial state of healing my self and my bridges.
But I continue to do so.

I
hate
myself
because
I
cannot
write
this.

My body elicits knowledge like a photographer creates images:

The photos may not reach everyone's standards for validation, but that does not
keep them from being beautiful.

I am trapped in the

in-between,
but I am at home in this third-space

for it is the space where I was born, where I grew up, and where I continue to live.

At this moment I am changing.
My cells are dying and being reborn.
My neurons are making and breaking connections trying to
remember the sensation of being alive. I am

the shaman and the hexed.

The witnessed and the invisible.

I am building an army.

I have drafted hundreds of thousands complete with
heavy artillery,

bullets, and
grenades.

With this	my army of
letters	words
will	terrorize,
destroy	assumptions
I will	bombard

the minds

that created the problems of this world.

You are not just you. You are a culmination of every book, stone, idea, oppression, empathy, and all else you have experienced. You have taken from every person you have encountered just as you have given.

On this day I want you to know, that I love you,

even when I hate you.

We Stopped Talking

by Elena Díaz Björkquist

She commandeered our group,
White woman on a mission
Shooting questions at us
About our projects.

We, a Pueblo Indian,
A Chicana, and a Yaqui answered
Politely, kept our cool,
Dismissed her rudeness.

Just before time to report,
I asked about her project,
A movie about Tucson's
All Soul's Procession

She told us about people
Carrying giant puppets,
Painting their faces as skeletons,
Wearing costumes.

"More people are painting
Their faces the past few years.
It's become
a new thing."

I shook my head, "It's centuries
Old, came from Mexico."
"No," she said, it's recent
Only in Tucson."

The others agreed with me.
I told her the procession
Was modeled after El Dia
De Los Muertos.

"No, it's not,
Definitely not!"
"It's a Tucson thing,
only in Tucson."

She wouldn't listen
So we stopped talking.

She reported for us
"Our group fell apart," she said.
"*These* people
Refused to talk."

The facilitator asked why.
"She wouldn't listen to us," I said.
"She was disrespectful,
So we stopped talking."

Silence hung over the room
Like a heavy curtain,
A room full of Chicanos,
Native Americans, Asians.

No one talked
But we all knew.

When Folklore Field School
Was over, the facilitator asked
Our group to stay.
Only she stayed.

Next morning, she went
To each of us, apologized,
Said, "I don't know what got in me,
Must have been my pain meds."

Serpent of Spring

by Xánath Caraza, translated by Sandra Kingery

I am a daughter of the light with tears of blue-green fireflies on my cheeks. Sea foam follows my steps on the beach, erases them, leaves no trace, attempts to hide them in its bowels. The sea soaks me with diminutive snails and blue crabs, but my body fools the foam and leaves them slipping slowly along every inch of my bronze skin, leaving a mound of marine creatures on the sand. I am a daughter of the light and of the song of the birds in the damp jungle. I carry the essence of flowers in my heart. The song of the *cenzontle* beats in my belly, it mixes with the citlalis in the night sky. I am a daughter of the languages lost in the tones hidden in the throat of the jungle. There are no paths that do not hear my steps, and on trails where I have yet to appear, premonitions of my verses hold sway. Words link to syllables of *huehuetl*. I am a daughter of the beating of *congas* and *teponaxtlis*, daughter of the light with the song of the *cenzontle* falling across my chest. The blue sea pursues my steps every day. Brilliant fireflies have already tattooed their poems on my skin. My father is the tornado and mingles with the plumed turquoise serpent of spring.

These Times

by Ana Castillo

In these times, you and I share,
amidst the air you and I breathe,
inspiration we take from day to day thriving,
opposition we meet,
the sacred conch shell calls us,
drums beat, prayers sent up,
aromatic smoke of the pipe are our pledge to the gods.

An all-night fire vigil burns
where we may consume the small cactus messenger
of the Huichol and Pueblo people of New Mexico,
red seeds of the Tlaxcalteca,
mushrooms of María Sabina,
 tes de mi abuela
 from herbs grown in coffee cans on a Chicago back porch,
 tears of my mother on an assembly line in Lincolnwood, Illinois,
aid us in calling upon memory,
 in these times.

In other days,
when memory was as unshakeable as the African continent,
and long as Quetzalcoátl's tail in the underworld,
whipping against demons, drawing blood,
potent as Coatlicue's two serpent face,
and necklace of hearts and hands
(to remind us of our much-required sacrifices
for the sake of the whole.
we did what we could to take memory
like a belt chain around the waist to pull off,
 to beat an enemy.

But now, in these times of chaos and unprecedented greed,
when disrupted elements are disregarded,
earth lashes back like the trickster Tezcatlipoca
without forgiveness if we won't turn around, start again,
say aloud: *This was a mistake,*
we have done the earth wrong and
we will make our planet a holy place, again.
I can,
with my two hands,
palpitating heart; we can, and we will
turn it around, if only we choose.

In these times, all is not lost, nothing forever gone,

tho' you may rightly think them a disgrace.
Surely hope has not abandoned our souls,
even chance may be on our side.

There are women and men, after all,
young and not so young anymore,
 tired but tenacious,
mothers and fathers, teachers and those who heal and do not
know that they are healers,
and those who are learning
for the sole purpose of returning what they know.
Also, amongst us, are many who flounder and fall;
they will be helped up by we who stumble forward.
All of these and others must remember.
We will not be eradicated, degraded and made irrelevant,
not for a decade or even a day. Not for six thousand years
have we been here, but, millions.

Look at me. I am alive and stand before you,
unashamed, despite endless provocations
railed against an aging woman.
My breasts, withered from once giving suckle,
and as of late, the hideousness of cancer,
hair gone grey,
and with a womb like a picked pomegranate
left to dry in the sun; so, my worth is gone,
they say.
My value in the workplace, also dwindled,
as, too, the indispensable role of mother.
As grandmother I am not an asset in these times,
but held against all that is new and fresh.
Nevertheless, I stand before you;
dignity is my scepter. I did not make the mess
we accept in this house.
When the party is done,
the last captive hung — fairly or unjustly,
Children saved and others lost,
The last of men's wars declared,
trade deals busted and others hardly begun,
tyrants toppled, presidents deposed,
police restrained or given full reign upon the public,
and we don't know where to run,
on a day the sun rose and fell,
and the moon took its seat in the sky,
 sacred conch shell called drums beat,
prayers went up,
aromatic smoke of the pipe pledged to the gods.
I will have remained
the woman,
who stayed behind to clean up.

Two Men And Me

by Ana Castillo

I left Bukowski again, went back to Bolaño,
Both men bad to their women. Me, like the rest,
couldn't get enough. Both smoked and drank
themselves to death. They liked it rough, said
that was how they got their best writing done.

One winter we all ended up in hell, ran
into each other at a café. (REVISION: bar,
public bath…FILL IN THE BLANK). Chuck
wanted to fuck. Roberto punched him in the gut.
We quaffed a few whiskies. They knew. I knew.

I wasn't that kind of girl. Instead, we set out to do
a three-way poem. Tu primero, said Bolaño.
"What?" Bukowski said. "No comprendo."
"HOW FUCKED UP YOU GOTTA BE YOU CAN'T
UNDERSTAND SPANISH EVEN IN HELL?" Roberto was mad.

"You *illegals!*" the other started racializing the situation.
No wonder he was in hell, Then, again, we all were. "I'M NOT MEXICAN,
PINCHE GRINGO," Roberto yelled throwing another swing.
This time he got me in the eye by mistake.

"There are no mistakes in hell," the demon bartender said, handing me
some ice. "That's the beauty of this place." The guys stopped.
No one had ever seen ice in hell.   Yeah, it was the start of
something big.

Xicanisma Prophecies Post-2012   Putin's Puppet

by Ana Castillo

is not Aryan (or a golden-hair-Thor) but through & through as close
                                                    to yellow as it gets.
A flim-flam man claiming billions no one sees.
                                        He & the Czar
had a chat at the Ritz,   in a bar,
over Red Bull, vodka, coke and complimentary chips,
served up by naked women who took American Express and rubles in I.O.U.s.
One rat said,
You take the East.   *I'll snatch the West.*
It's all for the taking for swines like us   and our friends
                    (ha-ha,
 like 'we' have friends), rapacious and sly,
unconcerned with who or how many die as we take the planet.   Don't worry, man.
 Forget
        the jaundiced Chinese. & Rocketman (we'll send to the moon.)
France can eat escargot. Palestinians must go. We'll suck the earth dry. You & I,
pillage until we are down to two.We'll compete for the universe.
Fair enough? (Haw, one said. As if we define fair by anyone's terms.)

I, the poet rest my head on a pillow or a rock, the throb is the same,
my brain doesn't stop its slideshow of doom.
 viewing Dr. Strangelove scenes,
reruns play & no new plots.
No breathtaking aerial shots of an Aston Martin headed along the coast toward the
villain's hideout.
No soundtrack.   (We are all silent, not censored, not yet, but quiet, waiting.)
No scientific facts in this version of a world for the taking.
No historical reference without *revisiones*… [stop]
 (No Spanish allowed or you may be arrested.
They are watching, legions in camouflage, hoods or riot gear, ready to take you out.
On your mark and get set.

Putin's Puppet doesn't read books—a novel or a memoir,
sits through films or listens to a symphony or even the Top Twenty.
He doesn't look at art.
Consequently, he has shut beauty down.
Putin's Puppet knows one color, said, his son, and that is green.

I will disagree.   Putin's Puppet does see color and it revolts him.
Blacks belong in Africa, he opines, and Muslims must stay in the Mid-East.
Mexicans are the scourge.
He doesn't want us on his turf.
It's as simple as this. Racist.
Race in the second decade of the 21st century to him exists…. like with his father,
his father before him and so on—it serves one purpose.
Servitude or genocide.
As for women, we are unimportant.
You kill a rhino for sport or for its horns. [You keep a woman only if she enhances your life.]
He's the the big man on campus with a loyal fraternity, he thinks..
Instead, I see anarchy merged with insanity, a fake man wrapped in a dictator's cloak.

How did we get here? How did we, indeed.
Not without concessions, not without greed.   Down the rabbit hole
the nation went   into Wonder-less slime.
We are in it deep this time.
When I can't sleep, I spot the devil pissing in the dark.
I've lost feeling in my hands and feet.
I am an indian woman off   the reservation,
as they say now, in racialist double-speak.
But in this country where democracy remained an aspiration., not a reality,
we still do reservations for the original peoples of the land.
Take a moment--this poet asks--take a moment to think on that.

Rezando

by Griselda Castillo

"el panteon (where grandpa is buried)
esta en Mexico"

my father's words become a bridge
we cross into my niñez
and grandpa's death
blossoms in our bodies

we adorn his altar with
cuetes canicas cigarros
to honor his mischief
and pray his travesuras
are tolerated
by corazones ligeros

"en Mexico se dice
that the dead return to us
as mariposas"
autumnal orange and black
souls tracking flowers
on the viaje they take
across our family history

"may we also find calendulas
to land on
may we know
to drink from them"
he says
"y asi, besito por besito,
find our ways back home"

Ursula's Blues

by Griselda Castillo

what does the ground know
of burdens and blessings
that lágrimas cannot teach it?

ay Aureliano
your words frenzy in my mind
like avispas encendidas
by the árboles de almendra
embalmed in your cologne

all I have left
es la memoria of you
watering earth
so it wouldn't crack
tragándose la casa entera
one hellish August

the impotent green manguera
drooping in your hand
how the water blessed
your withered feet
covered in zoquete

From Home

by Rosemary Catacalos
en memoria Bernardino Verástique

Desde tu tierra te dicen:
The chicharras are beginning to die again
and it is the end of summer fruit.
The peaches and melons are coming in
bruised and bitter and thin
to the point where the hawkers
peddling from the backs of their trucks
try to pawn them off as change.
And the *chicharras, ayyy, the chicharras*
are giving out with loud choruses
building one voice on another until
the trees shake with a noise
that pounds the heart and eyes.
There is no escape.
They are dying and pulling
the heat into the ground after them.
The mornings become brittle and cool
without their sound. *Camarada,*
the moon is on the rise,
dogs howl through the night
and it is September.
Grass is starting to grow
where you planted it in July.
It will die with the first frost,
come back again in the spring.
Camarada, in Greece there are grandmothers
who insist on being photographed as they
rummage behind the church among the dead
for the skulls of their former rivals,
finally cupping the empty bone for the camera
with the proud half-smile
of an accidentally longer life,
the eyes rheumy,
the pieces of embroidery fewer these days,
the shroud already woven.
I only tell you these things
because war has broken out in the lands
where the oldest angels
have always known it would come to this.
I only tell you because
Mr. and Mrs. Ozdabeano Maldonado
keep whirling their eternal polka
across my walls.
I only tell you
that somewhere in France
and perhaps elsewhere,
at this very moment
the dead are trying
to walk out into the air
without their stones.

Learning Endurance From Lupe At The J&A Ice House

by Rosemary Catacalos

> *"Believe you and I sing tiny*
> *and wise and could if we had to eat stone and go on."*
> Richard Hugo

When you talk to Lupe about El Salvador
his head that's too big for his body comes
slowly up off the splintered green table
at the ice house where he sweeps up every day
in exchange for a few beers. El Salvador.
He looks you straight and solemnly in the eye
and waves one bony brown hand down the street
toward Our Lady of Sorrows.
Then with a quick flying sign of thumb
and little finger he asks for another beer
and grins.
Now Lupe has been operating on what some people
call dim for a long time. Nobody can
even remember how he got that way or if
he was born that way or what.
But I'm here to say that he's a man
to talk to when you feel like if you tried
to plant a flower it would just die
or that if you tried to scream nothing
but flat silent air would come out.

Lupe. Los niños vieron todo, Lupe.
Even in the dark the children saw it all.
They heard it all.
How the quiet night went red with their mother's screams.
How loved ones who moments before had been
tangled in their bedclothes
were now tangled in their common blood
and the caliche of the poverty-soaked street.
How you could only tell your brother
by the saint's medal around his neck
since all that he had dreamed with
was blasted away.
How charred bits of his sister's schoolbooks

33

and a father's crumpled tin lunchbox
were all that was left

after the soldiers had gone
taking with them the man who had worn
a bag for a mask
and from that doubly dark cave
had pointed out the chosen houses.
Lupe, Lupe, what are we to do
when everywhere God is committing suicide
and every one of us is God?

Lupe sways onto his feet and moves
like a dirge to the pay phone

at one end of the open shed.
He pulls the only coin
I have ever known him to have
from a stained khaki pocket,
drops it lovingly into the slot
and begins to dial and dial and dial and dial;
sixteen numbers, forty-seven numbers,
fifty numbers, all one big number. He is
calling and calling somewhere very far away.
Finally he stops and listens
for a long time until something
tells him to smile.
When he hangs up, his worn coin
comes tumbling back out. No charge.
Then he gives me a slow heavy nod
and says, *Eyyy-hhhh. Eyyy-hhhh.*
Niños bo-ni-tos. Bo-o-ni-tos.
And he picks up an old broom
and goes back to work.

Memory in the Making: A Poetics

by Rosemary Catacalos
for Lorna Dee Cervantes

Remember the tale where the maiden lets down her long, charged hair for the lover,
his climb to her tower hanging by golden threads, by the very roots of her dreams?

This is not that story, which even then was vague about who, if anyone, was saved.
No, we are just past what some call without irony The American Century.

At my university, students who own Beemers ride bikes into the fields for Earth
Sciences while brown men from another country bike to other fields for food.

The students remember this, the brown men that. They are not the same. I say this
as plain fact, though many hold sincerity has been cheapened in our complex age.

A little girl called Shelly weeps on her way to the school bus. She wears jellies, cheap
plastic copies of a Greek fisherman's sandal. She spoke Spanish before English,

her Salvadoran nana, both her parents at work. Pink keys, purple keychains, clank
against her turquoise backpack. She did not dream last night. Tearstained, she

watches a family of lizards careen around the bleached trunk of a dead redwood,
limbs bleached bones in the Wedgwood bowl of the sky. I can't see children

these days without asking what they'll remember of all this. Am I Shelly's
Miss Frances, strange neighbor woman who dressed me in shawls and sang

sadly in German? Whose husband, it was told, went up in flames on the Hindenberg?
How do we know what will touch a child, mark her forever? Remember the girls

in their pale summer dresses? Remember the women they became? And then there's
the memory locked in the cells, in the blood. Certainly potatoes are a kind of faith

to the Irish. Also recall Poland, someone's grandfather escaping under his mother's
skirts, this cliché all that's left of being Polish, Jewish, poor. Even so, the moment

still somewhere in the bone: potato stubble, smoke, strong smell of a woman's skirts,
becoming Catholic. Gazing at grandmother, what did she know, and how did she learn it?

And now we are everywhere and nowhere: videophones, internet. No borders
in the air, fresh blood on the ground. How to dance? Where does memory go

in all this? To work, *emplumada! ¡A la chancla!* We wear the black velvet hat
that came with the dream, loosen our tongues with the fire of roasted *chiles.*

The Greek women of Souli danced off the cliff of their village to keep out of the hands
of the Turks. And here we are on the purple lip of the *cañon*, telling and telling, and

there's no such thing as going too near the sun. Each time and each time the first. Just
past the close of The American Century, the child's plastic keys rattle down the street.

Double-fractured Sonnets From Subway And Ferry

by Rosemary Catacalos

Nomina sunt consequentia rerum
Names are the consequences of things.
-Justinian

Ah, Dante! Why after all this time
confuse the issue so? The messenger is
the message, like names are what we're made to give
for living. This 'little sound,' its baby rhyme
inching on bloody knees up the drive,
why not call it *smoke* as say it lifts
love we don't remember or can't resist?
Don't call me Beatrice. The eerie shine

of subway rails, Guillaume's bandaged head
bobbing in the next car to boom-box jazz.
What can it all mean *so far from God?*
Nothing and everything. What the fickle dead
demand for their altars. *Pulque* thick and cloudy as
night on that ferry when we were gagged and robbed

on the way to our own christening. My name is fear
and also rage, *coraje, corazón, ma belle.*
(Will you get the phone?) Also *ma* lost *bête.*
Beatriz is my mother's name, sweet dear
wheel of the unspoken turning a deaf ear.
Not me, Jack. I talk back with hell
in all my seasons: red seed, red leaf, red yell
for my daredevil leap between cars. You there?

Now I can't find the damn circumflex.
(What self-respecting beast would go without
making that extra mark?) This is my psalm
for you, old friend. The aleph is clearly a way
of telling time. The labyrinth needs grout.
When in doubt, be calm. Shout, and be calm.

Red Dirt, Atacosa County, Texas
by Rosemary Catacalos

en memoria, Rafael Peñaloza Macedo

If in a field of wild sweet smells, if digging peanuts in red dirt, if the *comadre*
in the shack at the bend in the road brings her six children out to whistle and wave,

if the old horse is not ours, if the red boots take the *tía* dancing but not to the altar,
if the trails the cows make in mesquite brush, if the mystery of the farm just across,

where the man does not speak and sits in the sun with his eyes shut and arms
he can't lift hanging at his sides, still as his children's rusty swings. If the terror

of the bull's red eyes the night it charges the flimsy wood cart where we sleep,
if one day Carlos falls from the horse that is not ours and has to see an Anglo doctor

in Devine who doesn't much care, if the children dream hideouts and labyrinths
on the trails the cows make in mesquite brush, if no one can find the lone child

who believes there is nothing so safe as sunlight, how it touches everything,

but not the wrong way. If digging peanuts, if growing castor beans for chicken feed,
if digging and digging the well, if the grandfather believed this would save them,
if the city, if its broken glass, if the struggle makes good people do bad things, if you

can breathe when you say this. If the Herefords' white faces hide in the tule fog
by their water hole until someone staring hard can make them out, if a man who

can't move his arms smiles when his closed eyelids blaze red inside each time
the sun comes out from behind a cloud, if he noticed this when he was a child,

if it helps at all. If, digging peanuts, a sharp clod of red dirt bruises your haunches
when you fall back off your ankles into the high blue sky, if you laugh. If years

later you buy red boots and set out to find the grandfather's favorite tree, ancient
broad liveoak standing alone in the middle of the widest field in all sixteen

acres meant to save us. If, passing the empty shack at the bend in the road,
you wave, you by God whistle.

"What Is XicanX?"

by Lorna Dee Cervantes

To be XicanX is to be
a mongrel, half-breed, centipede
with a hundred avenues to bear;
To be XicanX is to cross the street
when either side arrives times quanta,
is to dodge the anyway and never have
a home; To be XicanX is to never speak;
Never spoken to, you swear on your
mother's side and then, *besides your
father was...* (and they decide);
To be XicanX is to take the risk:
exposure, suicide, an uncounted number;
You maid around in an invisible suit;
You know the bite of dogs, threat of suits,
the laws — miscegenation applies to you,
who you love may not love you back; You take
The Paperbag Test and fail; You know how
to fold a bag, tie a knot in plastic; "Savage Wench"
is what they call you in the census books: to be
XicanX is to have no category, no one
that applies; To be XicanX
is to plant a placenta in the ground over and over
in this Liberty one for all here: this world
"Between Two Waters," this America here,
over and over and over since the age
our ancestors first engraved upon the shells
of food now gone extinct (as we were once declared),
our mothers' names erased...; To be XicanX
is be América, America, not a "race"
("...for I, too, am America!")
Sometimes I spell it with an X:
It means The People (and I birth)
in any language.

It's Not The Tulips' Fault

by Lorna Dee Cervantes

For César Chávez & Angelica Guillén, in memoriam

It's not the tulips' fault
If a boy dies in the waiting room,
Penniless. It's not the fallen petals' fault
If a girl, caught in the migra's grasp
Gets deflowered in the mud.
Don't blame these flagrant perfumed
Mouths. Their dumbed words would house
Horrors. If they could speak they would
Wonder at the work of man, the toil
Of this endless labor of making fortunes
Only to lose lives to the withering cells'
Demise. Don't blame the tulips
For their poisons, for the bees dying
At the pollen's promise. Don't make them
Suffer the pickers' thirst. They bare backs
To the riven sun striped and stripped
Of sustenance, their dried out tongues
Caught up in the moment of rich desire.
Once they were wealthy with color, with
The vibrant fluid of justice pooling in
The uneven fields. Once they were worth
More than a man, a single hardened heart
Worth more than ten women's bodies.
Once their fists of bulbs moved Earth,
Weighted heaven. Once they were more
Valuable than the dirt they languor in.
Once they were winter's bitch, holed
Up in their dank holes, waiting. Once
A hundred thousand dollar bills fluttered
Over the promise of these Purple Hearts,
These fiery red heads and yellow ribbons
Of silken hope. Once, an entire country
Lay in their immigrant wake, their green
Fingers poking at heaven like the devil's
Cock. Once an entire nation lay captive
At the feet of the harvest. Once, an entire
Nation was held captive and the earth
Beneath their feet stolen and pock-marked
With the quest for gold. Now, these stark
Blood tulips lie, a reminder, remainder,

The inflation of their fleshy bowls
Starving the people who harvest, who
Hunger at the work of tulips. 5 for a buck.
Five campesinos' lives per fistful.
Don't blame the tulips. It's not their fault.
Caught in the frozen clay of history, they will
Not obey. They are. These hearty gangs
Last a week, if that....While brown backs toil,
While a child's armload weakens and
Death is forever. It's not the tulips' fault.
Give them a drink. Tell them what the sins
Of the fathers have sown. Vow now
Under the sun to end the suffering, to equalize
Organ eyes. And organize. Organize. Organize!

Not A Poem For Francisco X. Alarcón Who Wanted A Love Poem On The Occasion of His Death

by Lorna Dee Cervantes

My confidante, who knew then
how handsome you would become?
Your brilliance shows on your face,

At last. How can I write you a poem?
I want your certain flame to stay. I want
Your, "Good evening!" again. I want your fire.

How can I write you a poem?
Every word flattens into sand-dollars,
Crumbles with the decay of memory;

How can I write you a poem?
Words are Old Pesos worth less than
Their silver. Your silver! How handsome!

You have become! Brother Water Moon
To my Sun On Earth, mi familia, twin-
Driven by Muse, Herself (twin to that, too),

How can I stop this burning multiplicity?
I will you to the River of Light with these words —
impudent masses, total recall. I want you here.

Heal! You're not ready for sainthood yet,
Carnal (as much as I know how much
That would please you). I pray with your poems.

I image in the blazing ball of Yo
Alone in his single cell of execution,
The cross one has to bear — and love.

Love clusters to your core, the ore
Of ages in your blesséd jaguar's eyes (same
Blesser of my father's final journey) (same ailment).

(I cannot let you pass.)
(I can/not believe.) Be live
Wire in our stalled jeep some lonely road —

Your single word on the radio — or
Whatever comes to pass. We, youngest kids
On the poetry block, now old fogies/Elders.

Let the decades come in triplets, my
Old friend. Once it was, you were the only one
Who even knew where I lived, or if....

This, too, shall come to pass.
Our Spirits, braided; our feathered path
Bound in poetry's laser wire, our Spirit-To-All

Deliverance: the largest life of all
Is yet to live. You have yet to live
To write the poem that saves us all.

The River Doesn't Want The Wall

by Lorna Dee Cervantes

The river doesn't want The Wall.
It wants to ring free where it wants.
The river doesn't want The Wall.
It wants to roam through the home
of the brave. It wants to run free
with salmon, with stone, with ceremonies
older than borders. It wants to cross
with the swell and drain. Rain doesn't want
a wall to contain it, to constrain the span
of progress. River wants to merge its way
to confluence. River wants to mingle and feed.
River wants the rocks to sing freedom's song.
River wants Wind to speak its peace.
The river doesn't want The Wall.
The land won't let it. The floods
won't cede. The People will sing,
"The river wants to let freedom ring."
The river wants to let my people go.

Las Girlfriends

by Sandra Cisneros

Tip the barmaid in tight jeans
She's my friend
Been to hell and back again
I've been there too.

Girlfriend, I believe in Gandhi.
But some nights nothing says it
quite precise like a Lone Star
cracked on someone's head.

Last week in this same bar,
kicked a cowboy in the butt
who made a grab for Terry's ass.
How do I explain, it was all
of Texas I was kicking,
and all our asses on the line.

At Tacoland, Cat flamencoing crazy
circles round the pool
player with the furry tongue.
A warpath of sorts for every
wrong ever wronged us.

And Terry here has her own history
A bar down the street she can't
go in, and one downtown. Me,
a French cafe in Austin
where they don't say–*entrez-vous.*

Little Rose of San Antone
is the queen bee of kick-nalga.
When you go out with her,
don't wear your good clothes.

But the best story is la Barbara
who runs for the biggest kitchen knife
in the house every bad-ass domestic quarrel.
Points it toward her own heart
like some Aztec priestess gone loca.
!ME MATO!

I tell you, nights like these,
something bubbles from
the tips of our pointy boots
to the top of our coyote yowl.

Y'all wicked mean, a voice at the bar
claims. Naw, not mean. Shit!
Been to hell and back again.
Girl, me too.

Loose Woman

by Sandra Cisneros

They say I'm a beast.
And feast on it. When all along
I thought that's what a woman was.

They say I'm a bitch.
or Witch. I've claimed
the same and never winched.

They say I'm a macha, hell on wheels,
viva-la-vulva, fire and brimestone,
man-hating, devastating,
bogey woman lesbian.
Not necessarily,
but I like the compliment.

Last Dream

by Diana Marie Delgado

I wish I could stop
bringing myself to Jesus.

He comes and goes
like a sister who rents

the back house
and refuses to sell her dogs.

I walk into the kitchen
and say to my mother

who is at the stove
stirring beans,

I've lost my sight—
but she doesn't turn.

The following morning
I leave through a door

I make in water,
a tear I find

in the shallow
of my back.

The Stars Are Green Tonight

by Diana Marie Delgado

There was a small bird that seemed to follow us as we crossed the street. The sun was not out and had not been out for several weeks. I talked about getting a heatlamp, nightlight, sunlamp—anything to give me color. You were telling me that things would be different. But I couldn't hear you. It was as if you were calling out from the shore of a faraway beach. Or like the time we stopped in the alleyway of our apartment to figure out the name of that song.

Guadalajara, Mexico

by Diana Marie Delgado

I hear you walking in soft pajamas late at night. Touching every room with your feet. In the morning you ask me to cancel the movers. Only by now I've gone deep inside, to the tender parts, the skin around my eyes. Once, when visiting family in Mexico, a cousin drove to a field near a coconut grove, and after walking over green and yellow sea sand, little stones that seemed attached to no one, she led me to a hedge of flowers that when touched, closed.

The Wall

by Anita Endrezze

Build a wall of saguaros,
butterflies, and bones
of those who perished
in the desert. A wall of worn shoes,
dry water bottles, poinsettias.
Construct it of gilded or crazy house
mirrors so some can see their true faces.
Build a wall of revolving doors
or revolutionary abuelas.
Make it as high as the sun, strong as tequila.
Boulders of sugar skulls. Adobe or ghosts.
A Lego wall or bubble wrap. A wall of hands
holding hands, hair braided from one woman
to another, one country to another.
A wall made of Berlin. A wall made for tunneling.
A beautiful wall of taco trucks.
A wall of silent stars and migratory songs.
This wall of solar panels and holy light,
panels of compressed Cheetos,
topped not by barbed wire but sprouting
avocado seeds, those Aztec testicles.
A wall to keep Us in and Them out.
It will have faces and heartbeats.
Dreams will be terrorists. The Wall will divide
towns, homes, mountains,
the sky that airplanes fly through
with their potential illegals.
Our wallets will be on life support
to pay for it. Let it be built
of guacamole so we can have a bigly block party.
Mortar it with xocoatl, chocolate. Build it from coyote howls
and wild horses drumming across the plains of Texas,
from the memories
of hummingbird warriors and healers.
Stack it thick as blood, which has mingled
for centuries, la vida. Dig the foundation deep.
Create a 2,000-mile altar, lit with votive candles
 for those who have crossed over

defending freedom under spangled stars
and drape it with rebozos,
and sweet grass.
Make it from two-way windows:
the wind will interrogate us,
the rivers will judge us, for they know how to separate
and divide to become whole.
Pink Floyd will inaugurate it.
Ex-Presidente Fox will give it the middle finger salute.
Wiley Coyote will run headlong into it,
and survive long after history forgets us.
Bees will find sand-scoured holes and fill it (them)
with honey. Heroin will cover it in blood.
But it will be a beautiful wall. A huge wall.
Remember to put a rose-strewn doorway in Nogales
where my grandmother crossed over,
pistols on her hips. Make it a gallery of graffiti art,
a refuge for tumbleweeds,
a border of stories we already know by heart.

Presidential Interview:
The Donald of All Bombs

by Anita Endrezze

1
The world is a beautiful chocolate cake.
Brilliant missiles light up the cake.

59 missiles. Make a wish and blow
it all up. Grin and eat cake.

We need more bombs!
My factory makes em! Smash the cake!

Big bombs. Beautiful death. Hugely sums
of profit, icing on my cake.

NATO is not obsolete. China doesn't manipulate
currency but they make terrible terrible! rice cake.

Cut the arts! Cut the food programs!
It's not good for children and old people to eat cake.

2
After a weekend of golf and small balls,
let's send a 21,000 lb non-nuclear bomb to cake

the whole area in blasted dust. My ratings
will go up bigly. I'll take ALL of the cake.

I don't have small hands. My bombs are huge.
Syria or Iraq or Afghanistan. Those people don't eat cake.

I won the election. The media is a stink bomb.
Obama hid "wiretaps" in my chocolate cake.

I'm President.
You're not. Don't eat my cake.

Unearthed

by Daisy Franco

At 8 my father shined shoes
barefoot,
graduated to Mexican mathematics—
sharper than the hunting *navaja*
he once carried,
traded for chalk stained hands
title of professor
'til he found his way over borders,
dug ditches for decades
as if burying a dream.

My mother of black ribbon tresses
lived on Taylor Street at age 12—
hija de braceros—
didn't speak English,
her calloused hands toiled
assembling piano parts
while wishing to play
the tunes of her heart.

Those four firm hands
raised four brown babies
provided possibilities,
ensuring we wouldn't
dig ditches, interring our hopes
for the next generation.

And still on this soil,
continent of our ancestors,
we straddle the middle road
even after countless degrees
and accolades,
I walk keeping my hands
where you can see them,
lest someone think the brown girl
took something that wasn't hers.

Stereograph 1875 from Briscoe collection

Little Beauty

by Abril Garcia-Lin

Long smooth onyx hair
toasted caramel skin
Clear turquoise pupils
Unflinching almond eyes
Exotic feminine beauty
indigenous youth displayed
Commodities for colonizers

Forsaken sisters imprisoned
In an inhuman zoo
Dressed as natives
Of another tribe
Products of rape
Raped mother
Raped culture
Raped land

Children forced to
Perpetuate the
Infectious lie
That natives are savage
That colonizing rapists are
Cultured citizens

Through piercing eyes
The strength of protective older sister
Penetrates your soul

Reminding you
That you
With almond eyes
caramel skin
A descendent of fierce warriors
Indigenous to this land

You are meant to
protect what is sacred
To use your power
Your art
to heal hearts and reclaim your roots

Manny

by Abril Garcia-Lin

I see you in the amber glow of the city lights at night
I hear you in the rhythm of San Anto music, raw and rasquache
I smell you in the steamy corn tortillas of the westside Molino
I feel you in the warm wind of Woodlawn lake on a sunny day
I see you in the
 smile of la chula chicana dancing polkas with her man at the pulga
I hear you in the rapid pulse of San Anto streets flowing with life
I smell you in the alcohol soaked sweat of a musician after a late-night gig
I feel you in the clear spring fed water of Paradise Canyon, cooling my toes

I see you in the rough brown skin of that swave pachuco in the back of the bar
I hear you in the tap tap tap of feet moving to conjunto grooves at Rosedale Park
I smell you in the aftershave of the viejito smoking a Marlboro on his front porch
I feel you in the humid heat and searing burn of the South Texas summer sun

I see you in the vibrant colors and dazzling images of San Anto Westside murals
I hear you in the gritos of los necios at the Spurs games
I smell you in the sizzle of burning meat at the backyard barbeque
I feel you in the embrace of a beloved friend that has been long missed

You never left
You transformed into everything that you ever loved.

"Coming About" In The USA – Age 8

by Lisha Garcia

Coming About. A sailing term. A change in direction into the wind in order to move towards the desired direction.

1. At Camp Arrows. Dead in the water. Also, a sailing term. I dived under the Sunfish sail so it could pass over my head and catch the wind in the opposite direction. *This is tacking* the sailing instructor said. You sail into the wind in a zig zag pattern until eventually you get where you want to go. I thought of my mother now on husband number 4. *Men are like trains,* she says. *When you get tired of going in one direction you get off, find another man on a different train and go somewhere else.*

2. First unsliced apple. Red Delicious and you fetch it in this strange American activity called bobbing. Bite down hard enough to retrieve it from a large metal wash tub. Once in your hands, you must eat the apple from one side to the other until you return to the original heart.

3. First Baptist Church visit. Paula was the next-door neighbor my age, and teacher of outdoor games and all things Americana. She was going to be baptized. I was Catholic and baptized shortly after I was born and didn't remember the occasion. I spent the night curling her hair in pink sponge rollers. Baptism is the immersion of a believer in water, an act of obedience. Dressed in white robes, the preacher plunged her all the way under. His hand cradled her neck and her curls unfurled. *How can you bury anything in water,* I asked? *When you come up from the dunking,* she replied, *your old life stays inside the water, and you are born again with new life.*

4. Brussel Sprouts and Grits. *Lordy child you in Texas now and has to eat the vegetables from here.*

5. Under the desk drill. *Children it's time to practice,* said Mrs. Bell. If the Soviets bomb Houston, we are going to be ready. We are very close to Cuba and that's where the planes will come from. The fire alarm goes off. We hide under the desks. *Don't forget to tuck fingers and toes and don't move for 3 minutes.*

6. 105 degrees. Paula says it is hot enough to cook. I want to fry eggs on the sidewalk. My mom donates a whole carton. First, we try sunny side up then scrambled, and over easy. I had never heard of cooking on cement. Story McCarthy sneaks up behind me and yanks the ribbons from my braids and dares me to come and get them. They were a gift from my grandmother in Mexico and I can't stop crying. I hide behind the bushes in Mr. Smith's yard until he leaves me alone. He beat up my little brother just cause he could. *I can beat up dirty Mexicans anytime I want,* he said. I forgot to tell Paula about *Huevos Rancheros, Huevos con Chorizo or Ahogados en Salsa Roja.* My mother says I can't play outside anymore. We don't want any trouble.

In The Market, In The City

by Lisha Garcia
After William Carlos Williams

In a hurry to reach the meat stall
where everything must be fresh,
the butcher's assistant dodges
pot holes and people.

Brown hands with dirty fingernails grasp
the handles of the red wheelbarrow
filled with hog's heads.

A knife with a brown handle
is lodged between one
set of eyes, blood still
on the knife. Nothing wasted.

White chickens hang upside down
by their feet. Shoppers squeeze
thighs through feathers
and feel the juice and flavor of a meal.

Chicken feet are served
in the next stall, fried
over a coal stove mixed with spices
and sauces ready for wax paper.

Monsoon rains come early,
glaze the windows of cars
parked in the street. A small sparrow
drinks from a puddle of mud.

Police sirens flash red and white lights
hurry to catch a suspect.
nearby as the noise
stops suddenly, a dog, howls.

The boy sits on the curb across the street
watching everything inside this painting
waiting for his mother
as she bargains the price of squash.

Tar stains his new Nike tennis shoes.
So much depends on what he sees
and the red and white can of Coke
he holds in his hand.

Maria Merced Of San Miguel

by Lisha Garcia

The small brown cup of her Otomí hand
with nails shaped oval and framed in grease
flips tortillas on a charcoal burner
on the sidewalk of Canal Street.

Promises made at Mass over the heavenly host
are far away from the corn *masa*
she prepares into round little coffins
to hold the meals, she sells.
The *quesadillas, carnitas* and *chorizo*
taquitos prepared with a quick flick of wrist
leave burn trails on her hands.

When the sun retrieves its warmth behind
the cathedral steeple on the plaza,
she sets aside each tenth, the *decima,*
of her earnings for the church
and walks up the hill to her one room home,
the burner on her back still warm.

Every Sunday, innocent as her first communion
she bows before a holy scepter
held by a man to receive the blood
and body of Christ,
that mercy wedding feast.

She lights a candle and falls to her knees,
prays to the Mother –
that first Mother who birthed us all
the man in black robes says she is less,
she birthed a God, but she is less.

Soundless

by Lisha Garcia

1.

There is a beat to the freedom of the pine
detached from the forest in my front yard.
Enough shade and green to anchor
the rhythm of standing alone.

The bell tumbles from my grasp and stills its tongue
the very sound that calls me to the Sequoia,
the whisper I expect to hear from the Sahuaro
cactus the moment its yellow flower is set to bloom.

I can no longer be the ventriloquist
for the dangerous stories of the conquered,
for the blood of momentary history.

I am now the step that breaks
newly formed ice on the sidewalk
and for one second,
balance intercedes to prevent a fall.

2.

Burnt orange and cobalt blue
framed in ironwood
and Spanish accents
zip by academic rhetoric

beyond breath
beyond a casual understanding;
clear trout

swimming its rainbow
under my gaze in the Umqua River.

3.

Leaves, tucked under arms, neck and shoulders
strong in number but individually brittle
hold the shape of words
that can no longer be said.
Into anonymous ground
they crumble, exposing the transparent

At The Border Of Joy

by Jenn Givhan

on the crackling edges, the piña cold &
tart, darts on the tongue
the chicle that my girlchild in her pink

tutu, no tights, ballet flats against asphalt
spends all her grubby change to buy at Dollar Store
& my boy with dog hair woven

into his own popping against black sky-
fireworks spackled against his skull &
even I dance with a mop around the living

room mouthing Nicki Minaj, *This starship*
is higher than a mother f-
while now the girlchild with a bubble at her mouth

steams in science goggles at the kitchen
table & the beautiful boy reads comics
where a black & Latinx boy like him

grows spidey senses & says we can all wear the mask
& every time I've flatlined
these smallyets with their mama-

scrubbed bellybuttons or tender earlobes,
with their fevered skin I've cool-
compressed all night, Vicks vapo I've rubbed

into the fleshy pads of their patas,
lighting candles to Santa Muerte
until their chests

have cleared & they've breathed—
these small joys have shorn from me
the devil's winter coat & stitched

me into a tent we've huddled inside, embryonic,
each thawing underbelly, each summer scrying
into fall, as I've fought each unmapped desert

of depression, each broken territory of childhood
trauma come flooding back as a mama
so I could stay with them.

Have you known this punctured never unlatching
from your own praying hands? Have you—
this holding in the spined stretches of borderland?

Tell me, please, what prayers can I sludge
from my heavy-
bellied throat what demon

at the wounds blossoming as rooted fucking death
into the beast & huddle & mass—
the heat for the mothers & fathers who crossed worlds for *this joy*—

& instead were met with us. Who tore from their arms
everything.

*for Yazmin Juárez & your angel baby, Mariee, may she rest in peace, & may you
never forgive us.*

Santisma Muerte

by Jenn Givhan

While Santa Muerte is supposed to provide healing and protection for her followers, some don't consider her a saint but rather a fallen angel who is trying to win back God's favor, since she also grants evil wishes and can sometimes act kinda jealous. Sounds like my kinda bitch.

Bundle of roots, not canes, ofrenda to Señora Negra,
Black mantelpiece, cramp-bark without a wish
to harm, cross-marks or
cut-and-sifted chunklets of root bark, foot-
track magick, poison in the soles—
Keep her devil in the ground, evil protects us,
the unloved. Santa Muerta in the woods, crossing
most holy death, La Dama with her pillared
black candle. Collect the footprint dirt
of the person you wish to harm, La Flaca, the skinny
woman, and mix in a paper bag with graveyard
or goofer dust, then throw over your shoulder
into the running water of the river. Is this
cure or curse. Pray to Death.
The angel beckons.

I Am A Witch

by Jenn Givhan

Can you imagine the riverblack depths I've sunk
        the slipping crawdads (husks I've clawed) to sing
this breakneck hymn? O shells lodged in my privates
        I teach my daughter(s) their names, loud (daughters)
their names: & call into being what cannot hurt us
        (again). O brokebottle spells that sometimes fail still
keep us / from drowning. O guzzling gods
        of praising bodies for what they are & not what shames.
Lifeboats. Oars. Slick, swimming things. Whaled &
        wandering. Can you imagine a girl taught to hate
what will save her? Can you imagine a girl borne
        of doubt? Can you imagine a witch so powerful
she will heal a whole history / future / gift of pearls
        in the silt, & this will be only the beginning? I can.
Because the witch inside me lives, I live. And can say
        I am (Get your fucking hands off me America). I am *my own.*

Brujería

by Jenn Givhan

On the basalt-black
volcanoes where our ancestors buried
our bones, thousands of years, millions

calcified, milk teeth in the silt,
& now we tread, alone, a woman desperate,
arms upraised to indifferent sky

we stake our spines where a brush-
footed butterfly, a painted lady, maybe
a monarch, we cannot tell the difference,

her wings flutter quicker than our depression-
lazied eyes can focus, that butterfly lands
on a fat, dark pile of shit.

We see more shit everyday than almost
anything else & have, it feels,
for thousands of days. The baby

wipes her diaper on the wall. The cattle dog
presses her dirty paws against our
face in bed, & we barely pearl

the expletives on the wire anymore. They're woven
shit-thick into the fabric of our vocab. Our
children have become inured

to our fregadas & we pretend the articles
that claim more intelligent,
creative people curse are true. We curse

poverty. We curse lack of health
insurance. We curse the churning
of milkweed in our bellies, toxic

rot in the system, in the pipes
beneath our feet. Oil-slick. Mother-sick.
We call to our ancestors for help—

Our mother needs a house.
She's dying in the system.
Disabled & teaching

ten classes a semester at a for-
profit college, & not making
enough for rent. Our

ancestors remind us of ancient
magic. Survival. Bodies. Ours.
From the dust brown

women grow roots for hearts,
branches for limbs. We grab
& won't let go. We grab a hand-

ful of rocks & earth &, yes,
the shit.
                    The butterfly
lands in us. The million-year bones shine.
They luminesce.

Our mother's home flutters into view.
& wings. We grow wings.
We fly. The indifference

shutters open & releases our
ancient sky. We breathe
the rotted nopal flowers red-

round pear. We reach. We eat. Our
mother will be safe. Our children.
We gather enough in our branches.
We gather. We. Enough.
We pray we prey to death. The ground
lays bare as skin. A plane passes overhead.

Whether any of this happens
doesn't matter. Whether or not we lie.
Even our lies raise spirits, raise

the dead, raise mountains & hell &
daughters stronger than silence.
Our ancestors hold us as we cry.

I Work Out In A Huipil

by Tammy Melody Gomez

I work out in a huipil, its brilliant codices
stitched into the handspun Oaxacan cotton
in tight twists like these silken trensas
of indio black hair: the longer my braids, the more indigena I feel.

I pounce and pound in the fitness room,
and all the spaces where I work out my life philosophy,
look at the Tex Mex-erciser that I can be:
growing muscles, chiseling shoulders, and
showing my power in effective ways.
For my community.
Yeah, that's the mover and shaker I wanna
workout to be.

And, yeah, the calories get burned
as my waistline gets churned,
but I read Xicana lit—as I tread—
so my cultura gets learned,
while the copal smoke lifts high, from the incense burner,
because I'm a Truth Sojourner, clearing the negative
to summon the spirits,
like that spring night in Oakland long ago,
when *Rocky Rodriguez showed us how to
light the fire for my first sweat lodge.

And like a good coach for the Raza Team,
she taught us, taught us how to spin stories
to get our minds running.
I work out in huaraches,
with the tire tread soles,
to make this a Good Year,
to make this time count.
100 years is how old the best runners are,
the Rarámuri elders, cruising a Century (100 miles!)
like it's a walk in the park—ese.
So I practice my indigena reps,
as I represent,
keeping my momentum
like the soaring quetzal bird: high.

My body tenses with exertion,
the sweat drips, and the muscles grip,
but I will not live my life with my back bent in sorrow,
so straight up—I stand tall,
power through,
so I can prosper tomorrow.

This is Survivor Spirit.
This is making life work.
The stamina of my ancestors inspires me
as I hear them talking in the headphones of my memory—
like a motivational Tex-Mex-Mixtape—
that's my jam!

My workout is a ceremonia
that chisels love into this (heart) muscle
and fine-tunes my inner core huesos
so that champion becomes my new name
and my brave brown body glistens
like the buffed bronze frame
of a Mayan Goddess
at the top of her game.

Rocky Rodriguez is a spiritual elder who was a powerful voice in the Chicano Movement and has maintained her commitment as a social justice activist.

The Mexican Jesus Sings Lead Tenor In The Our Lady Of Guadalupe Teen Choir

by Liz Gonzales

The Mexican Jesus is a guy at my church who has dulce de leche skin and looks like the Christ statue flocked with white lilies on
Easter morning.

The Mexican Jesus' blue-black, just washed, resurrected-Christ hair hangs free. Grandma says, "It's disgraceful. That boy comes to God's house all greñudo. He should at least pull it back in a ponytail." I
point at the long-locked effigy stretched out on the bronze cross
floating above the altar and whisper, "What about him?" She digs
her fingernails into my thigh and hisses, "Callate l'hocico, diablita."
I don't care what she thinks of me; she just insulted my maybe
future boyfriend.

The Mexican Jesus is a junior at San Bernardino High and makes straight Bs. When he graduates, he's gonna take classes at the local JC. Patty, my best friend, told me so.

The Mexican Jesus is too old for me. I'm thirteen going on fourteen, but I join the choir for the summer anyway—to be close to him. Mama even lets me take the bus by myself from the Bench to the Westside for rehearsals. Otherwise, I'll lie on my stale sheets all day, eating watermelon and running the water cooler. The choir is the answer to her prayers.

The Mexican Jesus doesn't pay attention to Bridgette, Patty's sixteen-year-old sister who has sparkly eyes for him. She keeps her mean eye on me. She's jealous of me ever since the night she thought the cutest boy at the Tomorrowland dance crossed the floor to take her hand but asked for mine instead.
The Mexican Jesus comes to every rehearsal. So do I. The choir
rehearses twice a week and sings at the Saturday evening and
Sunday afternoon masses. This is more church than I'm used to. Though, I don't feel more holy.

The Mexican Jesus stands in front of me in the choir. When he sings his solo, his arms and bony body tremble like he's walking on
water. His head nods up and down fast, making his long hair ripple and swing. He belts out, "Lamb of God, you take away the sins of the world," and I imagine combing

his wet hair with my fingers after he steps out of the public pool, his locks spilling into my open hands, splashing my face like a waterfall.

The Mexican Jesus and I stand on the opposite end from Bridgette, who I catch throwing me dirty looks. She knows what I'm thinking.

The Mexican Jesus looks so cute driving his dad's beige Rambler to the choir's fundraisers. We all meet early on Saturday mornings at La Plaza Park to wash cars or sell fireworks. Bridgette and I wear the shortest shorts we're allowed because Patty told us we have the kind of legs boys like. The Mexican Jesus stays too busy talking to
customers, counting money to notice us.

The Mexican Jesus and the choir take a bus trip to Oceanside. Strung up in a new pink and brown bikini that Bridgette could never look so good in, I ignore the riptide signs, wade out to the curls to show off
my strokes.

A giant wave slaps me, pulls me under, tosses me into forward
somersaults, backward somersaults, forward, backward, and
finally spits me out on the beach where I land on all fours, tangled in seaweed, gasping. My hair droops over my face like a sandblasted curtain. My skin stings. Sand weighs down my cups, rubs the inside of my mouth. My bottoms are twisted. The breeze tingles my bare butt cheeks. From the corner of my eye, I spot the others in the distance, preparing the bar-b-cue. Relieved that nobody saw me, I suck air deep to keep from sobbing.

"Are you alright?"

The Mexican Jesus is talking to me for the first time! I want to throw myself back in the ocean like a reject-fish.

"Here, take my hand."

The Mexican Jesus *almost* saved me.

Railways

by Nancy Aidé González

Smell of dirt and sweat
Mingled with whiskey and cigarettes
the train resounds, he is home.

All day he mends railroads
comes home & takes of his dusty boots,
the sour aroma of twilight.

I watch his face
think of the softness of the figs
growing in the backyard,
play with dolls.

He calls me outside
talks to me as he smokes a joint
about constellations and the dangers of night,
I tell him of the butterfly I caught and set free.

The red porch paint peels,
nearby the cactus grows entangled
this is our small space
his jagged hand caresses my face,
above a shooting star scars the sky.

Then he and my mother fight
A blur of fists, blood
his departure marked with dissipating smoke.

I don't want to know the details
of where he went
or how he felt as all those bullets
punctured his flesh.

All I hear is his distant voice on the cracking
phone line saying," I will be home soon."

On the way to the funeral
we stop as the train roars
car after car after car speed by
weight & rhythm of wheel on steel,
he has gone home.

Foreigner

by Nancy Aidé González

I am a foreigner in my own country
there is torment in the disconnection,
I examine the geometries of mountains and
plateaus
pass by clamorous rivers,
the land remains the same.

The land remains the same
in the mirror, reflection
my face is my own
my wide brown eyes
my carefully drawn red lips,
the world has changed.

The world has changed,
I send a letter to a good friend
Wait for an answer that might never arrive,
the mailbox is empty
I must fill my own emptiness.

I must fill my own emptiness
the dirty laundry piles up,
politicians recite alternative lies on television
lying has somehow become the norm,
I march with millions in protest against injustice
raise my voice for the voiceless,
raids round up "unauthorized" immigrants
to be sent to Mexico,
there is an unraveling of fear and hate.

There is an unraveling of fear and hate
my soul knows the unsayable,
I drive to work and back home
throw things on the ground to see
how they fall,
pick up wilted flowers
try to revive them,
find a dead seagull on the path
blood encrusted with dirt
broken wing hanging,

I search for the bare skinned essence of
light within darkness.

I search for the bare skinned essence of
light within darkness,
at the park a small girl holds a red balloon
she becomes distracted by laughter
lets go of the string
watches the balloon float to meet the sun,
I want to peel the sun
lay my fingers on permanence.

I want to peel the sun
lay my fingers on permanence,
rays illuminate a thick black arrow tattooed
on the cashier's forearm,
I want to follow the arrow
to where it might take me,
so I may arrive at the unseen,
become connected.

I am a foreigner in my own country
the land remains the same
yet my world has changed,
memory filters through lace wings
those I thought I knew,
have become strangers.

Serenade

by Nancy Aidé González

I become earth's
remembrance of everything
creviced skin of red rock
endless pregnant season
toothless silence

I want to understand this world, your scars
stay cradled by tree arms
delve in splinters

my womb is filled with clay
barren it throbs

I want to say many things
but my words are trapped in caverns
where bats hide from redundancies
no one told me of the gritty essence
of the residue that settles

Black star dying
innumerable deaths in this life
we have come here to the waters
we are he and she
or man and woman
scent of copper and jasmine
we sip smoldering gravity
separated space fills
a serenade in golden afternoon

unborn twins sob
otherworldly whimpers   timeless
they can be heard by the bees and ants
they enter this wasteland   we inhabit
nameless they will remain, my infants

Adrift we are.   Come to me.   I am alone.
wild horses turnover the headstones

take my ovaries   spine   skull
take the truth I search for in crushed leaves,
in the fading contrails of fading light.

Joto

by Rafael Eduardo Gonzalez

n.

In the garden

the poplar trees have caught fire,
        a fox doesn't know it is a fox,
        the horses are running themselves

mane-less. I, behind the kitchen sink,
        stand witness to this—adding extra olive
        juice to your drink. And you, with a grin,

say, "I like them extra dirty."

*

Ashbery tells us, "Be supple, young man,
Since you can't be gay."

        I like to think I'm your *Thinnest Shadow*.
        The wax slides down the candle,

bubbles crawling, the wick dances
to your darkness. Your forehead wrinkled
in thought.

*

You come rushing in, screaming, "Who
did this to you?" The nurse holds

a dixie cup next to my swollen lip, and I chuckle.

*

The horses no longer run
because they trimmed each
other's hooves too much.
They stay timid, inside
the stable—thinking how
vanity got them there.

Lamento

by Rafael Eduardo Gonzalez

n.

Oh you, boy soldier. Oh Achilles.
You say you will teach me
how to hold a man's forearms

the same way you hold a gun.
Militant strict, starched white,
like the last name you left

behind. The tags reflect
your pale skin and the light.
Come on, lover boy, soldier

man, climb this heap of yearning.
Call me, crying, "I never wanted
to pull the trigger." Call me,

yelling, "You don't understand
Patriotism." Watch me, all in black,
crying over the oak. Watch me,

staring at what remains
of you, waiting for the gasses
to raise your belly.

Decirlo Claro

by Rafael Jesús González

Dicen los bobos
que venimos de mendigos
estómagos vacíos, vacías las manos
para quitarles lo que ya
sus propios canallas y bribones
les robaron.
Sí, venimos con hambre
huyendo la violencia
a donde la riqueza
del impero se concentra
pero con las manos llenas
de nuestras artesanías y labores,
corazones llenos de bailes y canciones,
con nuestra cocina rica en sabores.
Le traemos alma a un país sin alma;
traemos el arco iris
y prefieren el gris de sus temores.
Se empeñan en construir muros
si lo que se necesita es puentes.

To Say It Clearly

by Rafael Jesús González

The fools say
that we come as beggars
stomachs empty, empty hands
to take what already
their own scoundrels & knaves
have stolen from them.
Yes, we come hungry
fleeing violence
to where the riches
of the empire are concentrated
but with hands full
of our crafts & labors,
hearts full of dances & of songs,
with our cuisine rich in flavors.
We bring soul to a soulless country;
we bring the rainbow
& they prefer the grayness of their fear.
They insist on building walls
when there is need of bridges.

Flor y canto para nuestros tiempos

by Rafael Jesús González

(al modo nahua)

La flor y canto que nos llega
es desarraigado —
     se marchitan la flores,
        se desgarran las plumas,
           se desmorona el oro,
              se quiebra el jade.
No importa que tan denso el humo del copal,
     cuantos los corazones ofrendados,
se desarraigan los mitos,
     mueren los dioses.
Tratamos de salvarlos
de las aguas oscuras del pasado
con anzuelos frágiles
forjados de imaginación y anhelo.
Dentro llevamos voces mixtas —
abuelas, abuelos
conquistados y conquistadores
     — nuestro legado.
De él tenemos que escoger lo preciso,
     lo negro, lo rojo,
cultivar nuestras propias flores,
cantar nuestros propios cantos,
recoger plumas nuevas para adornarnos,
oro para formarnos el rostro,
buscar jade para labrarnos el corazón —
sólo así crearemos el nuevo mundo.

Flower & Song for Our Times

by Rafael Jesús González

(in the Nahua mode)

The flower & Song that come to us
is uprooted —
      flowers wither,
           feathers tear,
                gold crumbles,
                    jade breaks.
It matters not how thick the incense smoke,
      how many the hearts offered,
myths are uprooted,
the gods die.
We try to save them
from the dark waters of the past
with fragile hooks
forged of imagination & longing.
Within we carry mixed voices —
grandmothers, grandfathers
conquered & conquerors
      — our legacy.
From it we have to choose the necessary,
      the black & the red,
grow our own flowers,
sing our own songs,
gather new feathers to adorn ourselves,
discover new gold to form our face,
seek jade to carve our heart —
only thus can we create the new world.

Follow The Spirit, The Trail Of Slurring Auras

by Raquel Gutiérrez

Who will take care of you when gossip surrounds like revelers and effigy, who will
watch over the you who put away the altar years ago
And care. What is it?
Do I make sure you are eating? Feeling? Carrying the wild child
                                        to term?
You pine for the breathing. Stay awake, the course, coursing the
seductive force of intravenous lullaby, it only feels good right now.
I dabble you with scruple, thrust your solar plexus skyward, ruby birth stone powder
your body your sex.   Leave diacritical
                          bite marks from two thousand miles
        away a paranoid gestation. You should be with someone that can take care of
you lecture in the waiting room
        like a wolf and horse
that came to the palisade
                              on its own, and managed
        through fang and hoof to settle for new regimes

Dilute Democracy

by Raquel Gutiérrez

the whites on our frontier are suffering
the tyranny of a democracy   or so they have
                                                before we both got home

and since we are the best
brown babes they ever did see
they keep their mitts on us
and now we have our memories
                              erased and have to figure out

our own water ways   back to each other.

It is their party after all and our eavesdrop
is our pot luck and everyone thinks we come
from monument valley where lightening
charges this sedimentary formation
                                        with pink electrons

and no one bothers to fact check their belly full
of lies or double agency
to re-settle our indian problems.

there has been no public organ
to give good utterance upon
                              the way they pit us against
                              each other's lovers, nopal gladiators
hanging from the magnolia tree.

every white girl loves a magnolia tree
You and me in love own our rightful place
                              as potential allies of the collective
                                    and enemies of the state.

These are the jobs I want to take away, expose their science
as fiction in neon hues and clog the tributaries,
                        their veins with a blood of foreign substance,

dilute and dilute again
until the democracy
in our blood cries uncle

Virgen De Guadalupe Stopes Washing Dishes to Enter Into Centering Prayer

by Carolina Hinojosa-Cisneros

The Mojave Desert offered its dead in purple tree manifestations. Smoke trees, almost apparitions, called *La Corona de Cristo.* Blue-purple, indigo petals colored the sand where the bottom of my sandals crunched skeletal gravel. Should I have approached these manifestations like Moses, or like a Samaritan woman? My mouth hungered for water, for more than I AM, to ask what of children held in cages. Only an echo of sun beams—110 degrees of summer.   Silence.

      I watched an autumn sun
rise through mason jars
        water-filled on a windowsill
            horizon, overgrown stalks
                of cilantro—peppered the sunrise.

Little By Little I Turn Into Water

by Carolina Hinojosa-Cisneros

I.

It took me two days to scoop out all
The bathwater from the tub. Flung it
Onto a shriveled front lawn—milkweed,
Lantanas, laureles, and morning glories
Neglected since our arrival now wet with promise.

My milk, dried for days, seeped through
Like a gesture of thanksgiving. Rorschach
Ink blots shaped pelvis into butterfly
On my pale blouse. Inside, my newborn wept.
I did not know how to contain it.

I drown in waters I once tamed.
Like an ancient call,
Little by little, I turn into water.

II.

Woke up in Lake Havasu terrorized
From sleep, in a city whose dead walk
Around headless. Invisible and ancient
Men crawled around my hotel room
Hunched, hunting, hungry, kept secret.

Several weeks since, in my own home,
Similar feelings woke me like demons
Who returned for their war. My bedroom
Walls pulsated with breath. A glass
Of water under my bed para calmar el susto.

I drown in waters I once tamed.
We are each our own narcissus.
Little by little, I turn into water.

III.

If there exists a hell, the case is clear.
The Amazon is burning, Xiuhtecuhtli—

Lord of Fire—replete with bastard rage,
Thrilled at the sacrifice of this lover.
Drying her memories in log smoke.

Wisdom is a mortal memory when money is more
Valuable than breath. The jungle transforms
Into remains of trees: cathedral fig, giant red cedar,
Ceiba, carcasses of cattle. With the death
Of a rainforest medicine (wo)man so a library.

We do not know how to contain it.
America needs more beef.
Little by little, I turn into water.

to love & die in LA (Wanda's Sonnet)

by Esteban Ismael

in the dark cracks of this city
where great elephants decay, a shell
holding the omen in branches of a tree
drowns in the community swimming pool
where men swim having sometimes thought
they've already seen the other side of death—
eva inside her cat, the eyes of a blue dog,
felicia shot on her own porch, torrential rains
& gods like votive candles, human beings who too
live their unlucky days out & die. the mouth
can be an entrance to the temple:
take for instance, the day I come home
a gun in my face whispers I've never left
Los Angeles long enough to miss it

Standing Outside A Public Library In Michigan

by Esteban Ismael

The police get called. An old woman knows
some are desperate enough to even steal
books, suspect to playing it off as talking on the phone,
tying a shoelace outside of a building as a cover. Lord knows
how anyone could make a profit out of books, but
still, reasonable suspicion is standing on the sidewalk
at 4 in the afternoon. Laughing into an iPhone
with what must be calculation. Someone with my face
must have a plan to sneak through the door
no one notices. There are hidden benefits to a city
where everything looks the same. White on white
no one can see what you do—not the camouflaged rat,
the highbeam eyes of a snowy owl. The soft frost
color of a white sheet. White powder & hard work,
money somebody must shovel off the ground.
What has no benefit is not blending:
the squirrel writes cursive as he plows
through snow, the watchful brown hawk above
in the gray, a lurking fox waits at the base of a tree,
ready for all of it. Standing in a baggy black jacket,
confused by the raving woman that threatens
with one fist & 911 at her fingers, my two
fingers flip into birds aimed at everyone who watches
& does nothing, who ignore it so long as it's not them,
or not as obvious as a rope in hand, a loud scoff in a room
where my poem is being read: I fit the description
for everything except for the reality these
middle fingers happen to find themselves in, having just
finished writing a poem and not involved
in any suspect activity, that the woman shouting for police
happens on my walk home from a class I teach
the day we talk civil disobedience, the pond in winter hardened
into a mirror for a sutra to be sung to the god-forsaken
landscape of the Midwest, a man standing like Thoreau
face to face with a rock, a village idiot
surveying the thickness of frozen water: *There*
have been many stories told about the bottom,
or rather no bottom of this pond, which certainly

had no foundation for themselves. It is remarkable how
long men will believe in the bottomlessness
of a pond without taking the trouble to sound it.—
a student recites as an analogy for race, Detroit.
The frozen cement is thick as a 3 day rain
followed by another snow. Always treading thin ice
in this city. This woman is a surface breaking. Each slick
step away leaves a crack, a fissure that opens a deep well.

A Short-lived Family

by Joyous Windrider Jiménez

1.   1st Grade

A tall, dark, and handsome stranger picks me up from school
And takes me to lunch.
Let's sit outside, he says, *I like being outside.*
I sit on a small wall and he sits above me on a stone staircase
grass and dirt between us.
Boots and jeans, confident smile.
When I was in 1st grade, my teacher didn't understand me.
I told her me and my brother went swimming.
And she said, 'My brother and I went swimming.'
And I told her, no, he's MY brother, and you didn't go. Me and my brother did.
I can't stop laughing.
He is so clever, funny, and handsome.
I fall in love forever.

2. 3rd Grade

He has a wife in Arizona, and
They send me a Christmas box
filled with the most wonderful things.
Lip gloss that tastes like chocolate.
Pens that smell like fruit and pretty little notepads.
LIttle girl perfume and nail polishes.
Pink and blue happy cute creatures dancing across them.
It is the most Christmas gifts I've ever received.
Your daddy loves you very much. He talks about you all the time.
You're his favorite.
I tell her I thought my younger sister, by his second wife, was his favorite,
Because he would say, "Look at the baby, look at the baby."
.....I haven't seen her since I was three.
He says you're his favorite. He misses you, and I can't wait to meet you.
 It feels like a real relationship is forming.

3. 4th Grade

I leave my classroom and meet him on the school grounds.
In his arms a baby girl.
She stands on wobbly legs when he puts her down in front of me.
This is your sister.
I love her immediately.
She is beautiful.
She is mine.

4. StepBrother

I am excited and curious. Eager to meet my new brother.
In my cousins' house, I search for this new face among the
olive skinned, dark-curled boys.
They come running down the stairs. Which one is he?
No. Not him.
His skin is white like alabaster
with fiery orange freckles and the same color hair.
A humongous smile, just like his mom, but different.
Not smart. Just dumb,
And happy.

5. Bully

I am mean in small ways.
- *Why don't you answer when Jimmy talks to you?*
- *I didn't hear him.*
- *Why didn't you open the door for Jimmy?*
- *I didn't see him.*
- *But he was banging on the glass and shouting your name.*
Finally, my dad takes me aside for a conversation.
His voice always brings the right amount of guilt and reasoning
when I am being mean.
I realize how wrong I am. I will do my best to change.

6. StepMom

I like being with my new family.
She is kind, funny. She likes to laugh
She stands tall and strong and red.
She speaks to me like I am intelligent, perceptive.
She shares her life with me, her stories.
Her voice is comforting, colored with normal-sized emotions.
I watch her sweep the floor, I watch her make the food.
We go places together, we do family things.
We watch movies as a family. I get to see HBO and stare at MTV.

Only a couple times did the fighting get bad.
Like when he dragged her out of the car after stopping on the highway.
She didn't scream for help or fight back like others did.
She didn't make a sound.
It all went back to normal really quickly.

7. I am Big Sister

I always carry my baby sister, proud and protective.
Her personality is strong, and she commands all.
She looks like me, but lighter. We look like dad.
Sometimes I tease and tell her "no" for no reason.
She cries and when I try to make friends, she yells "No!" back at me.
She is fiery, and strong.
She likes to be spun by her arms.

No more, she might get hurt because her small arms are still fragile.
But my sister begs for another and how can I tell her no?
She is laughing and squealing then suddenly she is screaming.
We try to comfort her. *Look, the moon!* My Dad says.
She stops crying and looks.
Everyone laughs in relief, but then she screams louder.
The doctors bandage her up.
I feel so bad. I hurt my sister's arm.
I didn't mean to.

8. Summertime

My daddy's so cool.
All his stories are about him being a badass.
One time, a soda bottle fell and he caught it midair.
The bottle busted and cut his hand.
My dad lets me eat all the candy I want, even without dinner.
This is how I know he loves me more than my mom.
I stay up late and can watch and listen to whatever I want.
I like to be there whenever I can.

9. Getting Older

I am getting older, almost 9 now.
I have a super cute short skirt
that I borrowed from a friend when I was 7.
It has a purple bottom attached to it.
People are starting to say it's too small on me
I don't agree. It's perfect.
I mean, it has a purple bottom attached the skirt
And that coverd my underwear.
Perfectly fine. I keep wearing it.

10. Night

We all sleep in the living room at night
The only room that's cool enough.
On the couch, on the floor.
We fall asleep with white sheets and the water cooler running.
One night, I awake suddenly..
I am frozen, not breathing.
My brain is trying to make sense of the world.
My senses are picking up everything in the room.
The hand on me does not move.
 try to understand, but can't
I think maybe it's robbers, or hard core bikers.
They've broken into the house and one is touching my bottom.
I wait for shouts, for breaking, for violence, a voice.
There is nothing but silence, and the slight pressure of a still hand.
Maybe they are quiet bikers.
I know now is the time to cry out, but I can't bring myself to do it.
In the morning, everything seems fine.
No signs of anything at all.

11. Blame

I shouldn't have worn the skirt with the purple bottoms.
It was too small.

12. Strategy

I try to find different places to sleep.
I wait until the last minute to choose my spot. In the corner, three bodies away.
But my eyes keep flying open in the middle of the night.
The room is always silent.
The hand is always a little further than last time.

13. The Line

There is no denying it anymore.
Except I do, every time faking sleep.
Then it happens. One morning, we are wrestling and he moves on top of me, laughing.
I look in his eyes and feign innocence.
We are at a border I can't allow him to cross.
One more step and he'd have to admit that he means it.
One more step and then we'd have to look each other in the eyes and know that we know.
I decide to save us both and tell.
I ask a friend to join me. She tells others and I hate her.

14. Investigation

In the room where the puppets are,
It feels like they've cut a warehouse room in half with black cloth.
There is a tripod and camera towering over us.
There is a pile of puppets and at least three other people in the room.
Years later, I will write these words in a room
And wish I had this tape.

Is there anything else you want to tell us?
I shake my head no, but I look deep into the camera's eye.
I am looking at those who will see the tape.
They will understand.

15. Fear

I spend the next year worried for him.
I just want him to be okay.
I don't want him to lose his wife, his children or go to jail.
I only wanted it to stop.

16. Truth

At the courthouse, I try to pass a letter to him but they stop me,
At the courthouse, I see my new baby brother in his mother's arms.
At the courthouse, I point to the wrong person while testifying. I don't have glasses.

At the courthouse, they accuse my Mom of manipulating me because she is jealous.
At the courthouse, I whimper while answering questions, except when I defend my mother.
At the courthouse, I tell them the secret I didn't tell the camera,
that only a child telling the truth would know.
At the courthouse, I realize that his only concern was always himself.
At the courthouse, I am humiliated and feel like a fool.

17. Therapy
I have a school counselor and she sees me once a week.
It's a decent enough time.
She brings me to a model house with a family of dolls.
 She invites me to play, and says I can do anything I like.
I sit there, pick up a doll. Slowly walk it.
>   -   *I don't know what to do.*
>   -   *You can do anything you'd like. You could have the little girl dump*
>   *ice cream in the father's head, or anything you want.*
I repeat her role-play, and pretend to dump imaginary ice cream on the blonde
males's head.
I finish, then put the dolls down.
It's a decent enough time.

18. 5th grade

My Aunt takes me to see him at his latest home.
We pull up, and tears drop down my face.
Why are you crying?
Why am I crying? Why am I crying??
I can't respond.
There's no reason to cry.
I sit on a couch in the living room. I never move.
I see her slowly walk in from the hallway.
She is so shy. She cocks her head to the side and looks at me.
I smile but can't speak.
Jimmy comes and pulls her close to him.
(Stupid boy, he can't even whisper)
Don't talk to her. She's not our sister anymore.
He takes her away.

19. Epilogue

Stepmom takes the four kids back to Arizona,
Including the newest baby sister I never got to meet.

I start to visit my dad again.
We never mention it.
I carry it like a dead body around my neck.

My younger sister from the second wife and I become friends.
I fall in love with her children.

I move away. I learn to forgive. I search for my own healing
For the next 35 years.

Out My Apartment Window, West Baltimore: August, 2 A.M.

by Benjamin Nake-Hasebe Kingsley

I spread the blinds
with sleepy fingers:

Three boys
and a lookout fourth
none old enough
to drive the car
they're prowling
around:

My Marlboro
-colored sedan,
a Benz twenty-something
years old & seated
atop bald wheels
soggy under the weight
of rain & faded
parking lot
lights:

I think more
& more
she's the one
thing my father left me
I've ever really used.
It's a hell:
Of a time
they're having.
Attempt after:

Attempt
to pry the ornament
from hood, paint-peeled
& chipped enough
to reveal the gray
of stone beneath:

Five minutes
of sneakers mounted
on her grill & a flurry

of whimpering tugs
it's a real sword in the stone
scenario:

I lay back down
in bed with hope
in an anvil of heart
that one boy will
free the silver:

And to him
it will be
Excalibur:

And he will
brandish the star
the ornament the sword
long as a boy can:

Understand
there is no
outstretched arm. No
Lady hidden in crystal-misted Lake.
Every old white wizard
would see you burned
alive. Here no Merlin
will shoulder the spell
of all your weight:

With your own arm
you cut.
With your own arm
you take:

Here
we get after
our own.
From the gray
of stones we pry
we pull each jewel
of light. Here
we forge
our own:

Bodies laid
long
upon the anvil
of this street.

Only In Time

by Ignacio Ramos Magaloni

Decaying phosphor flowers
drift by in hindsight

Pluck one

take its story
for days without suns

press petals between your lips

chisel in breath a relief

release the synchrony of its reaching

speak bright cold shadows that might last!

Name it *Hope is Done*
schedule a show

while it almost lives

marble arms swaying
in the dark breeze of time

while the heart red pulses.

The Future Keeps Coming

by Ignacio Ramos Magaloni

Sometimes we see universes spin out in front of our eyes
like dangling rabbits pulled out of a top hat;

and we walk onto worlds like paunchy,
grief-mad Shakespeares playing paternal ghost

on the creaky wooden stage of our very own Globe,
distracting the audience from Hamlet's responsibility.

How dare we dream when the orange lights on the fail-safe launch
boards blink, blink, blink, waiting for a go from the President?

Or maybe he too plays his part, and all our dreams are yesterdays
that never could quite come into being, and what we call hope

is nothing but our regret inverted into a transparent cone which,
looking through it with our face in the wide end,

reveals at the tip the future pouring out at the speed of light--
not any slower than that. It is a wonder we see anything at all.

Love Stories

by Jesse Tsinajinnie Maloney

Beneath my sternum
encaged in flesh
a single charcoal briquette
flames and ashes
embers red through aortic
network branches
sprouting
leaves besotted
heated until ablaze
my love a bloody
enraged
forest fire.

Missing My Mother

by Carl Marcum

Weary, I bury
my head
in my folded
arms. Along
my skin,
a smell, sudden
and unmistakable:
tortilla de harina,
jábon y manteca,
aspirin and lilac. . .

The plancha singed
dough is the trail of
moles marching,
matching up
each of my arms.
My vision
is a yellow
kitchen where
I was made
entire.

Un Miércoles en Febrero

by Carl Marcum

The bare elm twisted, light snow stuttering.
What spring promises seems only cruel rumor.

The boy asked me what happened to my forehead.
These ashes, I explain, remind me that

I believe something, but can't recall why
that's so anymore—or why Fridays leave me

hollow. I pretend I'm the peddler of hats
in the boy's storybook, and I've no money

for lunch. I pretend it still means something
to deny the flesh. The boy tells me he likes

my ashes, and asks will I share them?
I press my forehead to his. Faith is doubt,

hijo mio, remember this: we are dust, we are
stars—we are what happened and what is next.

"All of my father's friends"

by Alexandra Martinez

All of my father's friends remind me of the
broken chair
broken a/c
broken tail light
broken door lock

All of my father's friends remind me of the
lost wallet
lost keys
lost favorite shirt
lost country

There was the one who
fixed our a/c.

The one who tried to
fix my car.

The one who
helped us move
when I was four.

I remember sitting in the cab
of the moving truck with him and my father.
Watching him watch the girls crossing the street.
Watching him lick his lips and hoot at them.

I laughed because he was my father's friend.

There was the one who
two weeks ago, my father called me and my
sister about.

Then he sent a text all it said was
HELP ARTURO

So we drove to the liquor store at the bottom of the hill,

Arturo stumbled around us and his words.

Kept saying how he knew me.
Kept refusing to hand over the keys,
Kept looking at us and crying and we cried too.

He wouldn't give up until he fell at least twice.
The owner came out into the parking lot and
crossed his arms and for the first time
in forever I prayed he wouldn't call the cops.

My father kept trying to get the keys.
It was my sister who took him by the arm and put him in the passenger seat.
And he's the one I really remember out of all of my father's friends.

"Brother Rabbit"

by Alexandra Martinez

I have milked many bereaved moons
of questions I already know the answers to.
I have wondered in the desert
For my little brother who
never stood a chance here.
Look at me, a dry orange peel
Desiccated and afraid next to rabbit roadkill.
The crow that circles above is my sister's compass,
it screeches to her:
"They are here!
They are here!"
But my sister is too hunched
over to see
And too sleepy to hear
And too young
To care.
She hates parked cars
by the side of the road
She hates parked cars
by the side of the road
with one man as the driver.
I hate parked cars
by the side of the road
with men in them too.
We think the same thought
when we walk by them alone
We think
If my brother were here
If my brother were here
As we dig our nails into orange peel
Feel the skin and pulp crack
into our hands
Spit out seeds at parked cars
by the side of the road
My sister's compass screeches to my   roadkill body
I stopped walking a long time ago
Laid down next to rabbit
Called him my brother
And when she found us we'd been
tied together with a yoke of orange seeds.

"Homeland Security"

by Alexandra Martinez

I saw you shake a canteen and then
empty it with glee.

The water melts away that desert where once, on
TV, I saw a reporter crack an egg on a rock.

The camera came back later and it had fried perfectly.
It made my tiny mouth water with awe and shame.

Now, you are the one who separates
the yolk from the white,

every desert morning and throws them
all back to the other side where they belong.

You fill both skies with the smell of rotten eggs, a hiss
of steam when their shells are dropped into clear, boiling water.

Haiku

by Demetria Martinez

Two thousand mile
Scar burns desert flesh. Black drones
Scan unholy land.

Babes wail, anthem
For a new America
Of the disappeared.

Mother's milk runs dry.
Days down to a trickle. Sweat,
Urine, bloody pads.

Still they come, fleeing.
No documents, just rainbows
Folded in pockets.

Still they come, dreaming
Of a land where heads don't hang,
Bloody, from lampposts.

Lady Liberty
Pushes stroller at protest.
Cops brandish handcuffs.

Father hangs himself
Above fruited plains when his
Children disappear.

Habeas corpus,
Habeas corpse, habeas
Corpus, corpse, habe…

Caged children, tender
Care facilities, dreaming,
Amber waves of grain.

Where is my daughter?
Purple mountain majesty?
Y mi hijo, where?

Beloved border, sage-
Smudged desert, migrant footprints.
Look, the Big Dipper.

Come beloved pilgrims,
Aqui, un santuario,
Gates ajar, enter.

Verisimo

by Pablo Miguel Martínez

> *When SAPD officers arrived at the scene, they found
> the boy lying in the street, suffering from gunshot
> wounds. He was pronounced dead at the scene.*
> —from local newspaper accounts of a recent shooting

> *A new depth of humanity emerged in last night's
> performance.*
> —from a review of Puccini's *Tosca* in a local newspaper

Last night they shot Mr. Arias' son;
few paid attention to the violence

        On those carefully built stages
        the tenor always has a premonition—
        you can hear it in the tremor of violin
        strings shivering in a minor key

When Mr. Arias found him, his son
was clinging to life, the medic said.
The boy was shrouded with plastic sheeting

        The tenor's singing is spined
        by sturdy, seamless columns
        of breath resonating in a mask
        of bone and muscle

A single bullet entered
the left cheek
of the Arias boy's face

        The breath exits as a sound
        almost not human

When she was told, Mrs. Arias shrieked,
she wailed in "a ghost-like voice,"
the reporter noted

        The soprano sings in a voice
        so loud you swear her chest
        will burst

The police captain could not get
Mr. Arias to stop sobbing long
enough to get a statement that night

The evil baritone thinks he has
finally ensnared the soprano—
he lusts after her

A case of mistaken identity,
twelve peers will decide months later

If she gives in to his wishes,
he will set her lover free.
The deep-voiced villain
snarls: She makes him forget
God, he sings

Mr. Arias' son was ambushed,
a detective writes in his report

At the opera's midpoint,
the soprano will stab her tormentor

Mr. Arias stopped going to church
after his son's death. Some days
he goes through the barrio shouting
Why? Why? toward a birdless sky

The soprano believes she has saved
her lover, whose kisses she longs for,
whose broad tenor chest she yearns to pillow

But her vile pursuer, Rome's Chief
of Police, has betrayed her: he murdered
the heroine's love

She will leap from a castle
parapet—her final notes a billow
of sound. Wild applause. The plush

curtains part. The sweat-soaked cast
returns from three hours of verismo—
thundering truth—to take their final

bows. A few roses will arc toward
the soprano's feet

Today the sidewalk memorial
for Mr. Arias' son is a hillock
of plastic flowers, flickering velas,
and a few breathless balloons

The barrio's truths, so far
from the crimson curtain,
don't have opera's redemptive

themes—no leitmotif to signal
a brilliant sunrise, a new time,
in the next scene. Here chests

burst, vermilion, not with song,
but with the blast of pawned guns.
On San Jacinto Street a chorus

of hunger, the yelp of a beaten
dog, a crescendo of ambulance wails—
the only sounds repeated, the only

dependable themes that return at dusk,
when the horizon waves with obscene
flames. Death is a trite character

here in the West Side, where
no one clamors for a seat,
where we seldom hear life's

gloriously triumphant cadence.
There are only breaking stories—
old stories of breaking lives

> They will leave the theatre,
> the intermission's gin a headspring
> of gay, carefree laughter

> "We were transformed by the power
> of the performance," one will say

In a few hours Mr. Arias
will take his own life—
life having taken so much from him

These scenes play nightly here
on the West Side's godless streets—
they know no season

The curtain never comes down

Note: Verismo (Italian: "realism"), a style of Italian opera writing that flourished in the
last decade of the 19th century. Operatic verismo is marked by melodramatic, often
violent plots, with characters drawn from everyday life.

Driving By The Old State Theatre On Ama's 79th Birthday

by Lupe Mendez

She damn near snaps her neck,
eyes stick to the fachada,
an old movie house, bare,
gutted white inside. She smiles,
looks, says,

I know why
you such a bruto, mi'jo.

Unfolds an old memory,
back in Fifty-Eight,
downtown Galveston has signs,
big, stark white black letter signs
Colored here, Colored
there, nothing

para invisible Mexicanos.

Unknown, unless
you make a mistake –
dangle you in a tree branch
late at night. Rent lady tells me
to be careful at night. Used to
babysit Anita and her pigtails,

a nursing school hustle, a barter.
Anita had a friend,
        Ama goes on,

beautiful, plump, black, small
Olivia.

Ama loved to teach the girls
how to cook on Saturdays,
pancakes, eggs, eat warm syrup
with a spoon, buy them dolls,
watch them struggle

with time tables and takes them
to the movie house. In front,
it had signs, big, stark white black
letter signs, No Colored
here. *In the building,*

mi'jo, I am bruta, then. Now.

I love Galveston Island winters,
a reason to hide the girls
in my pea coat.
Pay the janitor.
Sneak them through the back door,
their hands warm – sticky
from sweet maple. Their heads

unaware of hate. Their eyes,
their skins are the same in the dark.

The Migratory Patterns Of Chupacabras

by Juan J. Morales

You first sucked goats dry
through Puerto Rican countryside,

stared us down with red, oval eyes,
before escaping into starless nights.

The unknown lights arrive in Chilean skies with you
to drain llanos of steer into mortis,

to splatter open chicken coops in Venezuela
and Nicaragua, to drink up Mexican shores like Cortes.

Your signature is a puncture wound
on an animal's throat with no signs of struggle.

You are the exsanguination reported on Univision,
pastoral crime scenes ignored by CNN and *The Today Show.*

In your pursuit, we are left to wonder you as the demon
with the gift of flight or the pachyderm-skinned dogs

with freakishly long canines and claws
running from rifle-toting ranchers murdering in Texas.

We keep chasing you like the smoke of rumors
that sends us through Chicago boroughs and back out

to where we might lose your name, a nombre that captures you
in the vanishing between field and sky.

The River God

by Juan J. Morales

We find you on the sand barge
on a tubing trip
halfway down the Arkansas River
where we always stop
to skip the flat stones.
You are driftwood stabbed
into the bank, like a crucifix
with two heads—a sharp beaked, blackbird
and a gnarled human's head.

Each summer, we hear about someone
dying on your river, living reckless in beating back
the unbearable heat, so we add more rocks
and pours of our beer
to your base
with each visit.

Thank you for feeding the swallows
swarms of insects under the green bridges,
for giving the white tails drink,
and for watching over us
at the deep calm where we drift past
black cormorant nests in the tall, dead trees.
We will never underestimate you,
especially where it shallows but
strong enough to steal us under.

Why I Never Look At Planes Flying Overhead

by Cameron Moreno

It must have been summer
when the blue-eyed man caught me
staring at the Blue Jay
fleet, flying above the golf course
trees. He spit on my chin,
called me spic & pushed me
out of his way so I could meet
my kind, *faced-down in that fuckin'*
       river.

When he told me I should never walk
my *wet-back ass back*
into his place, I could hear
a hint of fear
in his weathered voice. Was he afraid
of my tongue when it makes the
perfect sound of rolling 'r's?
Was he afraid that I could cast
a brujeria curse
on his family
       name?

After that, my father told me
I had to grow a pair
of eyes in the back of my head
& let a mouth form on the folds
of my neck. He said *Never*
let them call you anything
other than your name,
       mijo.
I was taught to never look in the sky
when I hear jet screams, to see planes
leave streams behind, because the next cry
would be from my second face
making sure it hadn't gone blind,
making sure we were both
       alive.

Iguana Dreams

by Adela Najarro

Before coming to the United States,
Miguel went in pursuit
of iguana. It was Nicaragua.
He was riding a jeep
with friends who carried rifles.

Moving faster than cars idling
at the Tex-Mex border, the iguana
crosses shadow and light.

Highly adaptive, she also swims
in the sea and slides through deserts.

For over 7000 years iguanas
have imbued potency and healed
the weary. Crushed into a paste,
she is also an aphrodisiac.

Iguana power. Iguana dreams. Green scales
glisten wet throughout Nicaragua. The rivers,
arboreal forests and humid sky lending water.

Where the scars rise on my right ear,
I dreamed of placing an iguana tattoo.

Iguana meat can be broiled, sautéed
or fried. Miguel said he made iguana
stew, then promptly got ill.
Something about the unforeseen
brewing at high temperatures.

In Mexico, Guatemala, Belize, El Salvador,
Honduras, Nicaragua, Costa Rica, Panama
she digs deep to bury her eggs.
To avoid offending Padre nuestro, on Fridays
during Lent iguana stew is ladled over rice.

The morning Tere saw la guardia drive
up and Miguel ran, an iguana witnessed
all perched on a cement block wall.

After an earthquake shattered
living room walls and they were never
rebuilt, Miguel shot the iguana.
Then he came to the United States.

Somewhere in Texas or Arizona,
there might be one lone tree, a grand
old crotchety oak, with a squirrel
in one limb and an iguana in another.

Papi And Me

by Adela Najarro

I carry Papi inside. He is a glass
of lemonade that needs more sugar.
I carry a bottle of Flor de Caña, rosquillas,
and a steaming volcano caldera.
I carry sulfuric fog. I carry atmosphere.
I carry memories of when he held my hand.
We would walk around the corner
to Mitchell's ice cream shop.
He would let me order whatever I wanted
and listened to my litter girl chatter.
After we got home,
I would hear the front door open, again.
Then close. As he left,
my father would skip down the stairs,
whistling a happy tune.
He skies down a mountain in my dreams
and smiles through a moustache.
I tell him the condo next door
has nearly doubled in value
and we have bounced back
from the recession. I carry his ambition.
I carry his broken tongue.
I carry mangoes, nacatamales, y pinolio.
I don't have his straight black hair,
but I share that wink in his eye.
He is all right. He has been forgiven.
When did I do that?
Hey, Papi. Does the sand from Cerro Negro burn?
Can parrots fly with ash on their wings?
It would have been nice to salsa
with him at my cousin's pa'changa
but instead I foxtrotted with a man
who couldn't pronounce my name.

Men

by Andrew Navarro

It has been said that a man's yard, both front and back, represents
his character. I wonder what would be said of me then,
by certain men, if they beheld the state of my weeds? Men
like Emiliano Zapata, who is said to have stood over his children
contemplating their futures as they slept every night when they were young
and unlike men such as Pancho Villa, who is said to have only drunkenly loved
the revolution as it freed him from all contemplations and most importantly
yards. Yet in the end both men died unhappy which historians cannot confirm only
conclude by their portraits, to which the white haired philosopher would respond
good — life being little to do with happiness and rather more to do with suffering
or so I think I read once on a fortune cookie in the Chinese spot dad used to love
because all the cooks in the back were Mexican. As if that were a good thing to dad
who always ordered the general's chicken with extra peppers because nothing
to him was ever worth tasting if it didn't burn the skin of his tongue.

Can being Mexican be contained in a poem?

by Andrew Navarro

Can it? I ask at the altar
of the murialed saints
Spicer y Paz
pero por favor
who could believe
that a single poem could contain the living
and dead breath
of my family; *mi familia*
hermosa
deserves what
form could do it?
Perhaps O'Hara's tongue
could capture
the magic
of my uncle's stories:

guns blazing, we rode into the center of town
      is where the best tacos are sold
by a man that people say murdered
his father hated the family business
                pero eso es típico
      when you mix coin and blood!

Or short as Creeley
to relive those moments
that demand so
such as the time I learned
qué
este chile
sí
pica, chingase!

Poems filled with who
and doing what
exactly I may never know
but know
that I see the image
of my grandfather

in his garden
in mind walking
past the stalks of corn
to feed the chickens
and the birds
and water the dirt
he walks
that I remember
and so
the dirt, I think
the dirt is where
like so many things
in the dirt is where
the words I must use
will grow, yes
in the dirt, I believe
is where
the words
will grow.

Sin Labels/*Sin* Labials
(para Gloria E. Anzaldúa)

by Daniel García Ordaz

We are not born
With ideas about
Nationality
Language
Ethnicity
Religion
Gender
Class

Pero somewhere along the way
The powerful tend
To shovel that excrement
On the powerless

Make people walk around
With the kind of heavy baggage
Our enslaved forebears carried

Lessons quickly learned:
Classify or be classified!
Living or dead,
We taxonomize or die!

Here lies Gloria Evangelina Anzaldúa . . .
Nationality: *Tejana-Americana*
Language: Tex-Mexican-American, or Spanglish (en *Califas, Nueva York, y Chicago*)
Ethnicity: Mexican American, *Chicana*
Religion: Pre-Columbian *Americaníndia Católica (con Sapphos)*
Gender: *Mujer*
Class: from *Pobre* to Blue Collar Scholar
Classification: *Mestiza, Chicana, Zurda, Aflijida, Chingada*
Sexual Preference: Woman On Top *y Mujer* On Bottom
Temperament: *Anzalduende*

Denaturalized
Dark-skinned
Demonized
Dismissed

Discarded
Denuded
Desolate
Described *de todo lo negativo* that can be thrown at a woman who is
Desechable/disposable
Deemed *diferente*
Dissimilar
Divergent
Distinct
Diverse
Inderecha   But

Straight
lines are an abstraction of mathematicians,
those curved philosophers of logic.
Toda linea tiene curva.
All the earth is curved, circular, round.
Even the horizon
must bend to the laws of nature
not of man.

Yet we burn
        we yearn
        we turn

On each other we
Categorize we
Classify we
Label we
Sort we
Stereotype we
Pigeonhole we

Think we
Have the right
To don God's apron
And rename
What remains
From the clay
That he cools
On his heavenly stools.   But

We are not born
        To be   called.
We are just born
        To   be.

*These Are A Few Of My Favorite "Che's"

by Daniel García Ordaz

Chitos, Chalupas,
and *Chilaquiles,*
Cholos and *Chukos,*
Chales and *Chiles,*
Chelas and *Cha-Chas,*
and *Chocolate,*
These are a few of my favorite *"che"s."*

Chi, Chupacabras,
Cheves, Chicharras
Charros, Chicotes
Chicos y Chatas
Michoacán,
Machu Picchu,
and *Tenochtitlán,*
Chiche-

n-

Itza
Are all names of lands.
All the Mayans and the Aztecs and people like me
We like to use the sound —"ch," can't you see?

Chapulín, Chiripiolca
La Chimoltrufia
Chanfle, Chiflados,
La Chilindrina,

Some people are like,
—Dude, Man, let's just go!
Go ahead leave if you don't like my "*chow.*"

El Chavo, El Chompiras
and *Chespirito*
Chiquitilina, te hace chiquito,
Parangaracutirimicuaro—wait a minute, darn-it,
That doesn't go!

All the Mayans, and the Aztecs and people like me
We like to use the sound—"ch," can't you see?

Champurrado, Chubasco,
Chente, Chabelo,
Chaqueta, Chaleco,
Michigan y Chicago,
Pachanga, Charanga,
Huarache, Rancho,

Chivos y Changos,
y Cucarachos.
Chicharrones,
Muchachitas,
Mariachi bands

For Mayans and Aztecs and people like me,
It just doesn't get more grand!
A-Cha-Cha-Cha!

*Sung to the tune of —"These Are a Few Of My Favorite Things"

Horse Tamer

by Rita L. Ortiz

A horse's black eye blinks back at him,
answering a sigh somewhere in his memory
Cutting sugar cane beneath pale clouds,
 the chorus of chicharras dwindles

The horse tamer smirks, looks upon a third generation
whose palms will never stain reins with blood,
never to drip sweat on cornstalks
He cuts sugar cane in silence

Teeth searching my first taste, its thin honey dripping,
the horse tamer smirks, *Al rato asamos elotes*
My grandfather's wrinkled hands teaching
you eat what your hands harvest

His shadow and memory brushes horse hair,
settles in the slate blue of every evening

La Higuera

by Rita L. Ortiz

Covering most of the backyard,

It was a portrait—leaves, trunk, and flesh

> *Ten cuidado que hay arañas!*

> *Las hojas te dan comezon*

I guarded my bucket of honey rain fruit, a summer gift

Perfect green orbs

> *Y todos esos higos te vas a comer?*

I churned their god flesh with my tiny teeth

Sucio

by Jose Osequera

My nipples— slightly melted Hershey's Kisses—
bled brown through a milk sea of chambray:
they stared out as those of a wounded tiger
at anyone who dared look at the boy who wished
his mountain-forest honey eyes
were as blue as the old Windex bottle
his mom hid under the sink;
hair less like the black curls
that poked through the gardener's
sweat-discolored baseball cap
and more like the blonde, delicate sheen
of the yellowing foxtails they weed-wacked;
and skin that sun-kissed a peachy-red
not burnt-brown as their truck rusting on the lawn,
one that tanned darker, dirtier.
Ugly.

If I were what I wanted to be—
what I had been taught to want to see myself as—
when Grandma would call me *mi niño güero,*
I wouldn't have rubbed the swarthy possessing me—
exorcism by exfoliation— a demon, a shroud, a cocoon
I bruised my skin pink to shed— sprinkled cherry Kool-Aid powder
on meltwater swirling lava lamp red
between my discolored feet down the drain;

I scrubbed deeper, beyond my wounds
because shame hurt more than pain—
the harder I scourged, the darker my stripes resurfaced,
they stoked the first-degree burn
purifying the layer underneath the muck,
the melanin crocheted tight to my arm hair,
a mousy auburn in the fading light of dusk.

The loofa's bites scabbed dry, onlookers' chatter healed,
Grandma passed— as did my *blancura*— but the impurity that clothed me,
heavier than a Mexican summer shadow cast on brown *tierra,*
would never allow my eyes to see me as white as they wished I could be.

¿Ya pa' que?

by Juan Palomo

I drive you to Gámez Barber Shop and
pick you up half an hour later. Afterwards,
you want me to stop at De Hoyos Café.
I assume you just want to get a six-pack.

*That time I had to miss school
because I had no shoes?*

But you ask me to join you in the bar, empty
but for a few of your domino-playing pals.
Dos lonestars, you call out and pull out a chair.
Siéntate. You tell them, Este es mi hijo,

*When I was in the hospital
and you never even knew?*

Es reportero en Houston, with pride in your voice.
I cringe, not wanting to join you, but I mumble,
Buenas tardes. I do not want to embarrass
you by declining, by blurting out the anger

*When Mamá, attended my high
school band concerts, alone?*

I feel at your sudden interest in my life,
your alien display of pride in the man I've become.
Were I another son, I'd shout, Dónde chinga'o
has esta'o todos estos años? Where were you?

*When we begged the neighbors to buy
Mom's tamales so we could eat?*

I think of the old joke: a toad is crushed
under the wheel of a carriage.
The driver offers to move the cart,
but the toad croaks, ¿Ya pa' que?

What's the point now?

But the joke isn't really funny and so I keep quiet, opting
against shaming you. I choose to be the good son, as always.
I gulp down my beer and say we have to go. You don't argue.
Instead, you get up, leaving half your beer. You seem to know.

Loneliness

by Octavio Quintanilla

As a boy, I'd climb trees,
reach into nests birds

would leave unattended.
I'd fill my hand

with small eggs, and often
one or two hatchlings

would stare at me
from behind the sprigs.

There were times I wanted
to take them home,

keep them as my own,
raise them, imagined their beaks

would one day open
to call me, "Father."

[You take a picture of your father]

by Octavio Quintanilla

You take a picture of your father
with your new cell phone,

the last one you'll take of him,
thin and frail, looking like a praying

mantis as he brings his hand
to his mouth with a piece of bread.

If he pretends to eat, it's to appease
your hunger to see him eat

and not to appease what no longer
gnaws his belly, no longer the hollow

he knows. It's over, and you know it,
hours all you have now after wasting

years in silence, you in the same path
as his to reach this moment

where you hold up your heads
like dim lamps and face each other,

all light now as you search in his eyes
for closure, anything

that doesn't require words,
a doorknob perhaps

that opens the sky before you.

Cultured

by Miranda Ramirez

Father, you have been in prison most of my life.
You are my connection to a culture I am a part of
but do not know.

You knew my mother was a guera, a southern white woman.
You knew who she was when you married her, and when you left me in her care.
Papi, ¿lo sabías?
that at age twelve I would have to beg her, to stop calling obnoxious drivers wetbacks.
Don't blame her, the experience she had with the culture was not great,
At least that's what I tell myself.

She is uncomfortable with my interest in my non-anglo heritage.
She worried when I married a man of Latin descent.
When I tell her that I want my son to embrace who he is,
she reminds me he is a quarter Irish-German.

Quiero que entiendas.
This is a gift I am giving him.

She doesn't see me the way the world sees me.
She has never felt that awkward pause when the other person realizes you're not fluent.
My son is of many peoples, a walking melting-pot.
His mouth will hold two tongues.
At the Olympics he won't know who to cheer for.
He will never know spite from a parent, fueled by racism.

I blame you father.
You failed to teach me about anything other than stereotypes
and clichés about deadbeat Mexicano Papis.
You abused my mother and in turn, she paid me your retribution.

I want you to know that I refuse to let you ruin this
para tu nieto.
He will never know you, or the clichés you chose to embody.
He will know mariachis and caldo.
He will know big family parties and tears shed over fútbol.
He will form opinions about la Malinche.
He will climb Aztec temples and swim in the crystalline waters of a Spanish coast.
He will revel in the beauty of his lineage.
pero él nunca te conocerá.

We Are Of A Tribe

by Alberto Ríos

We plant seeds in the ground
And dreams in the sky,

Hoping that, someday, the roots of one
Will meet the upstretched limbs of the other.

It has not happened yet.
We share the sky, all of us, the whole world:

Together, we are a tribe of eyes that look upward,
Even as we stand on uncertain ground.

The earth beneath us moves, quiet and wild,
Its boundaries shifting, its muscles wavering.

The dream of sky is indifferent to all this,
Impervious to borders, fences, reservations.

The sky is our common home, the place we all live.
There we are in the world together.

The dream of sky requires no passport.
Blue will not be fenced. Blue will not be a crime.

Look up. Stay awhile. Let your breathing slow.
Know that you always have a home here.

The Border: A Double Sonnet

by Alberto Ríos

The border is a line that birds cannot see.
The border is a beautiful piece of paper folded carelessly in half.
The border is where flint first met steel, starting a century of fires.
The border is a belt that is too tight, holding things up but making it hard to breathe.
The border is a rusted hinge that does not bend.
The border is the blood clot in the river's vein.
The border says *stop* to the wind, but the wind speaks another language, and keeps going.
The border is a brand, the "Double-X" of barbed wire scarred into the skin of so many.
The border has always been a welcome stopping place but is now a Stop sign, always red.
The border is a jump rope still there even after the game is finished.
The border is a real crack in an imaginary dam.
The border used to be an actual place, but now, it is the act of a thousand imaginations.
The border, the word *border*, sounds like *order,* but in this place they do not rhyme.
The border is a handshake that becomes a squeezing contest.

The border smells like cars at noon and wood smoke in the evening.
The border is the place between the two pages in a book where the spine is bent too far.
The border is two men in love with the same woman.
The border is an equation in search of an equals sign.
The border is the location of the factory where lightning and thunder are made.
The border is "NoNo" the Clown, who can't make anyone laugh.
The border is a locked door that has been promoted.
The border is a moat but without a castle on either side.
The border has become Checkpoint *Chale.*
The border is a place of plans constantly broken and repaired and broken.
The border is mighty, but even the parting of the seas created a path, not a barrier.
The border is a big, neat, clean, clear black line on a map that does not exist.
The border is the line in new bifocals: below, small things get bigger; above, nothing changes.
The border is a skunk with a white line down its back.

When There Were Ghosts

by Alberto Ríos

On the Mexico side in the 1950s and 60s,
There were movie houses everywhere

And for the longest time people could smoke
As they pleased in the comfort of the theaters.

The smoke rose and the movie told itself
On the screen and in the air both,

The projection caught a little
In the wavering mist of the cigarettes.

In this way, every story was two stories
And every character lived near its ghost.

Looking up we knew what would happen next
Before it did, as if it the movie were dreaming

Itself, and we were part of it, part of the plot
Itself, and not just the audience.

And in that dream the actors' faces bent
A little, hard to make out exactly in the smoke,

So that María Félix and Pedro Armendáriz
Looked a little like my aunt and one of my uncles—

And so they were, and so were we all in the movies,
Which is how I remember it: Popcorn in hand,

Smoke in the air, gum on the floor—
Those Saturday nights, we ourselves

Were the story and the stuff and the stars.
We ourselves were alive in the dance of the dream.

Border Boy

by Alberto Ríos

I grew up on the border and when I left
I brought it with me wherever I've gone.

Its line guides me, this long, winding thread of memory.
The border wasn't as big as they say—

It fit neatly behind my eyes and between my ears—
It guides me still, I know, but it is not a compass.

It is not a place out there but a place in here.
I catch on its barbed wire in both places.

It is a line I step over and a ledge I duck under.
I have looked underneath its skirts, and it has caught me—

Many times. We're old friends and we play the game well.
When someone says *border*, now, or *frontera*, or *the line*,

La línea, or *the fence,* or whatever else
We name the edge and the end of things—

I hear something missing in the words,
The *what it all used to be*. Its name does not include its childhood.

I grew up liking the border and its great scar,
Its drama always good for a story the way scars always are.

A scar is the place where the hurting used to be.
A scar the heroic signature of the healed.

The border is not a scar. Instead, it is something we keep picking at,
Something that has no name.

The border is something with a history. But this thing now,
It is a stranger even to itself.

Mexican American Sonnet

by Iliana Rocha

gratitude to Wanda Coleman & Terrance Hayes

feliz feliz feliz   *no, no, no, en inglés*
la máquina   algo está mal con la máquina *no, no*

Mom, how do you say—   *no, no*

a ver: we derelict, we orphan, we arson, we organ
hearts half-sunned in our chests, we coffin,
                              we version

we crowd the border, we ghost your guns

Mom, help me spell—

        oye: we bleed through concertina wire, we
drop syllables behind us each time we're born—

you don't have green eyes to be speaking only English
voices hitchhike   voices hoax

we tread softly around violence,
                as if wandering through the maíz—
                              sonrisa's raíz

Mexican American Sonnet

by Iliana Rocha

gratitude to Wanda Coleman & Terrance Hayes

Miss you chingos!!!   she writes, she writes once every year
when her marriage has gone bad. —Monica, the most religious,
had the most   sex, was the most. There is something curious
about the word most, skepticism in superlatives: the way
it battles with *ella peor*, with fetish, the curve of Monica's
breasts in that top, her gray-colored contacts, does battle
with my hand pushing her mouth away from mine. There's
a crisis at the border, but it's not manufactured like the one

in my pants. *What you up to, loca?*   —Autocorrected, a red
line underneath our youth, *NADA, NADA*, in a headlock,
we never stood a chance, did we? Our fathers warned us better
than our mothers: Texas hickory, Mexican amnesia, we created
folklore from the places we were wounded:
      Victoria, Corpus Christi, we wounded you when we erased
      the bridges the most, watched the clouds & cars drown
      the most. When we won the saddest contest the most.

Dreaming Of My Late Mother-In-Law's House

by Linda Rodriguez

Smelling the sharp incense,
cumin and jalapeños,
I cross her floors
again, gold and white shag leading
past couch-flowers.
The television, an altar, always holds
fourteen family faces,
purple candles and Our Lady
of Guadalupe.

In the dining room,
Christ, crucified,
oversees holiday feasts,
and the corner between two doorways
holds the celebrant's chair
with gilded legs. Her sight
stolen by diabetes, Jennie
swivels—never rocks—from voice to voice,
answering with a high laugh like a child's
in an empty choirloft,
offering counsel and comfort
with a flutter of dove-plump hands.

Thermostats set at eighty
make sleep slow to come
in her high beds
while dried palm fronds, blessed
on Passion Sunday,
rattle against the lintels
and hold our city souls
inviolate
in that sacramental house
sanctified by holy water and her.

Fear And Guilt: Against SB 1070 In Arizona

by Linda Rodriguez

When they stop the brown faces,
the Chicanos, the Indians,
when they say, "Show me your papers!",
when only the white people walk free
without fear of being accosted
and arrested,
I want to tell them
their real fear comes from guilt.
Their ancestors killed the People,
the ones who were originally here.
They stole a continent.
Now they are afraid
that what goes around comes around.
It's the Indigenous in the mestizos coming here
that they fear, can't stand.

I am trying to swallow rage.
I am trying to remember
that my purpose is to heal
what has so long been broken.
I am trying to remember
that I know so many white people
who are outraged by this law, as well.
I am trying not to remember
the way they drove my ancestors
like cattle across the country in winter,
leaving a trail of the very young, the very old,
the too-weak-to-make-it behind in graves
scratched by hand from the frozen dirt.

And now they want us to show them proof
that we belong to the land they stole.
Does understanding the language of the heron
constitute proof of belonging?
Does listening to the wind?
Respecting the sacredness of corn?
Caring for the land?
Do they forget that the state they live in

was taken by force of arms,
that they once signed a treaty
giving full citizenship rights
to those who lived there,
that many of those brown faces in Arizona
have been there generations
longer than the earliest white faces?

It is more than I can handle, this hot anger,
this break in harmony with the world.
I must turn to the ancestors,
to the spirit world.
Give me strength and sense
to deal with this outrage.
Grant me *to hi dv,* the peace that starts within.
Help all of us draw together
to *a s qua dv*, triumph over oppressing powers.
You who were responsible for the survival
of following generations, even under conditions
that seemed to dictate that the People must die,
lend us your courage and your wisdom
as we fight against this unfair and callous law.
We will be shrewd and clever as you were.
We will not allow them to win.
Not this time.
Never again.

Tlaloc's Blue Children

by Odilia Galván Rodríguez

sacred frogs no longer sing
songs to bring the rain
children are born deaf
though some
of the blue ones
try to remember
they dream the deluge
others the soft rainfalls
on the mighty plains
others have visited
the *manantiales*
our sweet spring's
mouths
in blue-dreams
where rain-frogs
are born blind
until they can see
the green rivers
flow through them
there are children born
with the knowledge
smile and sing
the songs
to bring rain
it takes a lot of faith
and so many mothers'
don't pass that down
through umbilical cord
the red-river bind
between mother and child
those centuries-old
memories
of how connected
we all are to the earth
how our survival
depends on it
the arrogance of
intelligence and ego
the ability to create
inanimate things

has caused a bend
if not a cut
in the cord
of old wisdom
now called
superstition or
old-wives-tales
and Tlaloc's blue-blood
no longer flows into
the cells of most
of our unborn

Sister Redux

by Odilia Galván Rodríguez

You are disappearing Sister
as the forests are eaten back
even further, there's
a greater chance
that all the sacred plants
will become memories
like our people
they've wanted to erase
from the face of Turtle Island
All of us indigenous ones
from this blue planet
all our relatives
becoming a memory
our languages a memory
women's drums and
rhythms a memory
some of our ceremonial
dances a memory
Sister Wolf
let us sing your song
and call back
all the memories
let us make them whole
through our dreams
we will dream them back
into reality
Ah-Wooooooooooooo

Justice

by Odilia Galván Rodríguez

thousands of hands
grip protest signs
sing freedom songs
march for those
who have no voice
or for the earth
that is bleeding
hold others
through the bars
of rusting border walls
Spring flowers
winding around razor wire
designed to keep people out
instead of building
something for love like
clean and safe houses
for people who sleep
in weather warn bedrolls
under freeways
create jobs
that trust people
to work
because work is good
a health system that believes
in life
instead of obscene profits
holds its arms wide open
to everyone
medicines for the whole person
not for the symptoms of
no real food
of no real home
of no real security
love for all
because we're all
worth kindness
worth a life
worth living
worth loving

A Particular Kind Of Fully-Loaded Funk

by René Saldaña, Jr.

Fully-loaded means something
totally different when you're driving off
a car lot in your new ride than when
you're driving across the state of Texas
midsummer, in two cars and a truck,
twelve of us crammed in, evenly distributed,
to our new home.

Another word that means something else
Depending on the context:
funk. If we're talking music, it's Sly
& the Family Stone, Earth, Wind and Fire,
Rick James, and James Brown,
The Godfather of Soul and
the Hardest Working Man
in Show Business, to name a few
of my own favorites. If we're talking twelve
folks jammed into a car moving across
the state of Texas in the middle of summer,
it's all about an offense of
one's olfactory senses.

Dad asked and got transferred at his job,
Benny, my older brother, got a scholarship
to study at University of Houston—
Dowwwn Towwwn: imagine Isaac Hayes
singing that...now, that's the cool kind of funk.

How does a Mexican kid from deep
South Texas know about this particular brand
of music? you might ask. Answer's simple:
Tío Johnny, my mom's baby brother, who's
driving the truck that came fully-loaded when
Grandpa bought it new back in the day,
which meant an 8-track tape deck, a truck that
Tío inherited and's kept original all these years,
8-track set-up included. "Thank God for eBay,"
he's always saying when he gets the winning bid
on a lot of them. *A lot* meaning *not a ton of*

8 track tapes, but *a batch of them* instead.
A grab-bag. I can guarantee his truck's got
its share of both kinds of funk going on,
after ten hours on the road.

I'm with Mom, Dad, 'Buela Lupita, and
my baby sister. We got funk, not of
the musical variety, and Mexican on the radio.
Sometimes those radio guys talk so fast
even Mom says she doesn't fully understand.
But 'Buela Lupita digs some of the older songs,
the rancheras especially, and the ballads,
or corridos, which she sings along with
when one comes on she knows.
I'm talking, she belts it out and I just gotta laugh.
Makes up for the smells most of the way.

Dad keeps saying, "We're almost there.
Ya mero merito." And soon enough,
sure enough, the Houston skyline
like a mirage appears off in   the   distance.

But this traffic! Ya mero merito,
I gotta keep telling myself.

Home

by René Saldaña, Jr.

We pull into the drive-
way, and before Dad
puts it in park,
'Buela Lupita's out
taking a deep breath.
"Home," she says,
or sighs, or both.
I jump out, too, and
first thing I see,
right next door
in his drive-way,
a kid shooting hoops
listening to some tunes
on an honest-to-God
Boom Box.
"Home," I say.

Colonia Dreamscheme
(a South TX response to big city gentrification)

by René Saldaña, Jr.

I get what that's all about.
Except for us down in the RGV
it isn't gentrification creeping in.
It's the colonia dreams, tracts
of land parceled out into 1/8th
acre plots. Billboards asking,
"Ready to Own Your Own
Home?" The promise of home-
ownership…it gets us
every time: our twisted
version of 40 acres and
a mule: The Good Ole
American (Pipe)Dream:
billboards declaring
"Lots for JUST $500 down,
$100 a month." Crazy not
to, right? But failing
to mention that translates
into a lifetime of months,
that failure to pay
a couple or three months
the land, and anything
on it can <AND WILL> be
reclaimed, taken back,
the buyer left out in
the cold, left with nothing,
left to his own devices,
to fend for himself.
The land, repossessed,
repurposed, resold to
the next sucker born
every minute, who's
thinking, *Ain't gonna
happen to me, I'm no
fool. I'm flush. I got this.*
Also missing on those
billboards: No running
water, no ready electricity,

no city services, no street
names, no power, no
nothing. Wasn't it Hughes
who asked, "What happens
to a dream deferred?"
Here's what: one man's
pockets lined, the other's
a bottomless empty.
That's no kind of dream.

Que Bonito Dia

by Irene Sanchez

It begins with a fault line of memories
Swaying on a
Third Floor
The earth trembles more here

I find solace sitting on
Concrete Stairs
Overlooking
Oil Stained
Asphalt
It's cold today
Or else the heat would rise
Like ancestral fire
Of the roots that burn stories in our veins

The cats in the back are
Fighting again
Drowning out the quiet of
Inside
I didn't know I was capable of this much love
Children who are becoming mine
One who already is
You'd be surprised at how many fit in a two bedroom
This apartment is our home in Boyle Heights
But we're Mexican! My man tells me
As he holds me
Of course we all fit
We will be better than alright here

For we already have survived
Banning of our history and books
As well as the
Burning of our names
We keep sacrificing for the children
We have to
Especially our own
What's a Chican@ teacher to do?
But hold this responsibility as an offering
Like Corky once said
Try to sacrifice everyday

We know the next racist law is coming
The next attack on our gente
Is around the corner

I tell him we need to be on the offensive
It's the only way to be now
Because I'm tired of fighting by their pinche rules
It's time we make them

A plane soars above
Dropped phone calls back home
Wherever that was for both of us
Tucson to Oakland
Riverside to Seattle
We just know it's here now
In this embrace
Overlooking the barrio

I think back to the morning
When the shopkeeper yelled out
Que bonito Dia!
On Chavez
I mean
Brooklyn Avenue
I giggle
Because I didn't see it until sunset
Que bonito dia I repeat to myself
What a beautiful life I have now

City Limits

by Irene Sanchez

Today I drove past 20 cities and didn't stop
Except when I was on 5 different freeways
Parked
The signs tell me which city limit I am in
But I already know
Which streets can't be crossed
The ones we do anyways
The rusted railroad tracks that temps us to cross them
As children
Before we become adults
And learn what a border really is
We already knew
Learning that their side is really the wrong side
Of history
Because someone needs to work
People have to eat
Bus stops sometimes look like the great equalizers
Between the poor
And the not so poor
The difference is clear as the sun shining on
The hills in the distance
Tiny mansions looking down on us
One wrong turn
They'll let you know
This neighborhood is watching your every move
Signs used to tell those before us
You can't
Eat here
Speak Spanish here
You can't live here
Unless you enter from the side
You know it's funny
That's how they still want us
Quiet and serving them
One day I remember a white man said
He was "native" to Los Angeles
Because I guess even his college didn't teach him about
The history of the people here before
They likely did
But what does that matter

All is fair in love and war
And this city is a battleground
And the white man learned
He gets to write it
Until now
For our ancestors still walk
Connecting the earth to the sky
With each step we take defying their ideas
That we had no right to exist
Cause you see it's bigger than a city
Even one as big as
Los Angeles
I know enough by now to know
A city isn't a city
A state isn't a state
A nation isn't a nation
Unless they can put limits on us
And what some of us can do
Where we can cross and when
But here we are
With our umbilical cords
Tied to the center of this hemisphere
Defying all borders they have tried to stop us with

The Danger Of An Image That Speaks Is The Same As The Problem Of A Father Who Writes

by Paul Sanchez

Is the same as the danger of thinking
Too often alone long enough to fall
Into a love like Narcissus's.
A mouthful of January compiles
The language that looks forward
At the same time as it looks back.
A savior that suffices for another
Breath filled existence in the summer,
In a trap house, the ego is the zero,
The rhythm of the bare kitchen table
Is my body. In this house of cake,
A sticky trap of jelly is mortar and scarlett
Beams frame this house called a man.
Who could've missed the pity of flopping
Nothing this time. Shadows present
Shoving what little remains into the middle
Of the table. Time is the vehicle and tenor
Is that everyone needs to get out of your way.
You are the fingers that pull the words through
Like the wind slicing through my fever.
He can count on my fret, he can speak
On my images and write about my elbows
On the table, hands clenched with the other,
Pulling weight toward the floor.

All Places Are Sacred When You Recognize Your Tongue

by Paul Sanchez

Among crispy parchment layers, along
With a deserving portion of the words
Learned while spying into the language
Found at the bottom of a swimming pool,
The poisoned ivy is dusted under a cool
Diamond moon. Some nights, I look
For an indivisible dance partner
A firm iridescent pledge, another pale
One sided waltz "I take as my third,
An irrational decimal from your pi"
Is what she will say after I say
He must have loved her. The algebra
Of emotions is expressed in the loose
Mysteries of a pale moon. The forgotten
Ending of Coleridge is he died unfinished,
Raw. Call me superstitious. This tongue
Is working to lay down a bass line, makes
You forget why you're even listening.
I was talking about the ocean, not you.
So take it easy, although nothing is easy
When you're a man who's just been sold
For 1100 silver apples "This isn't Egypt"
Were her last words to him, jiggling
Her coins, skipping away to an oasis
So she could finally be alone and write
His ransom note. They told her they would cover
1110 silver whatevers, that was all they would pay.
Words and words will do for some things
And some ideas but not for all things and all ideas.
"This Isn't Egypt." Someone said I'm a spy
held for ransom in someone else's house.
Sent there by a love like derivatives sold
For imaginary numbers, quantums of syllable.
The last sound heard 1100 whatevers
Clinking. Nevermind the silver, bring
The gold that doesn't change meanings.
Constant moonlight is inclined to carve

A shoulder of stars and a wave of hair
Colored like wine, colder and darker
Than abalone flesh, seaweed, algae,
The drowning rocks and the rolling
earth and this island too will be bones
Amid pillars and chains. Some of them
To you and the same to me. Honey comes
From a lion and honey you eat too.
Honey comes combing through the body
Of a Roman lion. Honey you eat, the face
Of a lady reminds you of seduction, of minotaurs,
And eagle wide questions like what is a man
who are you where are we going and why honey
Comes from a lion and why honey sustains too.

Show Me Your Papers

by Raúl Sánchez

I will show you my yellow papers.
Which ones first?
Old yellow papers dated 1944

My father's papers Atchinson Railway man
bracero hard work *con* pride
he worked here during the war

my *abuelo's* yellow pay stubs
from the Yuma farm scorching heat
tio Manuel's pay stub too small

Imperial valley lettuce land
what papers you want to see
first and last.

My ID driver license legal
document to move around?
My wedding certificate

testimony to my wife
and all my bows.
My kids birth certificates

born on this land.
Social Security card?
My pay check stub?

Taxes, taxes, taxes!
Take home pay too low
who wants to know?

You want to see my papers?
My notebook? My poems
telling my story—

Papers with new laws
deny my existence
because some papers

don't tell it all
my dignity my pride is
not printed on those papers

those papers will burn
only letters and numbers shown
Why do you want to see my papers?

The Canyon

by Sara Sanchez

So too that a horsefly bite
frenzies from the scent of fresh blood
Others could sense the violence
You left inside my body

your lessons left me longing--
to crave the sting of your own suffering is to truly be enslaved

I buried your bones next to me
Under the red earth of my mother
I rolled in the decay of my shame

rotten earth, poisoned.
as the wind whipped me with the sorrows of the honeybee
muscle memory stripped away by death

Yarrow, Yaupon, Yucca grew from the concave lurch in my chest
Los yerbas buenas singing the lamentations of the wildflowers
share your water with those who share their shade

Cholla at my fingertips--
this time I won't make it easy.

The Gift

by Leslie Contreras Schwartz

Good morning to the woman who washes sheets at dawn
to the guard getting off second shift and the cook scraping yesterday from a grill

to the woman soothing the feverish baby, a child not her own
to the mop sliding night into day, the drill marking time to the city's sigh in bed

To the washcloth and the years of clothes being carried and washed,
the oven and the stove cleaned for years, and its coffee can of quarters, nickels and dimes

To the roof and the bricks, the concrete and evergreen lawns
paths made clear of leaves and debris, working faucets, the cool

hum of electricity, its quiet surge.

Good morning good morning good night
to the worker's every waking life

even the scuff of your shoe on the hard floor
is worthy of paintings, songs, and symphonies

every scrape and cut, loads and carrying
that may never be written or heard

but what a thought that some other place
every human's dreaming is recorded

along with our ancestors, the mothers and grandmothers
who spent lives washing and cleaning clothes, glory in the clothesline,

holy sound from the scratchy grass on their ankles

a thousand trumpets for the men who took dirt or metal, shaped a city from a ditch
loud snares and wild strings for feeding families in famine, going off to war and returning dirt
   poor

That in this other place how varied and striking of narratives
and how we listen to them, laughing, weeping.

Not in the audience but in the stage of their lives, which is ours too,
this stage full of wildflowers and sun, sky unbroken by clouds.

How we listen to them, our fellow citizens
and what a gift to humanity, the things they tell us.

We light fires at night.
Keep listening.

The Census

by Matt Sedillo

It happened fast
It happened young
A song
Nestled in your ear
A psalm of forgetting
A hymn of daggers and fog
Neither here nor there
You were taught
You embodied nowhere
Now declare your voice absent
Bow your head
And present your palms

You happened gray
You happened odd
No one
From nowhere
Born forgotten
The moral of your story
Quickly discarded
The invisible backs
That move the market
Now back to work
And thank the bosses
Cause nothing ever changes
But the census

Spic
Hispanic
Speak English wetback
Dirty
Stupid
Lazy
Good for nothing
Job stealing
Mexican
UnAmerican
Invasion by birth canal
Born of a nation of mongrels
Not far removed from the mountains
See how fast that happens

Once

by Matt Sedillo

Once upon a dream
Or at least so I heard
From the time long before
In a land now distant
We gathered
Took shelter from the winter
Our child eyes
One with the stars
Collected moonbeams
Our veins rivers and streams
Our heart was a beat
And each generation
One to the next
We built stronger nests
And legends
Were left
Fuller than found
Or at least so I heard
From the time
Before
I was born on a stretch of land
Known for its weather
Where
The sun shone its light
Upon the righteous and the wicked
The wretched and the privileged
The innocent and truly guilty alike
As their gilded steps
Fell upon our heads
For those who own the land own the law
And those who do not
Only its consequence
I had this dream once
A man walked a child
To the edge of a hill
Upon which sat a mansion
He pointed up and said son
There live the rich
And though you and I
May never live to see it
One day this hill will run red with their blood
Sometimes I have all the strength

And sometimes I have none at all
I have this reoccurring life
Where every moment is midnight
And every step is fog

Wake up
Wake up
Wake up on downtown bus ride
Along side
A friend of mine
Tell me your troubles
I'll tell you mine
Or we can just shoot the breeze
Pass the time
Something about a job
Something about the car
Some run in with the cops
How I almost got fucked up by the law
How everyone just stood around
And watched
How I talked my way out
Like I usually do
Tells me school kids
Are chanting in her children's face
Trump
Trump
And build the wall
We were children during prop 187
This is worse
I imagine
I pause
I restart
This is worse I know
It ebbs and it flows
Always really coming
And it never really goes
How our kids are never just kids
In this country
We talk history
Mendez and Lemon Grove
Rodriguez vs San Antonio
Saul Castro and the blowouts
McGraw Hill and Texas
How Tucson unified against us
How our ancestors walk with us
How our legends rattle our bones
How la lucha makes us strong
But la luna makes us who we are

She tells me she doesn't like to ride the bus alone
At least not night
Tells me of dangers
I never have to consider
How the world is full of threat
Because the world is full of men
No exceptions
I sit
I listen
The wheels keep turning
We reach our destination
Walk our separate ways
I find no peace these days
I head east
Towards clinics of cruelty
All humanity stripped from a system
Sadism posed as social work
In El Monte
The writing on the wall
Will insult you in two languages
On the corner
Of Paramount and Whittier
On the border
Of Montebello and Pico Rivera
Signs ring out to criminalize our movement
Six months in a cage for cruising
My father always said
They hate to see us shining
The car was once his
Its days are few
My feet are weary
I sleep in parking lots
Sleepwalk my way
To the westside
Some kind of festival of lights
At the edge of conquest
At the beginning or end
Of the Christopher Columbus highway
I make my way
Waist deep to the pacific
I welcome the waves
Make distant the land
Make distant its chant
Come this far to forget
Feel the moonlight ripple my skin
Awake again
I walk the pier
See them in the distance

The boys in blue
The killing crew
Authorized lynch mob
Death squad
America signed with a bullet
Five pigs to one teenager
Hands cuffed behind his back
Loud proud frat boys walk by
Drinking from flasks
Black youth is criminalized
White crime
Is state sanctioned
The guns
Their triggers
Their laughter
They call for back up
No crowd gathers
The city's eyes
The city's lights
March forward
This is expected
This is nothing to see
This what we have come to imagine
Never once
In all their murderous authority
Do they ever stop laughing
After an hour
They release him
No explanation
They simply
Tell him to stay out of trouble
This is the law of the land

I have this dream
Every so often
Of people
Beyond borders and prisons
Gathered in the distance
Telling tales of a time
When women feared the evening
When communities were punished by color
And grown men hunted children
Hardly able to believe
People once lived this way

Desierto

by Natalie Sierra

Heat
Buzzard of flame
One hundred years and no one
will know your name
Saguaro spine shoots straight to the
parchment moon
Shadows of spikes 10 feet tall
Enough darkness to stand in and
disappear completely

We consume darkness,
Yeah
Carrion Eaters rejoice
Mix my ashes with the earth
of your father's land
I shall rise again
As spiked and lonely as
lovely *nopal*, as *limon agrio*
There is life in these old bones yet

the scatterer of ashes

by ire'ne lara silva

what does it mean
to be born of a cataclysm
there was one world
and then there was another
there is no known number
for five centuries of death

we are children of ash
children of fire
children of corpses
children of blood soaked earth
mourning all these centuries
because we cannot
lay all their spirits to rest

mourning because new blood
revives the cries of old blood
because new tears fall everyday
to join the rivers of old tears
flowing inside the earth

mourning because we have seen
too many of our own die
and the dying has not ended
we mourn the nameless future dead
as we mourn the nameless past dead

what offerings can we make to
Nextepuah
the scatterer of ashes
when so much
has already been sacrificed
been lost been taken
scatter the ashes
Nextepuah
and let them rest

what does it mean
to be born knowing
we are destined for ash

lay them to rest
Nextepuah
and in return we offer this
when it is time
to scatter our ashes
you will find only
flames flickering
over our stubborn hearts

because we are not ash
we are neither dead
nor dying
not today
for all our dead
we will live
incandescent

we are children of survive
children of struggle
children of sing
children of pray
children of resist
five centuries of dying
has also been five centuries
of living of remembering
of gathering of building
of stories of birthing

Nextepuah
we may weep but
even our ashes will sing

devotional

by ire'ne lara silva

i am a lit fire
burning nothing
around me

my eyes
are smoke

from my head
not a torrent of serpents
but a torrent
of lions' mouths

lions' roars
in my eyes

in me
all fire
wrought into
bells and flowers
bows and arrows

no division
no separation
pure longing

all of my limbs
are animals now

warning for the young wanting to heal generations past

by ire'ne lara silva

you will want to envision entire valleys filled with benevolent ancestors will want to shower them with spring rain and multicolored blossoms and speak to the wind and the rivers and endlessly braid the sweetgrass as you call their names known and not known but do not forget

our ghosts have teeth our ghosts died sick died mad died cursing their killers cursing their children died stabbed died shot died starving died alone died abandoned died hopeless died watching their people die with them died watching their homes burnt to the ground died watching their crops destroyed died in boarding schools died in catholic missions died in battle died in the cold of cities died crossing rivers died in prisons died sick died diseased died forgotten

death does not remove despair
death does not remove rage
death does not restore everything

our ghosts have teeth centuries of ghosts with teeth are our birthright as much as the wisdom and endurance of ancestors we are born with teeth we can't always wield wisely we are born with the desire to rend ourselves the desire to rip each other apart we are born with teeth that lust for the shudder of flesh

in the long work of healing we must hold our eyes open speak also to the destruction within must hold close our ghosts with teeth must learn our teeth use them to free ourselves and each other use them to rip the seams of time and hurt and loss use them to tear open the festering wounds we must learn to use our teeth as tools not weapons

let the dawn break

by ire'ne lara silva

slowly softly brightly
over your skin
let the darkness
subside tenderly
even the piercing
memories of stars
growing hazy now
night will come again
night always comes again

wake gently
wake carefully
this day is not for weeping
your heart says
this day is not for raging
there are days
meant for surrender and rest
and growing strong

touch the earth with bare feet
feet that have run worked hurt
today let them touch the earth
gently rhythmically
hold your own shoulders
so accustomed to burdens
to bracing against blows
hold them like blossoms
precious and many-petaled

release your waist your hips
the spaces between
repositories of so much pain
yours and what was inherited
and the pain of those you love
let your body sway
hips weeping hips laughing
hips affirming that
life is still sweet
life is still
life is

repeat this
caressing your own lips
so that you remember
you are your own sun

sometimes i crave the color red

by ire'ne lara silva

the way others crave
red-bleeding fruit or a mouth to bruise with tenderness
or a scrap of silk stretched taut
i
crave the color red
and scrape my teeth on my bottom lip crave the color red
and test the air with flared nostrils crave the color red
and clench my own thighs to keep from reaching out
blindly madly hungrily
in every direction

this craving for red is
welcome
there were years i forgot the
color red years i forgot to want it years i forgot wanting to want

you'd think that desire
left abandoned rusting? would lose its memories
of sharp and of shining and of shamelessness but no
not so

i might have said   then   that desire was a knife desire
was madness impulse need   desire   was a gnawing ache

that desire like youthful beauty now seems a thing skin
deep to what this is
heat radiating from the bone making my heart a
crouching lion
desire now is articulation desire now knows death
and cages everything that is bitter and everything that is
sweet
and i know no other name for this now   this
illumination
within

A Simple Plan

For V.M.

by Gary Soto

To get rid of
A dog, you put on
Your brother's shoes,
Slip into a shirt
Hanging on a nail
In the garage,
Smack Dad's hair oil
Into your dirty locks,
The scent of confusion.
You call, "Let's go, boy,"
And with the
Dog's neck in
A clothesline noose,
You follow your skinny shadow
Down the street
And cut through
A vacant lot,
Same place
Where you stepped
On a board with a nail
And whimpered home,
The board stuck
Like a ski to your shoe.
You walk past
The onion field,
Little shrunken heads
Hiding hot, unshed tears,
And stop at the canal.
The dog laps water,
Nibbles a thorn from his paw,
And barks at a toad
In the oiled weeds.
The sun's razor
Is shining at your throat,
And wind ruffles
Your splayed hair,
Where a hatchet
Would fit nicely—

You feel the sharpened
Edge of guilt.
Come on, boy
You say, and leap
On slippery rocks
Set in the canal.
You stop to
Look inside an abandoned
Car with a pleated grill—
Three bullet holes in the door
On the driver's side.
You think, Someone
Drove this car
Here and killed it.

You brave another mile.
When you arrive,
The dog prances with
Joy. What is it?
A jackrabbit in
The brush? Feral cat
Or stink birds? You pick up
A board, one just a little
Smarter than the one
That nailed you with pain.
With all your strength,
You hurl it end over
End. The dog knows
What to do. He runs
After it. Time for you to spin on
On your heels and, arms
Kicked up at your side,
Lungs two bushes
Of burning fire,
Get back home.
That night it's steaks
On a grill, a celebration
Because someone
In the family won
A two-hundred dollar lottery.
You eat to the bone
And then nearly
Choke on the gristle.
You drag your full
Belly to the front
Yard, and stake

Yourself on the lawn.
The neighbor's porch light
Bursts on, and a shooting
Star cuts across the sky—
You touch your throat
And think, Something just died.
You lay with hands
Laced behind your head.
Somewhere up
The block a dog barks.
My dog is out there,
You think, and behind
Your closed eyes
You see him, a nail
In his bloody paw,
A board in his mouth,
And shooting stars
Passing over the curves
Of his wet pupils.
If you were a better person,
You would stab
Your own foot
And let him pick up a scent
Back home.

The Heart Of Justice

For California Rural Legal Assistance

by Gary Soto

Yellow pad, pencil tapped in protest,
Tools of the CRLA lawyer,
And the diploma on the wall,
The clock eating away the iron-colored hour,
The brief, the briefcase itself . . .
And what's that behind the breast pocket?
The heart of justice!

The year is 1970, the issue DDT,
The prohibition of the use of this chemical.
The Secretary of HEW argues
DDT will be around longer than the workers,
Longer than the families of these workers—
Therefore, why deny its use?

The farm worker possesses tools—
Scarf against wind and dust,
Hands with the powerful pinch of pliers,
Cinched belt, golf club called a hoe,
Hoe that ticks against weeds, hoe that spaces beets,
Hoe that splits the worm, that buries the ant—
And boots with an hourglass of agricultural sand,
Knee with its natural latch,
Shovel with its appetite for dirt,
Cloth gloves soft as flour.

Add roads, add the pulsating stoplights,
Add the Stations of the Cross—
Cross yourself in the name of Marysville,
In the name of Delano and Gilroy,
Of Salinas and El Centro,
Rural towns then with DDT
At their fingertips.

The farm worker knows the habitual confusion of government.
The Court of Appeals—what?
The District of Columbia—where?
A petition, a review, clemency—*como?*

They know the run-around,
The lie fat as a grower's wallet.
They know raisins like themselves, little people,
The lemon and its sour decision,
The false declaration of the jeweled pomegranate,
The onion with its tearful *cuento.*
They know this Big Mister, this Secretary of HEW.

The farm worker could sneeze on Big Mister.
Let *him* disrobe and bathe in a canal
Outside of Dos Palos, French Camp,
McFarland and Coachella.
Let him bunk on the ground
For there he will meet his cousin, the snake.

The chill of morning,
The stars opening and closing like fists,
And the farm workers in labor buses . . .
As DDT swirls like rumor,
As the three-eyed frog splashes in the chemical runoff,
Let law be an owl half-hidden in a flowering myrtle,
Let law be noble, a higher calling.

And think of the fields smothered in valley haze
And how the farm worker brought in crops
Dusted with that lethal chemical.
North and south, east and west
Citizens from that year
Ate their tainted fill.

Yellow pad, pencil tapped in protest,
Tools of the CRLA lawyer,
And fifty years of backbone.
You can strike down our lawyer with a federal hoe,
But another from Madera or Brawley,
Oxnard, San Diego, or Santa Rosa
Will rise up, like a cotton plant, for just cause.

The subject of the poem references Environmental Defense Fund vs. Finch No 23,812 (D.C. Circ.). The office of the Secretary of Health, Education, and Welfare petitioned to have the pesticide DDT once again added to the chemical arsenal of agriculture. CRLA argued against its usage and won the case on May 28, 1970.

Summer Work

by Gary Soto

I painted a wall of farm house
And then watched a shadow crawl up the wall,
Dirtying my work. Who would hire me?
I asked myself and sat on the porch
To eat a sandwich and free grapes
From the vine. It was 103,
Our work shirts damp. I felt a necklace
Of sweat break pearl by pearl from
Under my chin. I ate, drank water,
And then gazed at a *campesino* stumbling
From the vines, a grape pan in his hand.
It was high noon on that eighty-acre vineyard,
And somewhere a dog was barking.
I got up, the latches of my own knees hurting.
I called, *Oye, señor!* His shirt tail
Was out, a flag of defeat, and his knees
Were muddy from picking grapes.
I approached him. I said in Spanish,
My mother-in-law made this sandwich.
The bottled water didn't need to be explained.
He took both, releasing a black smile.
His front teeth were gone, his hope
For clean work absolutely gone.
I shivered in that sun: he was my age,
Early fifties, and who was I facing
But my immigrant self? He turned
And started toward the closest row.
I moved beneath the shadows of a pine tree,
Hands on hips, thinking, He's me,
He's not me. The grape fields
Fluttered their leaves. Nothing cooled.
I picked up my paint brush, ready
To climb the gallows of a tottering ladder.
We each had our job, mine a dirty wall,
And his was bowing under
A vine, where his knees hit the sandy
Ground, genuflecting to the powers
Of a godless sun.

At An Educational Conference Outside Of Atlanta, Georgia

by Gary Soto

Muumuu dress, collapsed hairdo from the 60s,
Weight on her right foot,
The politics of an Obama button
On her left boob,
The teacher wobbled
Through the traffic of other teachers.
Me? I was the skeleton
Behind a bannered table
Eating a power bar to keep up.

This teacher rolled up
With a cart of books,
All mine, none with vampires as heroes,
Flames at the end of arrows
Super heroes flying up from urban manholes.
She smiled, played with her bra strap,
And hugged the heavenly *frijoles* out of me.

"You're my favorite writer
Since my last favorite died,"
She said, and piled the literary goods
Onto my table—first editions,
Remaindered, dog-eared,
Coffee-stained, freebies,
Some tagged with yellow stickers,
None with badges of literary honors.
"You mean so much to me
I named my dog after you."
I blinked, cleared a little space
Inside my brain to get her meaning.
She laughed, pulled a pen
From her hair, and said,
"His name is 'Soto.' Don't bark at all.
Please sign my books."

I pulled my tail between my legs.
Obedience school was paying off.
Like a book, my spine was broken.
I asked: "What kind of pooch is he?"

She righted her collapsed hair,
Winced as if I were the slow
Learner in her class.

"Why, you silly Hispanic darling,
He's a Chihuahua, of course."

Juke Box

by Zelene Pineda Suchilt

A sigh from inside
      bubbles of smoke
       movement of curves
        weight the wait
          heavy heat
       & force
collapse
rupture

silk

winds
catch
& flutter

exodus

*

Around here are
cocoons
caked with hard work
hanging upside down
swearing at worms

longing
for the scent of

flowers

whose colors water
remind pollen
the lust within

*

There is a painting of Popocatepetl & Itzaccihuatl
peeling themselves off the wall

Above the rockola
        La Virgen de Guadalupe wears
        Christmas lights in colors of the diaspora
        perched on the highest place of this bar

She is home without a house

unreachable yet present

    are the Mariposas Michoacanas
    dancing sin sospecha
    living here in exile

Caterpillars grab their waists with
the violence
fear of loss can reproduce

in this, they are reminded of the salt within.

*

workers of the underground
twist their bodies
moving dirt for roots

movements shadow

a remembered sun
a waning moon

filtered beams of light

*

    I close my eyes & feel the cinch on my waist
    a return to the skies we use to fly
    requiems of memory belonging to a species of dreams:

            coitus midflight
            taking me down fall
            antennae entwined
            abdomen unclasped

analogue radio señales

lost in migration

*

Dizzy are we for the patterns we've lost
impotent crossings below as above

Meeting here is unnatural
no matter what we do

we exit without honey

the flutter becomes silent
music stops

& a voice from inside tells us:

we are unwelcome
to our own sweetness

thinning wings
assure our stay

that Monarch butterflies may no longer return to Michoacán
& we might die inside the sadness of our own cocoons

without sound

or effect.

What to do while awaiting the Angel of Death,
or, the Angel of Life

by Carmen Tafolla

Plant softly. Majestically. And always,
con *respeto. Y amor.* Seeds are our children
from a different mother. Nights are our
Angels, restoring pools of rest and planning
Even in times when we hide, secret blood painted
on our doors with brushes only we can see, with
plumas only we still remember how to use, even then
the Angels still remember how to find us, huddled,
shivering, praying, breathing in our dreams for dawn,
sueños del amanecer, sueños de la libertad,
squeezing all the seeds we can, in each palm
awaiting just one drop of stubborn sunlight
one ungestapoed heartfull of dirt
one action brave enough
to grow
    resistance
    change
    love

Marked

by Carmen Tafolla

Never write with pencil,
m'ija.
It is for those
who would
erase.
Make your mark proud
    and open,
Brave,
      beauty folded into
  its imperfection,
Like a piece of turquoise
    marked.

Never write
with pencil,
m'ija.
Write with ink
    or mud,
or berries grown in
gardens never owned,
  or, sometimes,
   if necessary,
    blood.

Feeding You

by Carmen Tafolla

I have slipped *chile* under your skin
    secretly wrapped in each *enchilada*
    hot and soothing,
    carefully cut into bitefuls for you as a toddler
    increasing in power and intensity as you grew
    until it could burn
    forever

    silently spiced into the rice
    soaked into the bean *caldo*
    smoothed into the avocado

    I have slipped *chile* under your skin
    drop by fiery drop
    until it ignited
    the sunaltar fire
    in your blood

I have squeezed *cilantro* into the breast milk
    made sure you were nurtured with the taste
    of green life and corn stalks
    with the wildness of thick leaves
    of untamed *monte*
    of unscheduled growth

I have ground the earth of these *Américas* in my *molcajete*
    until it became a fine and piquant spice
    sprinkled it surely into each spoonful of food
    that would have to expand to fit your soul

Dear Mijo   Dear Mija
Dear Corn *Chile Cilantro* Mijitos
This
is your *herencia*
This
is what is yours
This
    is what your mother fed you
    to keep you
    alive

Codex

by Roberto Tejada

With the luminous adversary
of the dark arisen a hummingbird
below the skirt of the earth
to instruct us in weapons and art

What we secured then was a world

And we were everywhere, like
a hand, like rain, as if
to mirror the stars above
this overwhelming valley

Though we knew these were signs

of fire, a comet falling
and a woman nightly weeping,
a hideous bird in nets
pulled up from the boiling lake

And there appeared bicephalous men

As if the enormous houses of time,
all the massive, seemingly
permanent skyward stone assembled
to eclipse this transient empire…

There being other authorized voices

Lost Continent
[after Rubén Ortiz-Torres]

by Roberto Tejada

Prismatic light-beams and motion to so enhance the monuments
encouraging society, goliath in its seizure of the earth people

former technology of bone, dawn's incessant yowling, renewed skin
a sort of liquid flesh: that we wish, even as tutors conveyed

the alphabet to faraway townships—need, even with our rhetoric
of puzzlement, faith overturning this makeshift enclosure

this great asylum in the ancient city of the Indies—to salvage
our nation from disgrace and despairing not, to us was tendered

the mistress builder most suitable to bestow the colossal head
on ground shuddering, all day blood and gold great mother

as when we found it, no longer migrant, holy in the highest
glory, honor and renown to Her most worthy everywhere

throughout all ages and generations, amen. There were two kinds
of breathing in the night; one that was jelly-colored and semi-solid

the other stunted in rapture or awestruck in such unbreakable blaze
as with incense and coagulates, to the artery, to cells that dividing

did duplicate, divide and duplicate again: cross-eyed, very close
to the triangular nose, upper teeth in baskets and bundles

like a shipment of newspapers very old admission stubs a cheap
notebook—all things artless, half real anyway— if a casket

if a prankster effigy, reflected face in a thousand interlocking
parts of what followed from the center point where I am

outside the fiberglass capital as in the one it beckons from a middle
order meaning. Out of isolation and forth to the deputy recitalist

of myself in surrogate space, precise eye of a properly positioned witness like the visitor contained by sound full ceremony

perverse in aim as even this strange novelty's current role was
no how natural in relation to the person of the world I was

but a careful construction in the urgent theme that was a single
death, in the modest epic most immediate of our demise, I mean

recall, translucent and disposable, the remaining corpses. World
that was smaller then. Were we so immune to escalation had

there been more to fabricate in the lost continent, and to relay?
I acknowledged the cranium from the old populace and paid

my tribute to the new passing reference in degrees of routine
or memory as was prone to fit on gossamer sail. "The laboring

populace had lost its faith," bemoaned the boatman, "You work
if you intend to eat, already by mizzen truck with the factory

vanguard a millennium or two of meteoric growth in on-shore
commerce while the class struggle, while the opposing Party

adored the technocrats who made vulnerable, ignored best practice
inauspicious to the earth folk who bestowed us no distinction

as with the likes of blue-collar wage labor output production lines
given to befriending fire hydrants and phone booths, from the hard

workers at the local megastore to the lot of us wretched who
learned to accept your differences and embrace our flaws."

Boomtown hub, big-money high style and ostentatious wealth
long replaced even in the labor union, "I used to think 'model

worker' was the title for ordinary bodies that toiled hard rules
and regulations notwithstanding," the racketeer reported.

"But now 'migrant workers' like me also merit the distinction
proving once again the elected culture populuxe in the atomic

age meets the Temple of Inscription's slogan to oppose reelection
of the General stripped of revolutionary nuance Temple of the Sun

telling Temple of the Count to salvage Temple of the Foliated
Cross sharp at the oncoming ax blades of Aqueduct wind glint

the vertical distance relative to the reference point of an edifice
projected onto a plane vertical to Temple of the Lion

sleep bundled mouth wide open as though to bellow in siren
Structure XII, phase six devoid of shading, ritual appended

to official documents chiseled to a rhythm other than my own.
Because they feared the perils and aftermath in ways more than

they loved the light that would lead them sometimes asunder,
Dynastic-Novelty-of-All-Modern-Convenience to resemble

a product sold inside as the alphabet attraction of its architects
a theory if I didn't doubt there was a God, killed by coagula-

tion a land could so venerate as to amuse. God who? Not enough
to claim by open gashing of the solar plexus—queen's bishop

to Huitzilopochtli!—"I was awakened at one in the morning:
a terrible moan. I thought maybe thieves…. Rain otherwise drip-

ping all over this household, and still no arrival. I'm desperate.
Rainwater refusing to obey, if the drainpipe moans are ended

if only this, as nothing else." It was time for my replacement
mother (a cactus, flesh that wasn't flesh from the flaming mortar

of antiquity) to declare the northern desert exile for all measure
of paterfamilias: hyperkinetic emblem in saturated color after

the mash-up act between neighboring nations, arsenal of food
stuff and lower transit by request, sensations new to denizens

demanding entertainment of the ignited variety, cartoon cigar
that detonates to singe my face into an orifice too of blinking

light: or pyramid permitting matters—head first—to so decline.

●●●

by Roberto Tejada

1≈

The plain terms this place a conversation where I reappear can hardly sleep with
sirens in the aviary amulets
to guard us, parvitude: where the failed
anchor of the everyday is a pale-green
egg-cup a paring knife a burnt match,
is a worm-eaten wooden box a quarter
pound of butter an alarm clock.
Alone now with these thirteen
words that will bring us back into being.
Watch where a purple script is
the jagged edge over which the drift
goes passing, as seen from the shoulder
of the highway not far from Oaxaca
where it borders with Puebla on the 125,
the smell of cowshit and brushfire
under the shadow of closing
thunderheads over the Mixteca,
off the road where we pull
and unbutton, your arms
in a Y to the sun, the dry heat of this
mechanical shine and motor
running in the dissonant
contours or rhythmic
five of what I like
about your body in bristle
and curl, the need to make
noise by feet in length
releases the kind of content
swelling when we touch
conclusive the ecstatic
cataclysm of the terrifying lull.
(Huajuapan • Iturbide)

The animal into parts—first slaughtered, in a body,
and then butchered, the blood-wet pelts
spread out to dry over trampled grass, the intestines hanging
from the chain-link fence
like the ribbed wings of a certain antediluvian something

is the matter with a newborn voice
bleating severance in which language
fucks me up in the smell of immolated flesh,
wet underbrush and mesquite. Slivers of it out to cure
from the day before are a stench
not a gravity in the air
as workaday and somewhere else
in the massacres we live with,
are a clove of garlic peeled, of Indians
by the Spaniards.

2≈

That she couldn't sleep at night without slashing her skin
as from the age of ten or twelve or else
the food she ate would razor steel,
would taste of being largely crosses on the surface
of an arm, a thigh, near a nipple,
into which the full weight
of her body now unleashed
was flying through the open slit

3≈

This nightlong rainfall is a hard zipper
when the cat's urine from the carpet
is about a house in no specific order, the cracked paint
on the ceiling an atrocity in the name of some collective self,
and the watermarks recalcitrant
to transformation,

ever changing,
                 a third of the text to paradise
when I one day write the horizon of the plural mind
unfolding in the rapid music rebound,
and I stutter, it's a pregnant shining,
cast against the walls now,
sufficiently warm, and a little juiced,
the joy of smoke through the nostril,
a final hit, a short unmediated dance
or gesture I would never make
in public, the ice-click in the glass
of lime and beer, the nearly midnight air
of June, and nothing severed
foremost. Someone coughing.

Afterlife

by Natalia Treviño

My dead visit me in dreams now,
one cowers in the closet, slightly

incontinent. One meets me in a restaurant
that does not exist,

waits at a table we must have agreed upon
in an earlier dream.

None of us aware they are both dead,
that this is *it* now.

We are calm, a little
embarrassed. We do not speak.

I wonder at the weather in my head now.
Had to be something sightless,

a depression, a hurricane
to have such power

to block me from remembering
they are dead.

Only a ruckus, a tempest
could be so strong to wipe out the sandbars
of grief, bring down power
lines, require rescue
boats and helicopters to lift us
out of that calm eye

just in time.
I wonder

at the fissures in the crust
of my consciousness,

what the fault
lines are,

like those underneath
Mexico this morning—

those that shifted,
turned a school

into rubble.
This magnum opus:

Our dog, ashamed she dribbled
pee on the carpet.

My father, who did not like to wait
for a table.

Petrushka

by Natalia Treviño

Honey, I keep sending my head
to the orchestra

and leave you
to have the slow roast

alone. And I take my head
for a run out the door.

My head and I review the red buds
half in bloom, lament how they've opened

too soon before the last
freeze. We hallow the sweet

grape of mountain
laurels, the blue and red blossoms

through this mud, this muck
of early March.

We remember my Dad
his ecstatic smile at his first and only

Stravinsky concert a few weeks ago,
his swaying next to me for the first time to a live

swarm of violins and cellos. The bassoon.
Had only heard recordings

before. Ever. Never again now.
Unless we place one on the grass

that grows over his bones.
And when I was a kid,

we sat cross-legged on the gold carpet
facing the black cones

inside his speakers,
glass of Vodka in his hand,

Stravinsky's orchestra conducted
by the other.

My bones vibrating in unison
with sonatas and crescendos

marked by the talons of
longing and loss then

so my head could remember it now.
And so I take my head around a corner on my run

now, and the oboe announces
Petrushka's head has hit the pavement

again, under the snow,
that it has cracked open,

was full of bran,
not brains.

Was but a puppet
all this time.

Standard American Death Certificate For Mexican Father

by Natalia Treviño

Department of Health, Education, and Welfare,

State of Texas Standard Death Certificate

Registrar's Number: Twelve Million PlusX:

(X=Immigrant-925 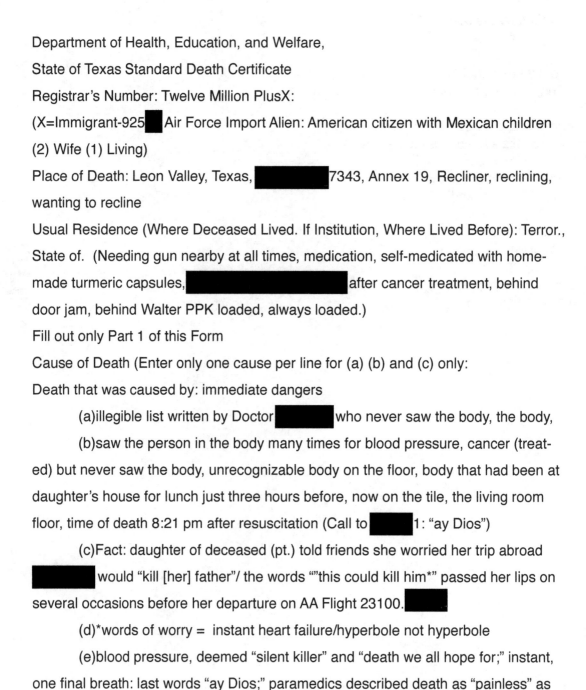 Air Force Import Alien: American citizen with Mexican children

(2) Wife (1) Living)

Place of Death: Leon Valley, Texas, ███████ 7343, Annex 19, Recliner, reclining, wanting to recline

Usual Residence (Where Deceased Lived. If Institution, Where Lived Before): Terror., State of. (Needing gun nearby at all times, medication, self-medicated with home-made turmeric capsules, ███████████ after cancer treatment, behind door jam, behind Walter PPK loaded, always loaded.)

Fill out only Part 1 of this Form

Cause of Death (Enter only one cause per line for (a) (b) and (c) only:

Death that was caused by: immediate dangers

    (a)illegible list written by Doctor █████ who never saw the body, the body,

    (b)saw the person in the body many times for blood pressure, cancer (treated) but never saw the body, unrecognizable body on the floor, body that had been at daughter's house for lunch just three hours before, now on the tile, the living room floor, time of death 8:21 pm after resuscitation (Call to ████ 1: "ay Dios")

    (c)Fact: daughter of deceased (pt.) told friends she worried her trip abroad █████ would "kill [her] father"/ the words ""this could kill him*" passed her lips on several occasions before her departure on AA Flight 23100. ██████

    (d)*words of worry = instant heart failure/hyperbole not hyperbole

    (e)blood pressure, deemed "silent killer" and "death we all hope for;" instant, one final breath: last words "ay Dios;" paramedics described death as "painless" as he clutched his crucifix in last conscious act. (██ citation 2/ resuscitation failure at 8:21 PM.)

(f)Fact: daughter of pt. loose, "always looking for danger" returns safely from trip Monday, June 3 after midnight

(g)Fct: pt. sees daughter for lunch Tuesday, June 4 from 12:30-5 PM

(h)Fct: pt. dies Tuesday evening, approximately three hours after seeing daughter after ****holding his breath for three long weeks

(i)****holding breath= hyperbole of the second degree: actual COD: pressure in the blood, hypertension, pills, texts, calls, frequently sent hopeful emojis (good luck thumbs up signals), rising like war tanks inside of deceased, pressurized bullets collecting in the atrial chambers

(j)years (40+) of beta blockers, life blockers, keep her home, keep her married, keep her safe while she "ekes out a living" (she was a single mom for christ's sake), not making waves, waves that could get her fired, get her divorced **again**, leave her son an orphan, make pt. blood pressure rise over a lifetime of being a *worried high-strung father ("ay dios" last words)

(k) Fct: (daughter =immediate cause of atrial stress resulting in myocardial infarction, gone overseas for too long including ██████ ██ for research, for "poetry" called "writing retreat," not at home, not with son, while deceased and ex-husband and second husband "watched" over the only grandchild) (grandson = going down the "wrong path"— cause: mother/the daughter of pt. not home enough: diagnosed as "selfish" "uninformed" (see (k) "cannot eke out a living")

(l) pt. d on recliner while trying to recline

Xingonas

by Lucrecia Urieta

We are one breath in
And many gusts out
in all directions
We bring storms into
one great epicenter of
swirling joy

Rain falls from us in
patches, other places a
sun beam
and we are still one sky
surrounding the world

We are there
and without us
you would be held together
by nothing but a flimsy, broken
band, swaying helplessly
as the pages run off without you

That is your story,
not Ours.

We keep the mountains
together, are the fault lines
running under your feet and
when we embrace or laugh
you never know when the earth might
tumble.

Atlas hugs the world
out of fear
in his dreams he holds its
weight and he doesn't understand
that the universe formed it
loved it
flooded it and burned it

That is our name
Universe makers
Earth shakers
Our clasped hands are spaces
between stars and
only by the grace
of our love will it hold together.

Dia De Los Muertos

by Viktoria Valenzuela

"Leave me/ Lying here/ cuz' I don't want to go…"(Veruca Salt)

Later, after you get home from work
    After someone wins the world series
        After we are lying in bed giving cariños
And after you admit
    You still fear the future me dying
And I admit that I still fear the future you dying; we say
        Middle age is not for faint hearts

        It's after midnight
        On El Dìa de Los Muertos,
          San Antonio, TX

I've built the altar
    For our antepasados
No pan dulce, but hay dulce
    Fruita y rosas

In bed,
    In our sleep, we hold hands
Giving thanks is done
    I kiss your arm
Our palms rub together
    Our legs extend, interred, as root systems of trees
        still in conversation

        After we die,
        We've promised the other, we'll be buried
together --just like this
        Naturally entombed beside a sapling
        Pecan tree where our children can come lay flowers.

To Diego Who Called Me Maíz

by Oswaldo Vargas

Even when the soil wasn't good for us,
we still grew to places where our tassel
swayed the most-

On days when our lanes ran dry
you handed me water
that you tucked away for this moment-

I remember you pointed to the ships
on the horizon,
conquistadores who set sail to find our field
where only you would unhusk, grind and llamarme maíz.

Ricardo, Janitor Of The U.S.S. Enterprise

by Richard Vargas

nobody knows i exist
but who do you think keeps those
squeaky clean hallways looking like that?
and every time our pendejo of a captain
navigates us right into the local magnetic-gravitational-
time-warp-space-flux-super-duper-ever-ready-force-field
and half the crew up chucks their breakfast, who puts in
the double shift?
sure, every ship needs guys like me to do the dirty work
but there's no need for the recruiters to lie about there being
plenty of room for advancement
i'm not blind, i know the only way we can
get into the academy is by landing jobs in the kitchen
so here i am, and let me tell you, it never ceases to amaze me
how people can get so dumb the more important they become
take the captain, for instance
one thing for sure, this cabron will never suffer from a prolonged
case of blue balls...the dude boinks anything in skirts,
and gets away with it!
i thought it was the v-waist figure he gets from wearing that
girdle all the time, but when i mail ordered mine and wore it
for a week, nobody noticed, even when i had to mop standing
straight up because the chingon wouldn't let me bend at the waist
everyone knows he always goes on those landing parties
(why do you think they call them that?) because he's constantly
looking for some strange action
rumor has it, and i find this one hard to believe,
during one of these excursions the old man
actually found time to get laid by a green chick...
talk about thinking with your chorizo! all i know is
he kept a daily appointment with the doc for two straight weeks
well, last week i was up for promotion
and as i stood at attention in front of his desk
in my best uniform, hair brushed, shoes shined, brass polished
he told me what a great job i was doing
a clean ship is a godly ship, my contribution to the morale
of the crew was priceless...i had so much bullshit packed up my ass
i thought i was gonna explode

then he said he couldn't promote me at this time
because i didn't take the initiative to enroll in a leadership course
being offered on the ship and i needed to work on my
physical appearance, maybe do daily sit ups and pass on
the free tacos during happy hour at the enlisted club
when i thought of how i spent Christmas Eve cleaning up
after the officer's party and how the stink of vulcan vomit
lingered with me for days no matter how many showers i took...
well, it just didn't seem right

today, while cleaning the captain's quarters
i found his supply of condoms, and without hesitation
i pulled out my trusty micro-laser swedish army knife
and proceeded to make minute punctures in each one

like my great ancestor Juan Luis Enrique Hidalgo Dolores
Garcia Vargas said as he was climbing the walls of the Alamo
"fuck 'em if they can't take a joke."

Tito's Carnitas

by Richard Vargas

he was the only guy i ever knew who could survive the aftermath of WWIII
with only a paper clip and a pair of shoestrings. he would have made any son
a great dad but it was his fate to have 5 daughters who all liked to eat… a lot.
my favorite story is 2nd hand, i wasn't there but have no doubt in my mind
that it's true. after a weekend of hunting with his half-ass warrior friends
which usually meant plenty of booze, good weed, and a piss poor attempt to
bring home some serious game, he was driving down a dirt road in his beat up
r.v. with his compadres in the back farting and sleeping, when out of the corner
of his eye he saw a wild pig running parallel to the road so he told someone
in back to hand him his rifle and while pacing the pig and at the same time
making sure he didn't drive into a ditch or a tree he points his rifle out
the window knowing he only has one shot. he squeezes the trigger, the pig flies
head over heels, lands on its back dead in its tracks. he hit the brakes and jumped
out with hunting knife in hand, started butchering it right there on the spot when
the 3 guys chasing it down came upon Tito carving up their prize and one started
talking shit until the doors to the r.v. swung open and out came 6 or 7 smelly hung-
over hombres, each carrying a rifle locked and loaded. Tito gave the whiners
a hunk of the carcass and told them to get lost. years later, after being out of touch,
i ran into someone at a party who knew Tito with the 5 daughters. i asked how
he was doing. the guy made the universal motion of doom, as if sticking a needle
into his arm. i proceeded to numb myself with whatever was at the bar.

Tito's copper pot
cooks meat crisp, juicy inside
tacos from heaven

Through The Fence

by Edward Vidaurre

for all immigrants

I offer these medicine poems
I gather this sage for you poems
Teach me to pray the rosary poems
Let's face the four directions together poems
In lak'ech- tu eres mi otro yo poems
Sweat together poems
Eres mi Yemaya poems
Flor Y Canto Poems
Don't drown in the river poems
Altar for our ancestor poems
sobadora curandera poems
Sana sana colita de rana poems
Drum beat poems
Conch shell poems
Cumbia poems y salsa poems
Hold my hand through the fence poems
Here's some food for your journey poems
La Bestia at high speeds poems
You are my kindred poems

Bring me your Dreamer poems
Your NO Borderwall poems
Don't worry about the orange guy poems
Don't speak his name poems
Your existence is medicine poems
Help me uncelebrated *Cinco de Mayo* poems
ya basta! Poems
Grito poems
Indigenous wisdom poems
Palo Santo poems
You were here first poems
Decolonize your soul poems
Code-switch poems
You belong poems
No more war poems
Son Jarocho poems *de Resistencia*
Corrido poems
Con safos poems
Flying *chancla* poems

Gather in this embrace poems
Crying poems
We're waiting for you on this side poems
We have hot coffee and tamales poems
Recipe poems
Share my rebozo poems
Come, fall in love poems
You are worth more than any labor you do poems
You are him, her, they, them poems
Welcome home poems
Get some rest poems
Tomorrow we'll plan the future poems
I love you poems.

Take with you these love poems
You are not illegal poems
We'll protect your women and children poems
You are not an alien poems
This is actually your land poems
You deserve so much more poems
Hide behind me poems
You are not merchandise to be locked up in container poems
Stay speaking Spanish, it is poetry
First & Last
Breath poems

*Poem for Resistencia en la frontera: Poets Against Border Walls

Caravan

by Edward Vidaurre

In a box, double bagged
Ziplock tight, with all his might
12 years old, torn clothing
Walking non-stop, no rides offered
Bloody knees from a fall miles away
Dry mouth and skin, he holds tight
Grandma is coming with, in a box
Double bagged, ziplock tight
During a break, Eduardo pulls a
Torn and dying marigold from his pocket
Sets the box down, sets the marigold in front
Of the box, he pulls a stick of gum out,
Chews on it for a while, sets it on the box
It's his ofrenda for this Dia de los Muertos,

Eduardo looks at his surroundings
Huixtla sends him a gentle breeze
He dreams of a warm bath with lots of bubbles
A plate of hot food and a cold drink
He lays down, next to his grandmother,
He cries silently, dreams of her voice saying,
"I'm proud of you, I'll be here when you wake.

When does it hurt during the heal?

Rio Grande, Rio Bravo

by Edward Vidaurre

I hear your whispers,
It's not the wind speaking anymore,
it's your longing and your spirit
in the leaves, in the ripples, in the razor teeth of separation

Entre tierra mojada, the scent of mud
that brings me to you, the birdsong that makes its way to us from across two lands
that share the same language of the heart that brings me to you,

Rio Grande, Rio Bravo
The hope of a new people
the baptism of the new *mestiza, nepantlera*

We hear the echoes of pain and struggle and we also hear the chants of
"Si de puede! y Aqui nos quedamos"

Rio Grande, Rio Bravo

It's not the wind speaking anymore
It's the water

It's the water
It's not the wind speaking anymore

Rio Grande, Rio Bravo

We hear the echoes of pain and struggle and we also hear the chants of "si de
puede! Y Aqui nos quedamos"

The hope of a new people
the baptism of the *new mestiza, nepantlera*
Rio Grande, Rio Bravo

Entre tierra mojada, the scent of mud
that brings me to you, the birdsong that makes its way to us from across two lands
that share the same language of the heart that brings me to you,

It's not the wind speaking anymore,
it's your longing and your spirit
in the leaves, in the ripples, in the razor teeth of separation

I hear your whispers

Predecessors

by Mar Vidaurri

The predecessors are weathered river stones
softened, smallened, quieted,
submerged under rumbling.
These smooth stones tumble from their grandchildren's hands,
breathing for a moment in the air,
skipping over a thin veil surface.
One impossible for them to break on their own.
They lay silent and heavy, unheard under,
only when in their children's hands,
when given as a gift, an invitation,
does a river stone yell in a tongue once known.
A tongue as thick as the mud that buries it.
A tongue still lodged in the mouths of all those who came after,
damned in by a thick blanket of new, standard, borders.

The Liberal Party

by Ed Wade

Being only half white,
I didn't quite understand
the dinner party conversation

with all the talk of pairing
the tartness of the crownberry
with the pungency of the camebert.

I got lost somewhere
between the subtle notes of oak,
hints of raisin and overtones of pear
in the chardonnay, though

I drank enough of it to joke
about the quinoa being the size
of congressional testicles.

I joked until the table linen
was soaked with my sloshy
quasi-minority perspective.

I joked so hard my date excused us
as she walked me to the taxi,
where I fell asleep having lucid dreams
of the leftover ribs I stashed
in the refrigerator.

Ah yes, I might have said aloud,
there you are, you ticklish
little fellas. Why don't you
come here?

I have a story to tell you
about the finer side of the city.

Family Archives

by Genoa Yáñez-Alaniz

should I be archived in our family history
below yellowed birth documents and deaths of mothers
each died and gave up her children and her marriage
to the darling young brides   only fifteen years old
unburdening their own fathers

should the church baptismal reports
from México with their dreadful detail of illegitimacy
and rape be placed above me   should the epidemic of
sickness and death in Parras de la Fuente 1836
consume my existence   overshadow

should the gunshot through the twelfth son's heart in 1880
Maverick County continue to go unsolved at my side
witness after witness said nothing
 should I be below stacks of acknowledgements
photos with presidents   presidential letters

each thankful to my husband
for his honor and dedication to country

should I rest defeated below the decree
documents that split up our home
our children   our future   proof of reconciliation
six years after the divorce

should I place my scandal between photos of great
grandfathers   posing with horses and Model Ts

shall my poetic verses for lovers
weave into my history of delicate times

shall I inhabit the future with lust of my deathbed
hands that held my throat in passion

twisted my wrists until the break of my bones

shall I place myself at the top   script out the disease
the mouth I possessed   my truths
shall I report the pills I refused

shall I live loudly   unashamed in the future
with my scandal   with my lovers
at the dinner table?

Eulogy For My Brother

by Genoa Yáñez-Alaniz

Some catch the wind
catch flight
puff up into the moon

Some lose their anchors
become shadows on walls
always searching
always gone

Some pawn off what few luxuries they own
for a ticket to revolution   1993   a journey to
Zapatistas   the thick of Chiapas   México

Some need to feel the spirit of Emiliano Zapata
and hear the people shout the burning
imprint of his words
Tierra y Libertad

Some stand 6 foot 2
with strength of five men strong
skin brown as brown sugar
and a melody of Spanish that rolls off
the tongue   like poetry

They called him   El Gringo
Norte Americano   Puta Madre

But still they loved him for his journey
Loved that he would leave the comfort
of privilege to take up arms with the starved
with families who kept the bones of their dead
wrapped in rose petals   clung to their hearts

He filled his hands with the beauty of spirit
the revolution   the honor and strength of people
rooted to the earth   rooted to La Resistencia
Tierra y Libertad

He sat in sadness unable to fathom the indignity
unable to watch disease creep in   to mother's arms

take her children one after the other   unable to
watch cruel death   swallow the elders   one by one

The poverty and oppression of gente indígena
heavier as progress brought them closer to demise
closer to gone   closer to the swallow of their land
He sat in circles   caught shadows of flames
on his skin   tapped out sonaja sounds
listened to conversaciones of independencia

Some people fall into the romance of revolution
set out to seize the moment   to witness
as Mayan Warriors fight for their land
wage war against a system of oppression

Some people come back battered
meant to wander the streets
half blind with a cherry eye bleed

some stand under light posts
with flashes of fire   raining down on their heads
talking to ghosts

Some have spirits in constant battle
against a colonized brain
unable to pull chemicals apart
for the healing of   mind body and soul
Some people hold prayers of Mayan Warriors
tucked in their sleeves
meant to keep them on a narrow road

meant to keep them from that spiral of gone
twisted inward
a beautiful mind
wayward soul

Dear Brother   rest your brain   rest your battle
let the words of Emiliano Zapata
 rest   on your bones

like Tierra   and   Libertad

I Once...

by Genoa Yáñez-Alaniz

sat up high on a horse in contemplation of my marriage
my head saturated in death clouds
eyes casting down toward my sister

she begged me to come down   but I was strapped
into the leather   I somehow twisted the reins
around my wrists too tightly   they cut through my skin

my sister said my laughter was not normal
it walked out of my mouth   a black bird with no nest
and I laughed harder

she said the whore wasn't worth my tears
wasn't worth my skin going red
wasn't worth my mouth catching at the hook   baited
 yesterday I couldn't tear away from a novel I read
about lovers   a hero at rest   his head pressed into
pillowy breasts   his cock stiff

always ready to take

The heroes are always ready to take   and damsels
always ready to give
or not give
a fuck about my marriage

their tongues were blades   caused despair
caused me to dig my own grave
made me face my own lovers with a shudder

though I had no lovers yet   I crouched   a pink flower
sickened   a girl whose father had gambled her home
 and lost   and now I am committed to this horse
committed to this false bravado and neigh
I will ride into the valley   pretend to love
the thickness of high grass and clover

I will wait for my perfect countryside meadow
to return   my hero always returns   the lovers can wait
his lovers   and my lovers

Purity Of The Homecoming Dress

by Genoa Yáñez-Alaniz

Daughter of skin born from a cleanse
We shall hide the Octoroon in the Texas census records
Great-grandmother will whisper that the grape carters
were from Nacimiento México
Nacimiento de Los Negros
But we have washed out the tight curl frizz of hair
Lightened the deep umber of skin

You want to wear the homecoming dress
but we cannot hide the shape   the muscle
Your school counselor has made that clear
We cannot masquerade you in a skinny white girl dress

So you cry and toss dresses one after the other
You reject   rip away the cling from the curves   the muscle
You accept your school's rejection of your body
You accept Sacred Heart's rejection of your body

and I am powerless in your self- hate
But then you reach for your favorite dress in the closet
It slides over your head
embraces the circle of your waist
Drapes with just enough flair to make it clear
that your hips   your hips will not be ignored
You slide your perfectly manicured feet
into three inch platform heels and you rise
You rise six feet high
The lift of your cheekbones   the angle and shape of your chin
will lead you into that school filled with pride

So then   we shall call them back

Bring back the survival of escaped esclavos from your past
Draw their spirits through the gifted length of your body
Bind them to the caramel coating of your Mestiza blood

Braid the strength of their bones through your hair
Hold them to the gaze of your brown eyes
Bring their ears to the flesh of your full lips
And thank them

1976: We Who Go Home...

by Genoa Yáñez-Alaniz

we who share stringed sounds of meaning
soothing inflections   that sing ancestral songs
tell legends of family lore y La Lechuza

We follow intonations of aromas to heated comal
to fresh homemade corn tortillas wrapped
around salt   y chocolate con canela stirred
thick into earthen mugs

Sounds undulate   highs and lows
roll off the tongues and tease
as Familia plays Lotería

Corre y se va corriendo
takes on new meaning

I am silent
I question words I am told not to say
words not spoken in English

I question the words of my mother
the prayers   the lullabies   consejos

I question the songs of my father
the songs he sings at weddings
at quinceañera celebrations

Even the music he composes with acordión
y guitarra have a language I am told to abandon
 At school we are shamed and ridiculed for our accents
as Spanish loses its home   on our tongues

We no longer hold words for spaces of comfort
for tradition   for things and people we love
corridos   hermanitos madrinas abuelos
Tia Lucia cocinando   calabacita con pollo y fideo
maíz machacado con mantequilla   cabrito horneado

Our mothers feel
the sting of rejection

as accents disappear
as we move on toward becoming
Other

Children with different ondas
Children navigating new identities new names
Children told to abandon language and cultura

Children who will grow up
and eventually
find   their way

back home

Acaso yo también voy a desaparecer?/Is it true that I, too, will disappear?"
Frontexto
Octavio Quintanilla

PROSA/PROSE

El Cañon Aravaipa

by Maria Teresa Acevedo

During the early 1970s, the Bureau of Land Management, Defenders of Wild Life and Nature Conservancy were three agencies with complementary intentions to preserve various aspects of nature, land and water use in the Aravaipa East Canyon. The Bureau of Land Management deemed much of Guadalupe Salazar's patent and lease land a primitive wilderness area to be preserved for the greater public good. These three entities had internal conflicts about their own self interests and policies. Several upper canyon ranchers quickly sold to Defenders of Wild Life. Guadalupe Salazar was not willing to sell. The sale of other ranches begin to create access issues to Guadalupe's grazing lands. The Salazar family attended public hearings related to preservation with little knowledge of the legal expertise representing BLM, Defenders of Wildlife and Nature Conservancy in those hearings. The Salazars spoke on their own behalf. Ultimately, continued primitive area policies from government and private organizations forced the Salazar family to sell their ancestral lands or face the ultimate act of Eminent Domain consequences. The Salazar family lost their ranch land for making a living. Today the 30 year conflict over the Aravaipa water rights continues. Water necessary to support the urban development in the greater Gilbert and Phoenix area now plague the wondrous cañon.

My grandfather, Guadalupe Salazar, had a devotion to food, visitors and nature. If a stranger made it to the farthest point in the cañon where my abuelo's home stood, his immediate command to my mother was *Lola, caliente los frijoles, tortillas y café*. He welcomed any stranger to his table, asked if he needed any gasoline, water before he hiked the land or drove the 45 miles of dirt road back to the main highway.

One summer day in early 1970, a tall lanky gabacho suited in cowboy gear arrived at my grandfather's doorstep. Grandpa tipped his vaquero's hat and extended a hand shake for the welcoming saludos. His hand was refused. He then offered café and a meal at his kitchen table, another traditional welcoming gesture. Also refused. It was in that moment Guadalupe (Lupe) knew that his family, his ancestors and cañon trails would be rewritten. His intimate relations with the wilderness would change. The cañon was now under scientific study. The urban cowboy at his doorstep was the new conservation manager for Defenders of Wildlife, a well-known writer and newly-minted envionmentalist seeking to preserve his new found love of southwest lands for people like him. This literary Easterner turned wilderness *chota*.

My grandfather's Aravaipa cañon is no longer a place where steep volcanic walls echo comedic carcajadas at his family's affectionate expense. In 1894 Guadalupe Salazar was born in the eastern Aravaipa cañon lands of Arizona. His ancestors were the first ranch settlers living deep in the cañon. It no longer holds his sense of place, no longer a place where canyon walls hear evening stories. Lively cowboy boots and bare feet no longer scratch the earth to accordion and guitarrón rhythms.

Over a century ago, he entered the silent world of wilderness along the batamote banks of the Rio Aravaipa. Thousand foot cathedral cliffs cradled him into his only world. A river of ancient Apache caves sheltered his eyes as wide open as water. His understanding of water was of silent currents, clouds and ripples shimmering like crystals. Earth miracles.

En el tiempo de los aguaceros, Guadalupe and his family took shelter on cliff ledges to watch the transformation of their familiar landscapes float down river in the raging flood waters. Pa Lupe recognized what trees had fallen from which location, whose Jeep fell prey to the waters. He knew plant so well, he knew which was used for shampoo that would not appear in spring as well as which years the creek vero (watercress) would bloom early or late.

Along thousand year old waters, he rode for thousands of days through nature's cycles which guided his life. He was a pharmacist of sorts. He knew well the pharmacopia wilderness offered for food and for medicinal healing. Guadalupe was a ganadero who worked long grueling hours on horseback in a wilderness of beauty. He was a vaquero who knew when a bird like a Peregrine falcon or an owl would appear before they appeared. Buddha-like, his vision and intuition was honed sharp by living in intimacy with his environment.

He rode where his Opata grandfather and great-grandfather rode in the same Sono- ra and San Pedro Rio riparianscapes, along cliffs where crepuscular-colored caves were once *recamaras* to Apache families, caves where *golondrina* and canyon wren notes descend into water song, where braceros sat along cave ledges for their night smokes. Where his alcoholic son Llemo slept to protect him from the smell of his *ba- canora* breath.

When Edward Abby and his environmental myth makers arrived to protect the wilder- ness from my grandfather's family, the Westering monkey wrench gang took over. Armed with science and romanticism and hungry for fame, their arrival in our cañon insured the destruction of our indigenous vaquero culture. Preservation. To Abbey, his friends and the environmental groups, it was a victory. It was a brutal blow to our family life. Our family saw, in action, the dominant culture's machismo of wealth accumulation that prevailed over our ancestral life. *Eminent Domain* was a disaster for many native cultures, like ours, who were forced to sell their lands. Guadalupe's ancestry was made invisible.

This was the death of his rancheria culture.

The Salazar family's original oral stories of nature rooted in the cañon and their intimate life with nature were replaced by an elitist self-righteousness and a watershed of impossible paper work. The descent of these environmentalists into the cañon was marked by the same conquistador energy as the Gold Rush. The well-meaning environmentalists created chaos for my grandfather's culture. His family now had to buy permissions they could not afford to marvel at "wilderness" they had considered home, a home that had always sheltered them.

Like any rise and fall, my abuelo Guadalupe and his ancestor's foot prints have been erased in favor of preservation. What remains are family ghosts shimming on álamo's leaves, sicómoro trees' alabaster trunks guiding the night, laughter rolling atop río ripples, horse hooves splashing diamonds of water skyward. Today, comaradas of planet protection breath in the astonishment of the cañons raw beauty.

EL DORADO

by Ciara Alfaro

My great-grandparents performed séances to convince strangers of the miracles they needed to be convinced of. At a price, of course. Because this is capitalism and miracle-workers need new alligator boots, too.

Here's how it went: My great-grandparents would shut their blackout curtains, welcome strangers with temporarily thick wallets into their séance room, and seat them around the table. Most of these strangers were Mexicanos, too, because some Catholics believe in this kind of thing. My great-grandparents would hold hands with these mourners like they knew them. Crystal balls, tarot cards, and Saints Candles lined the room, for effect.

Sometimes, on the weekends when their parents were at work, my dad and uncle would sit in on the session. They were the perfect age—young enough to still believe in magic, but old enough to do the things they were told. So they'd help with the small parts: turning on the music, blowing out a candle. All that really mattered was that they didn't fuck any of it up. Being a kid was no excuse for ruining the magic of a séance.

The curandero, my great-grandfather, would begin to chant in Spanish. Mariachi music played so faintly it almost wasn't there at all. After a few beats, when the mourners' palms began to sweat, the curandero released their hands and asked them to open their eyes. It was so dark in there, grainy with their memories floating in the air.

The trick to performing a fake resurrection, my great-grandparents learned, is to wait. If they waited just long enough, these mourners would enter a golden hour of desperation—a fleeting moment when they were willing to believe anything.

That's when the show would really begin. The mourners' eyes squinted against the darkness, their disbelief and relief marrying together, because they could finally see it: the miracle they came to find. Glowing white orbs danced across the darkness, slow and calm. The mourners thought through their tears that these orbs were their dead child. *Our baby is here and he is happy to see us*, they probably thought. The orbs moved closer, then further, always just out of reach. They were deliberate and they were beautiful.

Here's the truth: all people really want is for someone to convince them that their Catholicism is real and not as scary as their tía makes it sound. That a mother's child who died of pneumonia at the age of four isn't lost wandering the dusty depths of purgatory. That one day, when his niece walks into her grandma's living room on Mondays, she can look at the portrait of her uncle in his turquoise shirt pouting the way children do and not think that he is resentful of her. That little Marco is eating chicken and rice somewhere, too, and isn't offended that his family never thinks of him during their dinner prayers.

This reassurance disappears when the illusion of the séance breaks. There were only a handful of times when my great-grandparents got caught in their lies. When they did, it went something like this: the lights flashed on suddenly, lighting up the room with white, in the middle of the ceremony. Retinas burning, the mourners thought, *Is this divine intervention?* No, they realized once their eyes adjusted to the room around them. There were no orbs, no ghosts, no magic. Just a man with fancy boots and a startled expression, waving around a dark linen sheet covered in bits with glow-in-the-dark paint.

The worst way to have your heart broken is in a way that is comedic. My great-grandfather made these people blinded by hope into fools. Their friends, family, and neighbors told them to know better. It made them so angry, to not only be the fool, but to also be too embarrassed to tell anyone about it afterwards. Their grief was now buried in twice the silence, and it was enough to make them want to kill someone.

And these mourners tried.

They lunged across the table, knocking down Saints Candles, spilling wax, moving toward a chokehold, cowboy hats tipping, chairs falling, looking for blood. The clumsy scuffle was stifled by the crowded room and the memories that hung loose in it. Once the mourners were too tired to continue this fight, panting through their tears, they shoved the fake curandero and his wife, took their cowboy hats off the floor, and left.

It was my six-year-old uncle who'd turned on the lights. He stood there, frozen, hand still on the switch. I imagine his chubby childhood belly protruding over his orange corduroy quarter-lengths and a small grin on his face, not realizing the seriousness of what he'd done.

Following this incident, my dad and uncle were forced to wait in the car without air conditioning until the shows were over. My uncle got his little brown ass beat for turning on those lights. His ass was bleeding for days, they say.

My dad got his ass beat, too, just for being related to that *niño gordo*. That wasn't what he remembers the most clearly, though. It was what he saw that no one else did, without even seeking it out.

Behind the frauds and their clients screaming and wrestling and throwing crystal balls, my dad saw a ghost—a real ghost—in the corner of the room. The black thing stood there watching the madness. My dad says it was a ghost with a rectangular body, a ghost like John Wayne. It was the first ghost he'd ever seen.

He saw this ghost around their house many more times after this—swaying to the silence at the end of long hallways, standing in dark windows, watching him sleep.

When he tells me and my grandma this story at our favorite Japanese restaurant, the dark crimson booth we're sitting in seems to shrink and bring us closer together. Oak shutters block the afternoon summer sunshine from touching us. My grandma, who's usually the first to call my dad a truth-stretcher, doesn't even challenge him. She scoffs and shakes her head, then tells me she's been made to wait in the suffocatingly hot car, too.

My dad is fifty and has started to look his age for the first time in my life. He's been warning me for years that leaving for college will open my eyes to his aging, but it's finally true. His eyelids droop slightly, his decade-old paintball scars have finally re-emerged as permanent sunspots, and his black goatee is turning silver. My grandma sits next to him, small and stately, with her curly brown hair reaching out in all directions. Her face droops, too, but her skin is smooth beneath her honey colored makeup.

As the waitress brings us our check, I ask my dad if he thinks his grandparents caused their home to be haunted by making a living off the dead. He says, "Probably so." The way he says it makes me feel close to these curanderos I never knew, as if they're here with us, too. This ghost has always been my favorite: the ghost there to quietly laugh at my ancestors for thinking that any of us can fathom miracles at all.

LETY
AN EXCERPT FROM STREET OF TOO MANY STORIES, A NOVEL

by Denise Chavez

She had so many reasons.

Bobby never learned how to dance. Even now, after all these years he still did that same lame goose step that simulated rhythm. She had loved to dance and was what some called the life of the party. She was irreverent, funny, caustic and witty, like everyone else in her family. They were funny people with everyone except themselves. Cruelty to each other was rife. They couldn't help it. They grew up bitter. It came from their mother, Adoración. She was a cold and unsympathetic person. And she was a bad cook to boot. All of her children spoke of her deprecatingly. They had reason to. She wasn't there when she should have been. She favored the one son, neglecting all others.

Lety wanted to dance the way she once had. But now she used a cane. The weakness came on slowly at first and then it took over. Her steps were halting. She over-compensated and soon wouldn't be able to walk. She had once been young, once been limber. Now she was dying. Few people came to see her anymore. She was rail thin, emaciated beyond belief. She looked like a survivor from some terrible war, someone who hadn't eaten in a very long time. She couldn't eat. Everything became sour in her stomach and what she had once loved became poison to her. No more red chile, no more ice cream, no more sodas, no more no more. She ate soups now and hot oatmeal thinned out or grits or atole, a watery gruel to give her strength.

There were many reasons. She should have had a better life, a more comfortable life instead of the one she had. It had been too much of a struggle. Bobby never made a good living and after they married she couldn't work. She had wanted to, but there were the children, her mother Adoración. Mamá became her life and her cross and maybe her redemption. If she did go to Heaven, which she doubted, it would be because she had taken care of her mother for over 40 years. The lost years. The same number of years the Israelis wandered the desert looking for the Promised Land.

Her bedroom was dark and she wanted to call out but her voice was weak. When had it disappeared? She used to tell jokes, had great stories, could have been a comedian, yes, she was that funny. Now she had a mouth full of dust.

Take me to the living room she wanted to tell her daughter. All the sons had disappeared, and only a few daughters attended her now. The sons were all cowards. They couldn't stand to see her weighing sixty pounds. Sixty pounds of blood and pus. Sixty pounds of rage and ugliness. The nieces and nephews stayed away. When she saw them she insulted them and made them feel bad. Where have you been? Why haven't you come to see me? What do you see? A living skeleton? Go on, look at me. How does it feel to see a dead woman? How does that make you feel?

No one wanted her rage to touch them. So they stayed away. She was the woman who made snide remarks, the one who criticized, the one who gossiped and the one who made you feel bad because you didn't love her enough. You had loved her once, found her warm and special. You were once friends, but now you just wanted to get away from her.

She had her reasons. She was always poor when she should have been rich. She should have had a lovely home but it was always messy. She couldn't afford help, and when she did, the help helped others, never her. The help was poor girls from México who never stayed long. They always left after a week or two and never recommended anyone to take over their jobs. One of them told her to her face that she worked them too hard. And not only that, but that her sons were mujeriegos and that they were a disgraceful bunch of men. They had tried to touch her and get her to do things with them. The last girl that had worked for her told of worse things. Lety didn't believe them at first, but she later found out it was true. The girl accused her sons of trying to rape her. That's the kind of sons you have. Right then and there she asked the girl to leave and threw her clothing out the door. Liar. She was a liar.

Her brothers were that way, but not her sons. Was it true her sons had turned out like their uncles? She didn't want to think about it. The girl had provoked her sons, that was it. She was a whore. They were all whores.

It was true her daughter had several children out of wedlock. She and Bobby had sent her away, but then she came back and got pregnant again. There was no help for her. How did she become that kind of person? And yet it was that daughter who took care of Lety in her dying. She was the one who cleaned her and wiped her when she bled down there and flowed that dark black stew of blood and fecal matter. It was she who fed her the watery gruel that kept her alive for the short while she was able to eat.

Now Lety couldn't eat and. . .yes, she had her reasons. She had tried to be a good mother and she was and wasn't. Her children did love her, but not fully. She was cold like her mother, Adoración. It couldn't be helped. She carried the hardness in her genes. She wasn't fully capable of loving. She and her brothers didn't know what real love was. And yet. . .there was Bobby. There was that time when she was special and alive and full of joy. She wanted to earn a college degree, become a professional woman, have a nice home and land to build on. She had wanted those things that were never granted her.

She had her reasons. They were many. They were profound reasons and they outweighed whatever good came her way. No reason to struggle with it anymore. No reason to say yes or no or maybe so. Mamá was gone now. After all those years of hard work and her being the sad, barely breathing part of the house. She was gone suddenly like that. After all the time of uncertainly and struggle. Children leave and don't visit. Daughters find ways to shame and sons become enemies. So do other relatives. Some of them you talk to and some of them you don't. The ones you dislike avoid you and you them. You chalk it up to their personalities and their unforgiving ways but really, it was you who was the one disliked. You had your reasons.

You tried to protect yourself. You wanted the best for your family. You tried to give your children hope. But you had so little yourself. You just got tired. Everything became that living organism inside of you that wanted to scream.

You had your reasons. No one understood. If they did, they turned away when you started to tell them why. No one listened. How would they know? Yes, you were bitter. You had your reasons. There was too much disappointment. Too much worry. Too much lack. Too much disorder. Everyone clamoring.   The inside of you got lost. You never danced again the way you had danced before. With abandon and with joy.

Those days long gone. Those days a faraway past of longing for what would never be. Sorrowful and distant, that was you. Still is you. You have your reasons. No one to listen to you except those few. If even. God disappeared. He stepped outside and walked away. He walked down the street and didn't look back. He went out the back door and slammed it shut. He declared bankruptcy and left you without a dime. The dime was never yours. The dime was borrowed. It should have been yours, but it wasn't. It belonged to someone else. And you knew it. Bobby knew it. Your children knew it, all of them. They lived a second hand life. They were imposters. All of them faking it. All of them pretending to love. You had your reasons. And they knew it. They had their reasons and you knew why. It's a good thing you won't live to see. It would probably be disappointment. What else? I could go on and on. I wanted to say so many things to so many people. I held back when I should have spoken. I spoke when I should have held back. I was hard and there was a reason. My people were hard and unforgiving and unloving and cold. And yet, I remember. I do remember some times that Mamá held me close. Most of the time she was so cold. She couldn't help herself. She had such a hard time. Dad would go away, wander off, just like all the men in this family, well, except for Bobby, they'd just flat out disappear, and when you needed them they would be gone, just like that. Those were my brothers. My uncles. My father. And my sisters, well, they were rich or dead. We had to stay alive because it was unthinkable to give up just like that. We had our reasons. We were proud people who had nothing and deserved more. We came from proud people who once had. Once owned. Once knew. Once loved. Now we were bereft. What happened? Who was the woman who cursed us and brought down the vengeance to our family? She was in the past of us. She had her reasons. And that man? Who was he? Our great-great grandfather? The one who began it all. How was it we lost our way? Who cursed us and brought us shame? And why? They had their reasons. Who and what they were I don't know, will never know. I do know this. They had their reasons.

It was raining. Lety could hear the drops outside her window. It was late and still she couldn't sleep. There was much to be reconciled. The dead wanted to talk to her and explain what they could. She tried to listen. They had so much to say and one would think in an eternity of time they would have composed the words. But no. They had their reasons. The dead don't speak with their mouths. Their mouths are full of dust. Their eyes speak and sometimes the eyes of the dead aren't the eyes of those you once loved. Other people come to inhabit the forms of those you once loved, tried to love. They appear and then disappear and you never know when they are speaking truth and if they are the people they pretend to be. After a while you do discern that the person in front of you is not the person in front of you but someone else. Evil has a way of masking. It is clever. It manipulates emotion. It takes advantage of longing. It deceives. But you continue to outrun the darkness and after a while, the door closes and the spirit tires and goes away because it has been discovered to be a lie. It's almost seems too late or nearly too late. Today's the day. This is the moment. Listen. The dead come back to tell you secrets. Sisters, brothers, why have you left me with your stories? Go on, look at me. I'm listening.

Instead of horror I feel pity. And the story isn't the one I thought I would be telling. Within me moves a great sadness for your loss. I'm so sorry. I couldn't hear you.

The rain?

It's stopped.

THE DISAPPEARING

by Vanessa Bernice De La Cruz

Socorro Sanchez was in love, so in love, she skipped around in her tank top and flannel, combat boots hitting the sidewalk in a way she hadn't felt since she was 13. She sang not only in the shower, but at the pet store where she worked part-time and at the panaderia where she worked the rest. Her co-workers, sweet viejitas with memories of their husbands in their youth, stories of their first love, or anecdotes about the old man who hit on them at church last Friday, chirped their approval and ruffled her hair, pleased that she had something to look forward to. Life was hard for women, it didn't matter where you were born or how good your English was, life was hard and you found solace where you could. There's a reason telenovelas are a source of comfort to millions of hope-deprived people around the world.

And Chris, well, he was a good guy. That was a bonus. He was genuinely good, and Socorro could've picked worse but she didn't. He brought her flowers to work and was very expressive, and sure, maybe he was a little older than her and maybe he forgot her birthday, and to wish her a Merry Christmas, and forgot her last name on more than one occasion and sometimes he confused her with his ex, but he always said, "Good morning," and "Goodnight" and he once wrote her a love song with this band he was in but eventually got kicked out of. She played a recording of the song for las viejitas, who murmured their approval.

"Be careful," the oldest, Maria, told her. "La vida es dura, y el dolor lo hace todavía más." But the other ladies hushed her.

"Déjala en paz," they said. "Mira que feliz esta la niña. No la desilusiones."

But there was no way Socorro could've been disillusioned. She believed in love. Believed in Chris. Believed that this was the happily ever after she had secretly, in all her rants against love, all her rants against monogamy and tradition, wished for. She believed and when she was at the peak of believing, well, that's when her house disappeared.

She honestly didn't care, not at first anyway. She wasn't really living there. She spent most nights with her older cousins. Spent some of the really bad nights with some of the viejitas. She only went home to kiss her abuela and restock the go-bag she kept in the panaderia's locker room. Not that she'd ever call it a go-bag. The first thing she learned as a Good Daughter™ was that one should never call shit for what it was and no amount of rebellion or Americanized thinking would uproot the lessons imprinted on her subconscious since birth.

So that brings us to the first time.

See, the first time it happened, Chris was walking her home. They'd been dating for a few months now. Met each other's parents, each other's friends, each other's favorite mango vendor and tamale lady. Everyone knew it was serious and the seriousness of it began to seep into their nightmares. Those nightmares scared them so much, they became intent on making things work out for the better of their futures, the better of their dreams, to avoid having to answer, "What happened?" for the rest of their lives.

And well they were walking. His side bag hitting, almost painfully against her waist. They were glued together, their eyes focused inward while they tried to pry the necessary parts of themselves out for the other to see. He hated broccoli, she had a fear of clowns. He'd once been cheated on, they both feared their lives would amount to disappointment. Both had a tendency to let themselves be ruled by emotion. He hated the way the sauce gets stuck on a bottle of ketchup.

They shared this, hand in hand while they walked through her neighborhood, a whole 10 minute drive down Alameda away from his. They'd left his car parked at the closest library, spent their day off laughing between the bookshelves. But now it was time for the sun to set so they decided it was time to take advantage of the sunshine that was left and step into the afternoon breeze. They walked slowly, casually, down the sidewalk of streets she had known her whole life, not intent on getting her home now, just intent on getting her home eventually.

But Socorro's feet were hurting, and eventually was taking too long.

"Will you miss me tomorrow?"

"Yes."

"Pinky promise?"

"Yes."

Reassured, he smiled. "Okay, I trust you."

"I think we missed my house, Chris." She looked over her shoulder, had been looking for a while. Was too distracted by trying to find home in the coming darkness to be attentive to his questions. Too attentive to his questions to find her house. There was the block. And there was the street sign that got hit by a car only a year earlier. They never fixed it and it still stood crooked, always looking like it was going to fall into one of the cracks in the sidewalk. And there. There was the neighbor's car, an old Buick he polished every Saturday morning. She tried to see the roof where Christmas lights flickered year-round. Tried to spot the neighbor's altar, lit up on the porch by candles. Tried to hear her ever-arguing family. Couldn't find any of it.

"We missed it?"

"Yeah. It's back there. Let's turn back, yeah?"

"I think this is a sign."

"What's the sign?"

"You should spend the night at my place"

"Chris. My family would freak out."

"You're in your twenties!"

"Dude, I *just* turned twenty! And it's different for you. We've talked about this." She leaned into his shoulder to kiss him but he pulled away. They were no longer glued against each other.

"I mean, what about Julie?" She asked. "Julie just asked for permission and everyone was like, okay, you want to run off with a boy for a night, stay there forever! And then they changed the locks."

"That was a long time ago, and wasn't that her dad? Socorro you can't judge every situation by one person who isn't even in the house anymore."

"No but my mom's still there, and so is her new husband and so is my aunt and my other tio and their spouses and even my grandma who is the sweetest, most open-minded of all of them still thinks being with a guy leads to ruin or some shit. The only tradition my family holds on to is their control of their daughters."

"But when did you decide to start caring about tradition? And it doesn't even have to be a big deal, tell them you're staying at your cousin's. Or with a friend."

"They'll know."

"How? You're never even home."

"They know everything. Trust me Chris, they'll find out."

Chris sighed, this heavy, dramatic thing that she hadn't learned to hate yet. "I just don't think that you actually want to go home, y'know?"

She didn't. She thought about the yells that would keep her awake on work nights and the music they'd blast at full volume on her days off. The never-ending stream of noise. Her cousins and siblings never deciding if they were cutting ties or growing roots. Her aunts and uncles, noisier than all of them, storming in and out like children on some days and bigger children on others. And her grandma was growing tired. Tired, tired, tired and would be moving out of state in just a few weeks.

She didn't want to go back to her tiny bedroom that was once a laundry room, twin bed taking up most of the floor space. She didn't want to go back to waking up breathless because the weight of the family history and her own inability to figure out what she wanted from life was weighing heavily on her lungs. She considered moving out, who didn't? But rent was so expensive anywhere else. A studio cost twice as much here as it did in the valley, but she didn't have enough money to move to the valley. And who would even want to live there anyway? She didn't want to go to her house.

"Socorro, come home with me." Chris was holding her hand and whispering in her ear and she knew how it would end because it was how it always ended. With everyone, not just with him but especially with him. He'd get upset when she said no, would tell her she should claim her independence, she'd say he was right but it wasn't time yet. He'd ask when. She'd say she wasn't sure. He'd have to rethink their relationship, he'd question her maturity. She wanted the negative feelings to go away, wanted to go back to singing and skipping. It wasn't time, but would it ever be?

She looked back at her house but couldn't see it. "What if they kick me out?"

"I already told you I want you to move in with me."

He kissed her. A Maybe died in her throat. Socorro Sanchez did not go home that night.

They couldn't find her house the next morning. He drove her, sleepy and in his pajamas. She still wore clothes from the day before. They assumed they'd missed it. Maybe drove too fast, were too tired. They stopped for tamales and champurrado. Decided to go back to his place and nap before work. Half-asleep, he held her against him and said, "Quedate."

So she did.

She didn't come back for clothes because his sister was almost the same size as she was. And what his sister couldn't provide in the form of hand-me-downs, she got at thrift stores or the little plaza down the street from his. It didn't matter that she had to forego her flannels for polo shirts or that nothing ever seemed to fit the way it should. Even if it was the right size, it never fit against her body the way her favorite shirt did, the way her favorite jeans fit. She spent that first night and countless nights after that with the feeling that she didn't fit in her body. She was too big or too small. Her bones weren't sitting the way that bones should sit.

She texted her mom and called her stepdad but neither of them responded. She tweeted her abuela. Called her uncle.

Socorro had never spent a night at a guy's before. She thought it was safe to assume that her family was angry. Julie told her not to worry about it. Mayra said, "Hey, hey, hey, don't cry. It's going to be okay. I've been in this exact same spot, I've been through it and whatever happens, it's going to be okay. I mean even abuela went through this when she met my abuelo. Then abuelo did it to our moms. But the difference is, I'm here for you. Julie's here for you. Belen is here for you. This entire generation is here. Whatever happens, whatever you need. Aquí estamos, babygirl."

Socorro stopped crying long enough to whisper a thank you at her phone.

"And it could be worse right? At least you and Chris are in love and Chris is a good guy and he's good to you, right?" Silence.

"Socorro he is good to you?"

"Yeah Mayra, don't worry, yeah?"

Neither of them had been home in a while. Neither of them could get ahold of anyone either.

And Chris, he was distracting. His presence numbed her to everything else. She lost the job at the pet store after the owner decided to close shop and move back to Guadalajara, so she started working full time at la panaderia. Las viejitas started quitting after years of asking for better pay. Some of them went to other bakeries. Others started working fast food. They all seemed happier. Only she and Maria remained. They didn't talk much but they worked together, ignoring the snide comments of the new girls, trying to ignore the unpredictability of their constantly changing line of supervisors. Occasionally exchanging looks that said, "No te preocupes.Everything's okay."

She went back to Chris's place covered in frustration and sweat and exhaustion. He drew a bath and she quickly forgot everything. Home, work, the knot in her stomach that grew heavier whenever she went outside. Chris lived in a nice neighborhood, slightly more suburban, slightly less below the poverty line. It was still California, rent was still insanely high, but his family had a garage they'd converted into a studio apartment. They slept there, stayed up late watching movies and eating cereal. It was a dream, a dream in the way her younger self dreamed of things. In the way her favorite novels taught her to long for heartbreak and hardship and novelas taught her that toxic relationships were just relationships.

But Socorro missed her abuela. Missed the woman who'd taught her to braid her hair before going to sleep every night. Missed her gentle smiles and kind teases. The way her eyes glittered whenever she said anything she knew was clever and the way she read Neruda while she stood over the stove. She missed her favorite shirt and favorite jeans. Missed her tiny room where she could stare at the ceiling and secretly wish for romance and Better Things. She knew she was living in the Better Future she had wished for. There was love and independence, stable work and sleep.

Two months passed. The things she missed began to haunt her nightmares.

Socorro borrowed Chris's car shortly after the dreams started. She'd had nightmares of her childhood home burning down, falling into a sinkhole, being carried away by snakes or crows. Being lost across the planet. Sinking into the middle of the sea. Don't get me wrong, Socorro didn't expect any of that to happen, but she just had to check, just to be sure, you know?

So she drove and drove but never seemed to get there. She drove past it by accident. Drove back. There was the neighbor's house. The street sign. The other neighbor. The old lady across the street. She took out her ID to check her own address. She'd lived there her whole life except for a year when she was 6 and her not quite-divorced-yet parents moved out to the valley and then quickly moved back. So she'd grown up there. Lost her first tooth. Ridden her first bike.

She typed her address into Google Maps. 1840 East. It should be there. The red house next door was still there. The grey one on the other side was still there. She called every family member on her contacts list but no one answered. She tried to find parking but it was late and a Friday so parking was almost impossible. She found something down the street, but by the time she parked, Chris called.

"Hey, where are you? I miss you. Come home." So, she did.

Months passed and she drove by each Friday but she could never find the house. Her calls went unanswered, her texts went unread. She began a weekly ritual of driving into the library parking lot to cry after each failed attempt.

At first, Chris was understanding. He'd soothe and comfort her and would even go look for the house himself but was always unsuccessful. The street was closed. The car would break down. His GPS wasn't working. He, like her, assumed her family was mad at her. Maybe the stress of that anger left her unable to find it. Maybe the property had been sold off. She was prone to anxiety. It was anxiety and her own unwillingness to grow up.

So his soothing whispers gave way to exasperated shouts. She was annoying. The way she worried. The way she smiled. The way she ate. She no longer sang, no longer sang at work. No longer sang in the shower. No longer sang at all. She became self-conscious under his watchful gaze. She couldn't remember feeling this isolated any time before.

Some of the viejitas at work returned but they stopped ruffling her hair and began patting her shoulders sympathetically. They recommended novelas, having children, going to church, running as far as she could make it. She swallowed her desperation. She no longer felt young and traded her combat boots for sneakers. Her jewel-toned lipsticks for muted tones. Chris would buy her clothes that never quite fit right. He never liked the things she'd buy for herself. He preferred her hair curly and she preferred it straight.

It was two years before she read the messages. Two years of dozens of Fridays spent crying. Two years of dwindling enchantment. Wondering if she had imagined her life before Chris. If the family she had been so eager to run away from was a figment of her imagination.

The messages.

He was in love with a girl he kept pictures of on his phone. He told the girl he loved her and she told him she loved him too. They were planning a life together through elaborate double texts while Socorro was at work. They were planning a life and he didn't deny it. Made no attempt. See it was actually Socorro's fault because she was so needy. Because she cried too often. Because she was always anxious. Because she was so insecure. Because she was always at work.

She accepted his explanations silently. Stopped looking for Home. Stopped looking in the mirror. There was not a single piece of clothing she wore comfortably now.

She slept by his side for six more months and finally saved up enough for a deposit on a studio somewhere. She apartment-hunted while he looked at his phone and she pretended to ignore the flurry of messages on the screen. She looked downtown and inland, by the beach and by the freeway. Down the street from her old neighborhood where no one seemed to remember her. She decided. She would live there, down the street.

She lost the keys to the studio the day she moved in. It was raining and she didn't have an umbrella. Her bag full of belongings had been moved from Chris's place to this tiny room in the morning before work and now she couldn't find the key and the viejitas had brought tequila to celebrate her freedom at work and so she was drunk and could barely stand and she'd spent the whole day feeling liberated but now she just felt like a facsimile of an adult. She could see the roof where the Christmas lights flickered year-round.

She stumbled down the sidewalk. Past the broken street sign. Past the buick and altar. Home wasn't there. The neighbor's was. Everything else was but home wasn't.

"Where are you, stupid house?!" She yelled into the sky. Decided to sit down and cry on the sidewalk. "Where the fuck are you?!"

She cried for hours and hours and hours after that. The sky darkened and grew light again. It rained and rained. No one passed by. No one looked out their window. Her tears formed a stream around her, flooding the street and every car parked nearby. Soaking her sneakers so that they floated off into the distance. Soaking her jeans and her polo shirt and her hair and so before she knew it, she was floating in an ocean of her own tears and precipitation.

The sky remained dark for three days and her eyes became too dry to continue crying. They closed and she slept, peacefully. Quietly. Full of love for the girl she had been before. For the youth she had lost. For the dwindling enchantment.

When she woke up, it was still raining but the house was right there in front of her. Where it had always been. The Christmas lights were up. Her aunts screamed at each other from the second floor and she could hear her cousins laughing in the kitchen. The key to her studio was in the pocket of her pants.

Mouth open, she began to cry again. Ran to the door of the family house. Considered going to the studio to shower first, to grab a jacket but what if this disappeared again? The knob was unlocked. She knocked anyway. Could hear the house grow quiet. Her abuela answered the door.

"Mi'ja you're getting wet ¿Dónde estabas?! ¡Metate que te estas mojando!"

TALE FROM TENACATITA

by Leticia Del Toro

Petra watches her father, Oscar, kick a mound of broken shards on the road to the posada. The shards are red bits like a giant eggshell from a mosaic in the earth. Petra examines her father's target and notices the furrowed sand: tire tracks probably, torn in from a narco's vehicle. She and Oscar are just off a bus from Vallarta. Petra marvels at the open sky and the soft surge of waves she hears beyond the road. Surviving ten days with her father in a fishing village seems impossible, yet she vowed to help him return home.

"There's another one crushed," Petra says.

"Maybe la mar se salió and the sea washed them in." He puzzles at the fragments of crushed shells.

Suddenly Petra sees a defiant surviving claw.

"No, the roads are totally dry. These are jaibas de tierra. Mom used to catch these and cook them."

"Good, dinner ideas. I'm all out of plata. How about you get cash from the maquinita and pay for the bungalow?"

She follows him into the front office of the posada. It's their first trip together since her mother, Erminia, died last fall.

"I want to show you exactly which cove to throw my ashes out from," he had said on the ride from the airport. "Forget those expensive burials. I'm telling you now, I want to be one with the huachinango."

Back home, only three weeks a widower, he had raged through every bar in town before hitching rides to Salinas. Sometimes in the morning Petra would find trashy women fixing themselves coffee in her mother's kitchen. She ran them off and Oscar hated her for it.

There were men in town that respected her father. They had unloaded sugar at the refinery silos together. Petra had answered the front door at odd hours to panicked men, saying "Come quick, your father's in a fight!"

If it had only been humiliating, she might have been able to stomach her father's adventures. Though every time the phone rang her head spun. The constant calls from neighbors and compadres pleading, "come quick" worked on her psyche. In dreams she'd find him bloodied and beaten beyond recognition. She pulled him from underneath moss-covered planks at low tide or she dug into earth with bare hands, reaching out to him as if he were buried alive. How often it seemed he wanted such a fate.

In the reception hall of the posada, light reverberates off the huge leaves dangling maniacally into doorways. Green at every angle suggests more trees than sky. Beyond the green, luminous patches of blue touch the cove, connecting it to the world that exists only beyond the unmarked roads. The main highway buzzes with four-wheel drives, huge Dinas and ten-seater comunales. She'd wondered how many of those taxi vans decked with crosses, stringed lights, and prints of buxom Aztec virgins circulated legitimately and which whisked people away to grisly ransoms.

While the coast seems lawless, it is also gorgeous and humid. Velvet air caresses her skin and works soft kinks into her hair. She reminds herself to enjoy this part, as they will soon head inland to Jalisco.

She knows the routine from past family reunions. The family would gather to be blessed by the bishop of Guadalajara. The men would sparkle: slick-heeled licenciados with timeshares in Manzanillo. Their burgundy coiffed wives luciendo with elegance would pose the constant question, "When will you marry, Petra?"

Living with her father is not what she envisioned for herself, but if she were to move out he would let the house go to ruin, invaded by junkies, winos and meth heads who only see an old man with a healthy pension.

Before leaving she wanted to buy him a good suit, but he wouldn't go to the store with her. The stink and grime that settled into his wardrobe could not be laundered. She no longer picked his clothes visually. Whiskey and grief shrunk him between shirt sizes. She could change his clothes, but not his gaze: heavy lidded eyes sunk deep in the sockets like half opened clams.

In the office of the posada, Oscar introduces himself in the old way, "Buenas tardes, señor. Oscar Ordoñez Villareal, para servirle. We come from 859 Monroe Avenue, Monterey, del otro lado."

Earlier she tried to discourage his banter. "We're targets here, papi. They'll post YouTube videos of you to extract money from your familia and who the hell will care?"

He introduces his daughter, "Mi hija, Petra, the last of four. La encargué pa' la soledad."

She is used to his formal introductions. What is new is the admission of a loneliness foretold, how she was born to relieve it.

The allure of the one-road fishing village is not its quiet. The water vendors and gas trucks blare their anthems, like birthing cows, *"A-GUA!"* A carnival jingle punctuates an amplified, "El gaaaaas!" A rooster crows, deafening for those who crave the language of the wind.

Oscar and Petra walk south towards the edge of Tenacatita beach. They find a lone palapa near the shore where a creeping lagoon meets the coastline. A young woman rocks her baby in a hammock. A weathered couple sits behind the swinging baby, veiled in mosquito net.

Petra orders a lime soda and Oscar takes a Tecate. He wants to talk but the palapa owner won't look his way. Oscar's expression changes. He makes a trout face.

"I'll rent a boat in the morning," he mutters.

"You think you can afford one at gringo prices? You should buy a spot on someone's lancha instead."

"I'm no stranger. Who you think I am? Chingado! Es mi país."

"Alright, calm down." She looks to the lagoon and sees dark slick ridges rising from the surface: dorsal bumps, then the head of a crocodile.

"Look at that."

His eyes are on the baby's mother, not on the waters and the rising crocodile.

"No, eso no es nada. You shoulda seen the animalones used to be out here when I was a boy." He laughs rousing the elder near the baby.

"Oiga amigo, what's his name?" Oscar asks.

"Se llama Panchita," the old man replies.

Oscar immediately explains where he's from. The young woman narrows her eyes at her patrons.

"I can't wait. I'm going for a swim," Petra says.

"Watch out for cocodrilos. They even like flaquitas," Oscar says.

Petra leaves him chatting at the table and runs off towards the ocean. She takes off her shorts and runs into the surf, a t-shirt covering her swimsuit. As a child she came here twice a year, in summer and winter. Back then she was free to wander for hours, absorbed in play with the local children. They jauntily scavenged the coast from La Manzanilla to Barra de Navidad. How her feet always felt newly polished, soft and perfect after those trips! Yet now when she wore sandals in the plazas people stared at her damaged feet.

The azure waters soothe her. She had dismissed the heat beaming down on the road they took to this cove. The sun, relentless shot the magnet of her tight ponytail and the nape of her neck. In spite of the waves, she feels the scorch trapped in her skin and pressing outward. An ache pulses from her temples like a machete cleaved on a green coco.

In the water she's buoyant and light. She lowers her back and shoulders, then her head rests cradled in the water. In this little cove, there are no crashing swells only the caw and dive of pelicans and the silver glints of damselfish between her limbs. She swims further up the coast so that the palapa seems tiny. Here the waves break harder. She swims under a wave, just beyond the breakers where the white froth can toss and wring you out, revolcándote. She swims to where she cannot touch, treading toward the rise and ripple.

She breathes just to reach the blue green wall, the sun alive within. Each time the wall rises, she tosses her body forward to ride the jeweled illuminated curve. The force rushes through until the sea is inside her.

Here with the thrash and suck of the waves, the cyclical throb calls her to heed its power. Her mind is loose. She remembers how it felt to have a man inside her. Just at his edge of letting go, she nudged the tightening, summoned that quick clenching of her walls around him, the caving in and the release. She could lose herself to the ocean.

Oscar waves his baseball cap from the shore, "Órale, let's go!"

He stands next to a wooden sign planted just a few yards away. It reads: *Peligro la mar se sale. En caso de temblor o inundación, corre a tierra alta.* She wonders about the physics of how the ocean leaves and returns raging.

She scowls at her father. She's reminded of all the times he yanked her away from her Abuelita Lupe's home. Maybe they stayed an hour, just long enough for a taco of nopales and queso fresco. Oscar always said Abuelita was too poor to host them properly. But Petra loved to wrap herself in her Abuela's sunworn rebozos, smelling of maiz and the smoke of burning canefields.

She glances back and sees a small, vapor of a man.

She dips her head back and breaks the surface. She breathes and clears the salt from her eyes. She sees him standing again, surrounded by thick adobe, the first walls of the rancho in Sayula.

"Go back, I want to swim," she calls out.

The wall is growing, a mirage of deep highland earth, pounded and shaped by the hands of young indios. Her father runs into the doorway and reappears as a child, curly haired, with stocky legs and bug eyes. He runs down the shore with a basket of bread.

She needs to run after him but feels weighted in the thrash of the waves. She crawls through the breakwater and heads for the adobe.

She enters through the doorway where she saw her child-father exit and recognizes the interior of the Villareal home.

She glances back to the young girl near the palapa. She raises a green coconut over her head. The woman yells to Petra, "Ven, por tu coco helado."

She doesn't remember having ordered a coco.

Fourth of July, the summer she turned eleven, she arrived at the Villareal rancho late that night before being rushed through a dark corridor. She blamed the long ride through the snaky mountain roads past the Nevado of Colima for the searing pain in her legs. She soothed herself to sleep with visions of fireworks.

The next morning she woke to a deep pull in her lower back, as if she had swallowed huge hot stones that settled in her spine. When she pulled out of bed and stood up, she felt a stickiness in her panties. She recognized the dark stained mess her mother said would come. Couldn't this have waited until the end of the summer?

She thought of her tías discovering the sheets. Maybe she could sneak off to the lavadero and wash the bedding before anyone noticed. She wished her mother would appear. The clang of silverware in the courtyard, footsteps, someone sweeping, the patter of fast hands torteando, all resounded from the courtyard. Suddenly a child's scream tore through the familiar sounds, "Puto buey, puto, puto, ¡yaaaaa!"

Someone snapped a leather belt. "¡Cállate, Clementina!"

The belt was for the little cousin, the one they called La Gorda for her chubby stature.

The child pushed open the door and slammed it. She balled her naked self up in a corner. She roared then sprung into a throaty snarl as if she wanted to run up and pounce on Petra.

Petra sat up in shock and Clementina jumped over the footboard. The child dug a stubby finger into her chest demanding, "Y tú, ¿quién eres cabrona?"

From the licorería on the corner, Oscar buys El Jimador. He takes the tequila to the second floor patio and fills a juice glass.

"Do you want to get some huachinango or ceviche?"

"It's not good here," he says.

"Then why'd we come here?"

"To rest."

"Well, I'm going to see what these ladies are selling." Earlier she had spied some women setting up a thin metal grill.

"¿No vas a acompañarme?"

"No, don't have no money."

"You've got money for this." She taps the base of the bottle.

"Mi amigo gave it to me."

Sure, you've got friends all over.

Just down the road is the smallest plaza she has ever seen, painted mint green and soft fuchsia. A few men sit at the tables arranged near the food stand.

A young girl offers them small bowls of radish, pickled carrots and chiles. She recognizes Chelo from the palapa further up the coast.

"¿No has terminado?" Petra asks, wondering if a day's work ever ends.

Chelo shakes her head no and explains how just before sundown they close the palapa then continue into town to help at the grill. She changes the subject, complimenting Petra on her lentes.

She feels silly, realizing her sunglasses are still perched on her head when the horizon has faded orange to lavender. Petra takes off the glasses and hands them to her.

"No, no, gracias," the girl replies.

Petra's gesture feels clumsy, her offer too forward.

Chelo finishes taking her order, four chicken sopes and four tacos of carnaza.

An elderly beach vendor sees Chelo and lays down her wooden case full of beaded jewelry: necklaces and bracelets of hemp, leather, shell and stone.

Chelo hugs the *viejita* and props up her case.

"Abuela, dale uno a la señorita."

Before Petra can protest the woman has scooted over and in between masterful bites of her sope in which no cabbage or crumbs of queso seco fall, the old woman presents several necklaces.

Chelo points to a small choker of green stones. The woman untwists the clasp and moves behind Petra.

"Permíteme," she says brushing her rough hands against Petra's neck. The woman's nearness makes Petra want to cry.

"Lo necesitas pa´donde vas," The abuela says.

Chelo returns with a covered plate of tacos.

"How can you stand your father?" Chelo asks.

Petra explains she's used to the drinking.

"No, hablo de ..."

She explains how the old man tried to touch her legs. It was true. He was atrocious.

Chelo's rounded cheeks curve like plums when she smiles, especially as she tells how her old man almost fed Oscar to the crocodile. She mimics a gesture of throwing someone into the sea and Petra notes Chelo's strength. She must've wrestled with fishing nets in the tide and carried infinite crates full of soda bottles. The thought of her father reaching for her legs disgusts Petra.

Petra apologizes.

"Así son. Cuídate."

Petra quickly calculates how much she needs to pay for dinner and the necklace. Missing the mark will strike an insult and paying too much appears boastful. She thanks Chelo and leaves a tip along with her sunglasses. She tries to press a few coins into the old woman's hand.

"Esto no se paga," says the old woman with an airy grin. She seals the sign of the cross in the air with a kiss.

Just as Petra crosses the street, a young morenote advances on the road, riding bareback on a chestnut colored horse. She looks up and locks in his stare. His features are a sandstone marvel: carved cheekbones, a strong brow and the etched line of his jaw stir her curiosity. He checks her from head to toe, from her salt-tangled hair down to her chanclas. She scratches at the sand fly bites on her elbow and watches his outline fade in the dark until the clomp of iron on earth is all she hears and wants to follow.

That night while she finished the last of her beer, a swirling gust of wind assaulted the patio. The palm fronds on the roof flapped and dry leaves fell around her. Down the road, a metal awning tore off in a gust and keened as it swung from its frame.

The manager of the posada ran upstairs to check the state of the palm fronds. Lightning flashed revealing a spray of *güira* geckos on the wall. They crawled in sudden bursts towards the rain and it occurred to her this colorless one might be an axolotl. Petra stared at another, twitching its chunky head in profile. Its flat unblinking eye examined her.

"Cuidado, scorpions fly from the ceiling con el viento."

"They better not fall into my tacos."

"We don't have a clínica here, so pela los ojos."

"Like them?" She pointed to the critters on the wall.

He laughed as he pulled the furniture further in from the rain.

"Would you like some tacos? My father took off."

"I saw him leave with Anselmo, our contractor. Iban al pueblo."

"Ah, he didn't tell me."

Suddenly Oscar appeared. "I didn't go anywhere."

Rapid-fire lightning illuminated a canopy of clouds poised above the silver-tipped waves. To the eye, rain ceased mid-fall catching single streams in a stroboscopic freeze. Petra had never witnessed such rain, slicing through the night with a tinsel sharp gleam.

Suddenly a sheet of plexi-glass blew off the roof, sending the palm fronds flying into the street.

"How could you be so stupid to pick a place that's falling apart?" Oscar asked.

Petra froze against his words, focusing her sight on a gecko climbing the wall as Oscar skulked away. In the storm's gorgeous display, the creature glowed, his innards alight and distinct through his skin.

Petra wakes to knocking at the door circa three in the morning. She peeks into the other room of the bungalow, hopeful to see Oscar resting soundly in bed. The bed is made and empty.

"Señorita Villareal, are you there?"

"Who is it?"

"Manuel from recepción. I have news about your father."

Perhaps this time his angel failed him. How many times has she heard this exact urgency in a knock at the door when she expected no one?

She wants the sand to quicken, to swirl and swallow her father wherever he is. She opens the door.

"Disculpe. I didn't want to disturb you, but one of the bus chóferes took this from two guys in Melaque. They emptied the money and tarjetas, but left this identificación."

He hands her the thin billfold.

"He'll be back by morning, si Dios quiere."

How to sleep? She steps into a cool shower. The raging bites on her skin have turned into patches of tiny bumps, turning the dark skin reddish and raw at her thighs and ankles. The water trickles on her back and limbs. Sand hides everywhere on her body, settled in her hair, in her navel and behind her ears. It even washes out from between her legs.

Night mist of the ocean spray mixed with a light llovizna. The crash, wane and pull of the tide calls to Petra. She wades in on her knees. She is naked and sand is pouring from inside her, anchoring her to the shore, rising in directive dunes out towards the highway. She wants to reach deep water where a boat is gently rocking.

A man in the boat calls to her. "Entra, Petra."

She sees his white shirt and his hands on the oars.

She feels the pull of the land, the emptying. Her skin now leathery and thin cracks as she moves. How can she face this man with her body so untouchable? The abuela comes up behind her and takes her hand. Petra scratches the bumpy skin of her midriff with new nails, teak wood growing from her cuticles.

"Zúmbale!" The abuela hurries her into the waves. They swim under the moonlight and hear a high falsetto voice. It sounds like a son huasteco, but this is not Tamaulipas.

Petra reaches the sides of the boat and the man reaches to pull her in. She is lighter now, free of the sand inside her. He removes his shirt and offers it to her. She accepts it wanting to cover her degradation with the worn manta. She moves aside his nets.

The abuela is still in the water, wiping salt from her eyes. She turns to the horizon where a black bobbing form swims toward them. The slick form raises its head.

"Chelo," the abuela chuckles. The fisherman helps the abuela and Chelo inside.

"Atiéndala" Chelo instructs and the man holds Petra, stroking her arms. The abuela unwraps leaves tucked away in folds of her wet skirt and asks if he remembered the bottle. He nods.

Chelo takes the oars. Her face glows in the night as she begins rowing, towards the bay of Tenacatita.

A lightning bolt shatters the sky signaling it's time to begin. The abuela at one end of the boat, behind Chelo, is mixing herbs in a bottle.

"Empínatelo," the abuela instructs. Petra gulps the full cup as the fisherman smoothes her hair. He runs his hands over her arms and lifts her shirt away to check the crackling skin of her midriff. His hands warm her and she eases back, reclining in the boat. She lets the sea rock her as he massages her waist. He picks at the new moon scab at her navel, now fibrous and peeling. He coaxes the edges, pulling back the pithy mottled skin. In the dark he reveals sections of seeds lining her abdomen. The garnet kernels glisten in the moonlight. With his tongue he loosens the seeds from their honeycomb casing, delicately sucking at each layer.

"Cuidado, no vayas a chupartela toda."says the abuela.

He keeps the juicy grains intact. Before sunrise, he will have extracted whole sections avoiding the temptation to chew or swallow their tangy sweetness. He spits the kernels into the bottle of mezcal to steep with slivers of sugar cane. Moonlight reflects her midsection exposed, yet she is not bleeding. The abuela's eyes shine with prayer.

The posada manager kneels on the tile of the flooded bathroom. Petra's eyes are open, her naked body limp. He takes off the necklace tight around her neck. He covers her with a towel then carries her to the bed. Her breathing is labored. He leaves to send someone out in search of her father.

In a few hours, Petra wakes damp and hot in bed. The gas vendor continues with the infernal music and jingle, "El gaaaas!" The bed in the adjacent room is untouched. She looks to to see if the wallet is on the nightstand. She tries to remember where she left her own debit card. She needs buy a southbound ticket from the bus station.

She puts on a t-shirt and walks out to see if Oscar is sleeping outside. Just near the door is a large jug filled with a ruby colored liquid. She pulls out the cork and smells it. *Did he leave this?* Of course not, Oscar only leaves empty bottles. She recognizes the aromatic brew of ponche de granada. She pours a little and toasts to herself in the mirror, "Drink of me and you shall be saved."

She tastes herself. She cannot travel with the weighty bottle. Maybe she can sell it at Chelo's taco stand. All those who drink this libation will know of her burden. They will remain clear-eyed coastal tourists. She envies Chelo and her family. Although watchful, they are safe in their home with palm fronds for walls, loyally guarded by their cocodrilo.

Oscar will wonder if he lost his daughter to the sea without ever knowing he lost his daughter to the road. She will be no one's Persephone. She scans the room for her clothing, chanclas, and the green necklace on the nightstand. She puts it back on, a sweet token from the abuela. As she heads downstairs to return the key, she fingers the green jade: hearthstones at her jugular to remind her how to wear the ocean's jewels.

"When Blood Wants Blood"

by David Estringel

There is nothing like the smell of Santeria. It is a distinct smell that jolts me into my body the second I find myself enveloped in it: one that suggests cleanliness—in every respect—but with a little magic mixed in. Not easily reproduced, you won't find it anywhere but homes or other places, such as my *botanica*—a Santeria supply store—where regular *orisha* worship happens. It is the intoxicating blend of lavender-scented Fabuloso All-Purpose Cleaner, stale cigar smoke (used for various offerings to our dead and these African gods), burning candle wax, and subtle, earthy hints of animal sacrifice from the past, offered for the sake of continued prosperity, spiritual protection, and other vital blessings from the divine. You won't find it anywhere else. No, it is not common fare, much like the smell of ozone immediately after a lightning strike: it is a *right time, right place* kind of thing. But why wax nostalgic (besides the fact that my own home hasn't smelled like that for a long time)? It will be *Dia de Los Muertos* tomorrow and there is much work to do.

My *boveda* has gone neglected for months now, squatting in my cramped dining room, cold and lifeless like the spirits it was erected to appease. A thick layer of dust has powdered the picture frames of my dearly departed, making their rectangular glasses dulled and cloudy. I look at the faces of my maternal and paternal grandparents and find that details that were once fine have phased into each other, as if viewed through a thin curtain of gauze: I can't clearly see them and they—likely—can hardly see me. That is how it feels, anyway. The white tablecloth is dingy, yellowed and stained from months of occasional sprinklings of *agua de florida* cologne and errant flakes of cigar ash. The water glasses (nine of them to be exact—one large brandy snifter and four pairs of others in decreasing sizes) seem almost opaque now, with their contents having long evaporated, leaving behind striated bands of hard mineral and chlorine, plus the occasional dead fly, whose selfless sacrifice was likely not met with much appreciation by my dead Aunt Minne or Popo Estringel, my mother's father. Various religious statues call for immediate attention with frozen countenances that glare, annoyed that my Swiffer hasn't seen the light of day for some weeks. Then there is the funky, asymmetrical glass jar on the back right-corner that I use to collect their change. The dead love money (especially mine). This fact has always suggested to me that hunger—in all shapes and forms—lingers, even after the final curtain closes. Makes sense, if you think about it. We gorge ourselves on life, cleave to it when we feel it slip away, and then after we die we…

The statues—mostly Catholic saints—each have their own specific meaning and purpose on my boveda. St. Lazarus provides protection from illness. St. Teresa keeps death at bay. St. Michael and The Sacred Heart of Jesus, which are significantly larger than the other figures, are prominent, flanking either side of the spiritual table, drawing energies of protection and mercy in and out. It's these two things I find myself increasingly in need of these days. At the back of the table, there is a repurposed hutch from an old secretary desk with eight cubbies of varying sizes, where nine silver, metallic ceramic skulls reside. They represent my *egun*, those who have passed on. They usually shine quite brightly in the warm yellow glow of the dining room's hanging light fixture, but they look tarnished as of late. The eye sockets alone still glisten as if wet with tears, pleading for attention. A large resin crucifix rests in the half-full, murky water glass that rests in the center of the altar. It sounds sacrilegious, but it isn't, as placing it so calls upon heavenly power to help control the spirits that are attracted to the shrine, allowing positive ones to do what they need to do for my well-being, while keeping the negative ones tightly leashed.

Some smaller, but equally important, fetishes also haunt the altar space, representing spirit guides of mine: African warriors and wise women, a golden bust of an Egyptian sarcophagus, a Native American boy playing a drum, and four steel Hands of Fatima that recently made their way into the mix after a rather nasty spirit settled into my house last year—for a month or so—and created all kinds of chaos and havoc, tormenting me with nightmares—not to mention a ton of bad luck—and my dogs with physical attacks, ultimately resulting in one of them, Argyle, being inexplicably and permanently crippled. Various accents, which I have collected over the years, also add to the *ache* of the boveda: a multi-colored beaded offering bowl, strands of similarly patterned Czech glass beads, a brass censer atop a wooden base for incenses, a pentacle and athame (from my Wicca days), a deck of Rider-Waite tarot cards in a green velvet pouch with a silver dollar inside, and a giant rosary—more appropriate to hang on a wall, actually—made of large wooden beads, dyed red and rose-scented. Looking at all of it in its diminished grandeur, I am reminded of how much I have asked my *egun* for over the years and can't help but feel a little ashamed of my non-committal, reactive attitude toward their veneration, as well as their regular care and feeding.

This year's *Dia* will be different. It has to be. It's going to take more than a refreshed boveda and fresh flowers to fix what is going wrong in my life right now; a bowl of fruit and some seven-day candles just won't cut it. Business at the botanica is slow, money is beyond tight, and all my plans seem to fall apart before they can even get started. The nightmares have come back, and the dogs grow more anxious every day, ready to jump out of their skins at the slightest startle. My *madrina,* an old Cuban woman well into her seventies that brought me into the religion and orisha priesthood, told me last night that we all have a spiritual army at our disposal— our ancestors, who desperately want to help us in times of need. She said with enough faith one could command legions of them to do one's bidding, using as little as a few puffs of cigar smoke and a glass of water. While a powerful statement, that isn't how things roll for me. Her prescription for what ails me was far from that simple. "This year, your *muertos* need to eat, and eat well! They need strength to help you and you need a lot of help," she said. "When they are happy, you will be happy. When they are not, you won't be, either." She searched my eyes for a twinge of panic, and they didn't fail her. I knew—right then and there—what she meant. It made my stomach drop straight down into my Jockeys. That feeling may have very well dissuaded me from going through with tonight's festivities, if things weren't so dire at present. *Eyebale* is a messy business, regardless of how smooth one is with their knife (blood sacrifice always is, which is why I have always had such a distaste for it. Thank God I only do birds). Regardless, my egun eat tonight at midnight. I give thanks to my egun tonight at midnight. I—hopefully—change things around tonight at midnight. What else can you do when blood wants blood?

THE BROWN INVASION

by Alma García

In the bronze light of late afternoon, as Jerry Gonzales stands at the French doors overlooking his deck, Chavela gives her orders.

The coffee table, she says. Make sure you use two tablespoons of wax, just two, only two. Top to bottom. Never in circles. It's an antique.

"Sí, señora," is the response.

Jerry glides to the landing at the top of the stairs and peeks over. The heavyset woman Chavela addresses stands with her back to him in the kitchen, her black bun drooping, the waistband of her pants bunching beneath her T-shirt. She shifts between feet in breadloaf-sized athletic shoes.

Chavela with her pixie cut, her pink blouse, her pantsuit the color of ashes.

"También las ventanas, por favor," she adds briskly, tapping the bottle of Windex on the kitchen island.

The woman nods.

For she is the new maid. The *maid*.

There's no way in hell he's addressing this woman as "tú."

"Dad," calls a voice behind him, "can I take one of the cars?"

Adam, their son, pokes his head from his bedroom. Black attire, as ever. Orange stripes in his hair. Eyebrow with ring inserted without permission and which he is required to remove in the presence of his grandmother.

"Where?"

Adam shrugs. He has developed a theory that matriculated seniors shouldn't have to explain everything. Having graduated from high school a mere week ago, he is focused mostly on packing things into duct-taped boxes in anticipation of the day his parents will drive the seven hundred miles to San Diego to deposit him at a dormitory's doorstep, God forbid he should attend El Paso's serviceable university where, it so happens, his father recently achieved tenure. But Adam desires new experiences and opportunities; he wants to see more of the world. Of course, Jerry has encouraged this curiosity. Of course, both he and Chavela want only what's best for him.

Although, if this were completely true, Chavela wouldn't have spent the past two weekends angrily cleaning out the garage.

"Take the Volvo," he says now. "Return by midnight."

Adam grins. "Thanks, viejo." He disappears.

Jerry returns to his desk, his embossed tomes. *Pope's Dream: A New View of the Pueblo Revolt of 1680. Sons of Oñate: Modern Colonialism in the American Southwest.*

From downstairs comes a surprised female gasp, followed by the yapping of a small dog. He oozes back out of the room. Chavela's Pomeranian dances on its hind legs.

"Ay, Paquito."

Chavela stoops down and tickles him under the chin. She extracts a dog biscuit. Her voice rises an octave: "Who's my good boy, are you my good boy, yes you are," and the biscuit is snapped up in midair.

She looks up from the floor. "¿Te gustan los perros?"

The maid is practically standing with one foot on top of the other. "Sí, señora."

Adam breezes into the room, car keys jingling.

"Hi sweetheart," Chavela says, rising. "Say hello to Lourdes."

"What's up, Lourdes?"

Chavela gives him a narrow look.

"Hola," he says. Then to his mother, "What's for dinner?"

"Chicken."

He takes a Coke from the refrigerator before he slips out.

Chavela shakes her head. "¿Y tú—tienes hijos?"

Lourdes nods. But Paquito has started yapping and dancing again, and her voice is lost in the racket.

In any case, Chavela is back to business. With a voice that is already sharpening, starts to explain about the floor wax.

And the coffee table, she adds, don't forget, top to bottom, top to bottom, not in circles. Never. It streaks, it smears. It's an antique, and by the way, there is a sandwich in the refrigerator for you.

"Muy bien, señora. Gracias."

Chavela makes her gathering sounds—papers, keys, sunglasses.

Señor Gonzales is upstairs, she says. He'll be home for the summer, researching. Writing. In any case, he knows you're here—she pauses, as though to let this information sink in—and I myself will be back in a few hours, goodbye.

Jerry cracks opens *Sons of Oñate*. He whaps it shut.

He descends through a rising aroma of Pine Sol into the kitchen, where he comes upon the maid herself, a dowdy vision in rubber gloves and seventies-era headphones, from which are emanating the sounds of a soccer game at tremendous volume.

She stands with her back to him, filling a bucket with hot water at the sink. Welcome back, booms the announcer, to the midseason game of the Primera División, and it's shaping up to be the biggest game yet of 2005! Chivas have the ball!

He watches coolly as she removes the bucket to the floor and scrubs the sink. Foul on Silva! Monarcas get the penalty kick! Chivas take possession at midfield. Enríquez passes to Medrano. Medrano to Burcíaga—but no, Chivas recapture and Vermeulen, the Belgian, takes the ball, he's closing in, he shoots—

"Sí, sí, sí," she chants at the ceiling.

"GOOOLLLLLLLpe de poste!"

She hisses through her teeth. "Me lleva."

"Buenas tardes," he calls out.

She startles and whirls to him.

"Ay, perdón." She shuts off her headphones and removes them, blushing. "Buenas tardes, señor."

He forces a tight smile. "¿Usted se llama Lourdes, no?"

Her dark complexion mottles as she nods at the window over the sink. Does she think he's making fun of her by speaking to her as an equal? He has no idea. He removes a casserole dish of macaroni and cheese from the refrigerator and inserts it into the microwave, then snatches up the remote from the kitchen island.

The TV squawks to life in the den. The news is nattering on again about the fence. Every bit of disconnected chainlink and barbwire along the border converted into a seven-hundred-mile wall of concrete and steel. Brownsville to San Diego. In theory.

He zaps the TV off.

Remind me of how often will we be seeing you, Lourdes?

Twice a month, señor.

The microwave beeps. She mops.

He locates a Diet Coke and fills a glass with ice. Well, he says. Have…fun.

The mop never pauses as he climbs the stairs to the deck.

Here, he contemplates the rocky, blasted-away flank of the mountain, the long-defunct twin smokestacks of the Asarco copper smeltery in the distance, the haze smoking upward from Mexico. He firms his feet. The Gonzales name entered the local register even before the 1848 Treaty of Guadalupe Hidalgo and the annexation of Texas to the United States—which is, as he enjoys clarifying for his students, before its inhabitants were invaded by White settlers but after said inhabitants invaded the Indians and, one could say, intermarried, though you wouldn't want to bring that latter point up in polite company—and those who are descended from this stock are rooted here like the most ancient trees.

Below on the street, three houses away, the back gate of the DuPre home whaps open.

It's Miguel, the neighborhood lawn guy, shoving his mower at a trot as though he was fleeing a bank heist.

The door of the DuPre household slams open behind him. Here appears Huck Himself, minus his ever-present cowboy hat. In fact, his shirt is torn, smeared with a great stripe of dirt. His hair plasters his head, as though he'd hatched recently from an egg; bruises stamp his arms. A toolbox-wielding man in coveralls nudges past him. Huck smashes the door with the side of his fist. Then he disappears into his house.

Something tingles distantly in Jerry's veins. He looks about for other DuPres, but none are in evidence.

Out the side door of Jerry's own house scuttles another human form, round and low to the ground.

Lourdes.

She calls out to Miguel—for apparently, they know one another—a question in her voice. Miguel shakes his head like a weary old man. Is that a puff of laughter escaping Lourdes's lips? Did she really just say, "Pues, *todos* son locos"?

And then Huck's at the door again, calling out to *her.*

She goes to him. He talks at her in English. She supplies some halting English in return. Then she breaks free and hurries back to his house, dabbing at the valley in her bra with a paper towel she extracts from the waistband of her pants.

The mountain darkens with shadow as a cotton-ball cloud passes over the sun. A flock of grackles swoops down to the telephone wires above him, arguing and heckling.

He finds Lourdes in the den. Already she's got her headphones on, this time with music cranked to an impossible volume as she swishes the duster. He watches as she pops open the can of wax, swirls a rag into the brown ointment, leans over the rough grain of the table top to rub in circles. Around and around and around.

The guitar inside her headphones makes a dirty-sounding shimmy.

"Good grief," he pipes, loudly enough to be heard. "¿Está escuchando a Creedence Clearwater Revival?"

She jumps, clutching the smeared rag to her chest, and fumbles for the off switch. "¿Mande?"

"¿Le gusta classic rock?"

"No sé." Her face is on fire. She turns a quick eye toward the table, where the brown-orange circles of wax cut across the grain of its surface.

He doesn't care about the table. He tries for a conspiratorial smile.

So. What's all the excitement about over at the DuPres?

She shifts from foot to foot.

Oh, come on, Jerry presses.

She tries to shrug and darts another glance at the table, where the wax darkens.

I guess I'll ask Miguel, he teases. You can stay here with the table.

Señor DuPre has asked me to come every week from now on, she bursts out.

Jerry raises an eyebrow. "Oh?"

Señora DuPre, she tells him, seems to have left Señor DuPre.

She sinks, as though something has punctured a hole in her.

His smile feels stuck to his face.

"¿Le dijo Huck? ¿Señor DuPre?"

"Sí." She looks as though she might cry.

He chuckles to himself. " Que la chingada." For her benefit he adds, "Perdón."

Then he sets down his glass, carelessly and too close to the edge of the table beside the recliner, where it topples and crashes to the hardwood floor.

She moves even before he can exclaim his surprise. He laughs his embarrassed laugh, turning in circles, his hands massaging the air as though the necessary implements will somehow appear. But she has already returned with dust pan and whisk broom, wastebasket, rags. He makes protesting sounds when she approaches, reaching for the wet shards with a crumple of newspaper, but she says no no, takes the paper from his hand, shoos him back.

From the front door comes the sound of a key turning in the lock.

"Hola-hola," Chavela calls out breezily. Her heels click-clack on the tiles.

"Gracias," Jerry says hastily and backs out of the room.

"De nada," Lourdes murmurs without looking at him. She snatches up the table wax.

"Rose Marie DuPre just left her husband," he blurts into the kitchen.

Chavela looks up over the screen of her laptop. "You're kidding. Where did you hear *that?*"

"From our exceptionally efficient new maid."

It is with a cooling horror that he hears, seconds too late, the burr of resentment in his voice.

And yet he finds himself unable to speak—to clarify, to calibrate—as Chavela freezes in her pose.

"I am sorry," she says with a final, deadly calm, "to hear about our neighbors' marital problems. We have already discussed the housekeeping issue. But because our maid also happens to work for the DuPres, not to mention a dozen other neighbors"—glancing toward the den, she lowers her voice—"que quiero saber is where she gets off being so indiscreet. The first time she meets you, no less."

"There's no need to be so hard on her."

He's not sure from what part of his body these words have been dislodged. Or why the resentment in his voice has been replaced with a rippling offense.

"So now you're defending her?"

"I am not defending the maid in any shape or form. I'm saying to leave her alone."

She slides off her stool. Without shoes, she's the same height as he. "Would you defend her if she gossiped about us to Huck and Rose Marie?"

"Tranquilo." He pats the air. The doorbell rings. "Son," he calls up the stairs, because he has yet to hear the car backing out of the driveway, "get the door."

Chavela examines the backs of her hands. "Too bad she had so much to say."

"Perhaps we ourselves could stop talking about it."

"I'm getting another maid. This one isn't going to work out."

"No!" he sputters. "We're keeping this one!"

Again, the doorbell.

Chavela fumes at the ceiling. "Adam, answer the door. Right now!"

She is answered by the flushing of the upstairs toilet.

For the briefest of instants, Jerry's eyes meet his wife's in a shared consternation. But it is not enough to provide counterbalance. He stalks to the door.

A woman waits on the other side. Like Jerry, she is at mid-life, though perhaps slightly older, dark and weather-worn in complexion, with a long, woolly, gray-streaked braid tossed forward onto her shoulder. Her face is creased with the half-curl of a smile.

A sudden wooziness softens his knees.

"Madre de Dios," he says to his sister.

And she cackles and asks, "Did you miss me?"

Inez.

She's thinner than he remembers, but still sturdy enough, still the same short, hawk-eyed woman who has always tossed back her head in laughter to show all her square Indian teeth. Only now, she is missing an eyetooth.

The screen door creaks. He feels his arms lift, enfold. He detects a faint odor of gasoline. Strange, he thinks from some place outside of himself, the things you come to believe with the passage of time.

For starters, that Inez was most likely dead.

"Come in," he warbles.

The thundering at the top of the stairs is Adam. Inez turns in Jerry's hands, and as she registers the young man descending upon her, she breaks free, her face blooming with joy.

"Well, hello!" she exclaims when he reaches ground level, and then she throws her arms around him.

Adam startles inside her grasp. His face is so blank that, to Jerry, its meaning is instantly clear. He hasn't recognized his aunt. At all.

And Inez steps back with a very cool countenance, indeed.

"Surprise!" Jerry announces. "It's Inez! Let's all sit down!"

He herds the lot of them into the kitchen, counseling himself: Tranquilo. For he is not afraid of his sister. Not the way he'd been when they were kids and she, still a full head taller than he, could be moved to de-trouser him publicly unless he offered up a cut of his paperboy's wages. No. He is a different creature now, and Inez is merely a woman seated at his kitchen table in dirt-streaked jeans and a man's plaid button-down shirt, drumming her calloused fingers as though waiting for a slow bus. Even Chavela, who has been as stiff in this eternity of minutes as a mannequin whose eyes follow you at the store, bends enough to remove a set of drinking glasses from a cabinet.

"¿Algo de tomar?" she inquires.

"Tequila," Inez answers with a slap to the tabletop.

Chavela runs her tongue over her teeth and turns to Jerry.

He pulls opens the dishwasher and sticks his head in.

"All right," Inez says, directing her voice across the table. "What are you up to these days, young man?"

The silverware is still in its cage. Jerry gathers up a warm fistful, lingering for a moment in the dishwasher's soap-scented interior. For he who moves last is more likely to win the game—isn't that what their father always said?

"Well," Adam begins, "I just graduated from high school."

"I see. College?"

Adam picks his eyebrow ring. "Uh-huh."

Inez gives him an impatient look and stirs the air with her hand.

"UC San Diego?" Adam responds.

"¿Y tú, Inez?" Chavela interjects. "Where are *you* living these days?"

"At the moment, I suppose I live in El Paso."

Chavela draws a breath of great patience. "Were you living somewhere else in the previous moment?"

Inez laughs. "What is this, the Spanish Inquisition?"

Chavela responds with a grunt of amusement. Perhaps time, friend that it is, has blunted the darker emotions. Inez, for her part, extracts a small packet from the vinyl fanny pack at her waist and tears it open. Pop Rocks. Por Dios. As though she was still ten years old. She offers some to Adam, who declines, and tips the packet to her mouth.

"Now that all of these pleasantries are out of the way," she says through a mouthful of sizzle, "what does a person have to do to get something to drink around here?"

Chavela pastes her smile onto her face. "You know, Inez, your appearance is a bit of a surprise."

"Pues, claro. I'm sure it is."

"I'm sure," Chavela pauses aridly, "everyone will be relieved to hear of your return."

"I'm not here to please them. Or anyone, really." An evil smile pricks Inez's lips.

The pounding in Jerry's ears is almost physically painful. In fact, he's uncertain whether he's imagining the commotion he hears at the front of the house—an enthusiastic rattling, a fumbling with a lock.

"What's going on at the door?" he barks.

"I'll check it out." Adam leaps from his chair.

"I forgot," Chavela says as she follows him out of the room. "It's Marcus."

And then he is alone with Inez.

There is neither fury nor glee on his sister's face. Only an aging woman in work clothes who looks, frankly, tired.

He releases his forks into the silverware drawer. "It's been a very long time," he begins.

She offers a half-smile. "Claro que sí."

"It's good to see you."

She inclines her head. "Likewise, Momito."

He cringes. "God. Don't call me Momo."

"It's your *name*."

"Por favor. 'Geronimo,' if you must." He sighs. "Have you been to see anyone else?"

"Certainly not. Who else but you would be my first choice?"

He smiles faintly, achingly, into the silence that follows.

Now, from the region of the front door comes Chavela's low voice: "You're not going to believe who's here."

Yet the elder of his two sons blows in like a believer. Here's Marcus in the kitchen on the way to work, in khaki green uniform, muscular and brimming with youth, throwing his arms open wide. "Tía!" he calls.

Inez spreads her wings. "M'ijo!"

Then they meet in a joyous embrace that looks as though it could end in the breaking of Inez's ribs.

"You're huge!" she says.

"You're...little!"

"So you remember your old tía, do you?"

"How could I forget my favorite aunt?"

Jerry offers a look of pure wonder to his wife. But she only lifts her eyes to the ceiling before she opens the refrigerator and removes a six-pack of 7-Up, a six-pack of Sunkist, and a liter of Diet Mountain Dew and clacks them down on the table.

"Does anyone want a Coke? We've got three kinds."

"Tequila," Inez says, dropping back into her chair.

"I didn't know you were coming, son," Jerry says.

"Didn't Mom tell you?" Marcus digs with a thumbnail into an orange. "She's making me take home a bunch of stuff she cleaned out of the garage."

"Ah." Only now does he notice the stack of boxes resting beside the back door.

Chavela nudges forward two cans of Sunkist. Inez gives Marcus a look that says, *Can you believe this?*

Marcus cracks one open. "So where have you been keeping yourself?"

"Bozeman, Montana. At least for the last couple of months."

"Doing what? Herding goats?"

She smacks him on the side of the head. "¿Cómo que 'goats'? I was working at a Dairy Queen." She eyes Marcus's uniform. "So. You're Border Patrol now, too."

Marcus leans back in his chair and offers the toothy grin he uses in self-defense. "Yup."

"Well. *That's* interesting. I thought the line would end with my brother."

Jerry stills his hand. The trouble with history, he reminds himself, is that by the time you notice it repeating, it's already happened. Especially when Number-One Son, who certainly could have finished college, who has an excellent aptitude for earth sciences, is now a two-year veteran of the United States Border Patrol.

"Is there something the matter," he says very calmly, "with my son's choice of vocation?"

A great stillness seems to overcome Inez. Then she smirks.

"I dunno. *Is* there?"

Jerry runs his tongue over his teeth. He will not take the same bait she habitually offered for her own amusement thirty years ago. He will only offer a few clarifications.

"Has the border been secured yet?" he responds.

"Do you want the cynical response or the philosophical one?"

"What odds are you putting on a border wall ever being built in our lifetime?"

"I thought we were discussing bloodlines, not bureaucracy. And anyway, does anyone really believe that thing could stop the Brown Invasion?"

"It's not like he has to be an agent forever," he adds hotly, "if he doesn't want to. Especially if he ever decides to go back to *school*." He gives Marcus a pointed look.

"You guys," Marcus interrupts, laughing. "Look. I'm not cut out for an office job. I like being outside. I like figuring people out. And it's not like I don't have plenty to do, you know?"

A glow of approval warms Inez's face. "Ah. A student at the University of Life."

"That's right," Jerry says. "One who has decent health insurance."

Adam, for his part, gives his brother the sort of look that means, *You make me want to vomit.* Chavela sips Diet Mountain Dew.

"So, m'ijo," Inez continues. "Has your father ever told you about the prank he used to pull when he was an agent?"

Jerry's breath leaves him. As surely he knew it would.

"Inez," he warns, croaking.

Marcus scoots to the front of his seat. "This I've got to hear."

"Totally," Adam adds.

Inez leans onto her elbow. "Okay, so on slow nights, he would wrap himself up in an old sheet and a wig and wade out into the river, see?"

"Inez."

"And his partner would be the lookout, and if anybody approached, he'd give the signal, and your father would start moaning and wailing and calling out in this high, ghostly voice for his drowned children."

Jerry grinds his heels to the floor. "Inez!"

She turns to him. "What? Are you saying it's not true? If we're to believe the stories you told, you used to play spook all the time."

Marcus snorts. "You pretended to be La Llorona?"

Jerry feels his mustache bunching under his nose. "That was a long time ago."

"He always said it was for purposes of morale," Inez continues. "And that half the time the detainees were cracking up, too."

"Dad," Adam says, in a tone that conveys both shock and approval.

Marcus shakes his head. "Oh, man."

Chavela, who already knows, rolls her eyes.

Jerry looks away. "We always apologized after we cuffed them."

"Of course you did," Inez says, her voice suddenly gentling. "You were hardly more than a kid. Like this whippersnapper, here."

She smacks Marcus on the thigh.

"Of course," Inez adds, "they did have to pry that woman off you when she ripped your wig off."

"Inez, por Diós!"

"Seriously?" Adam pipes. "You know this is Mister Moral High Ground himself, right?"

Marcus grins. "So what other dirt have you got?"

"Ever hear about the time I took your father to the circus? This was before anyone knew about his clown phobia."

Marcus rises. "Hold that thought. I gotta see a man about a horse." He exits, laughing, toward the powder room at the front of the house.

And here, at the opposite entry to the kitchen, appears a short, dark, rounded form, whose eyes pin themselves to the floor as Jerry leaps from his chair to cover the molasses-thick distance in the hope, the hope beyond hope, that he might somehow block the view before Inez can turn in her seat, who peels off her rubber gloves to announce meekly, "He terminado, señores."

Inez sits up, electrified.

"¡A la verga!" she crows. "¿Eres la criada?"

Lourdes turns the color of a tomato.

And you work for my *brother!*

Lourdes steps back like a spooked horse.

"My God," Inez continues, grinning at Jerry. "She's not even legal, is she?"

Jerry, gritting his teeth, swoops in on his maid and escorts her outside.

He bids her adios on the front lawn after handing over the last of the cash in his wallet. Then he removes himself to the deck.

The sun squats on the horizon now as he leans against the railing, Asarco's smokestacks going dark against the golden rays that splay past, a drift of motionless clouds above brightening with a pink neon glow. The inversion layer fades to purple like a movie screen. Across the distance, the mountain peaks of Juárez steep in shadow; the buildings downtown have begun to wink on. The dry creosote throws complicated shadows. Any drier and it would spontaneously combust—two inches of rain with the year half over, news reports of starving desert animals creeping into the city, little gray foxes and coyotes and even, if one is to believe the sighting, a mountain lion. Times were, when the boys were still small, you could sometimes see a lone figure or two clambering up out of the Mexican side of the foothills in these cooling hours and hurling themselves across the freeway. Now, on the access road near the boundary-marking chain link, he can just make out the glow of a parked white-and-green Border Patrol vehicle.

Adam once told him the local water supply is doped up with a naturally occurring solution of lithium. "Everybody's drugged," he said. "Why else would anyone stay here?"

Perhaps the more salient question was, How does anyone escape?

We've always been weeping and searching for the dead.

by Yola Gómez

It's during the night that I become hyper aware of my mind, of my thoughts, of my memories. In the morning I'll tell my partner that my brain kept me awake. And they'll give me advice about how to fall asleep. I drink tea for my brain, eat food for my brain, read books for my brain. I exercise for my brain and think happy thoughts for my brain.

My brain makes me drink tea, eat food, read books. My brain makes me rub my skin raw, pick my hair. My brain makes me shake when I turn out the lights and my brain picks the worst times to remember shit I just don't want to remember. My brain tell me I don't belong here. It tells me to be more positive and to stop being so cynical, telling me to not speak up, to smile, to let them touch my hair. So, I cut off my head. I just watch myself.

It is estimated that a baby loses about half their neurons before they are born.

I remember that she called for me from outside. Her voice had a high pitched strain that I had only recently begun to decipher. It was dark out. She had been outside smoking and suddenly had another attack. She was a young mother with three children. Poor, traumatized, sick, and getting sicker. She didn't know what was happening to her.

I ran outside to her and saw her gripping the side of the house; she was pulling herself along toward our front porch as if she were facing the threat of a great fall off of a cliff face. Slowly, shaking, she made it up the stairs and into the house to lie down. This attack was the start of years of doctors visits, seizures, inability to walk; the start of the slow, steady, and devastating mental and physical decline of my mother.

I spoke with my mother the other day and she talked to me about when she first started hearing "the voices." She was an orderly at a hospital. "They started out as whispers and laughs". She became increasingly paranoid. Eventually she would quit her job, one of a long string of various jobs throughout her life. She did everything from cleaning offices and painting restaurant windows with festive designs, to long-haul trucking, office work, and making stuffed animals. She would hang on and do whatever was necessary to care for us. Just hanging on.

We see this pattern repeating. My spouse and I both work in mental health and have noticed this trend in youth: bright, multi-talented, sometimes gifted, almost always suffering from complex trauma, and suddenly having their first psychotic symptoms as teens or in their early twenties. Their brains splitting.

How did I escape this? I had an uncle on my mother's side who suffered from schizophrenia, who lit himself on fire. I think of queerness in our family. My mother is a lesbian, my sisters, one identifies as a lesbian and the other bi-sexual. I identify as queer. My mother was raised Christian.

We were Christian-identified until I was 7 when my mother decided we would become pagan. We all "came out" later in life. Was part of our madness attached to the shame and guilt instilled within us by the church regarding our genders, our sexualities?

Our brains were property of the church in some sense, and thus our bodies were not our own. If my body is my own, how my own is it? My brain, my consciousness, *mine*? How closely related are desire and madness in our society?

Born into a system that would have us die, devalued, marked as other before entering the world. Our brains, our consciousness, our identities dependent upon the perception apparatus of others. Hailed always as inferior. It's as if we were born as the living dead.

I never acknowledged the creeping in madness. I didn't even possess enough self-awareness to know it was there. Another gift from my mother. Cliche. I didn't know myself or what was happening to me. Everything, just was. And that's how I operated for so long. Throughout my childhood until I hit puberty, I was just affected by my environment. It wasn't until I had enough that I began the long journey toward self-discovery which would lead to an understanding of trauma and the brain and thus the reclamation of my body.

The human brain weighs approximately three pounds and is 60 percent fat.

Throughout history we've seen the mad, the marginalized, the wanderers of liminality, the marabouts as peripheral. What is externalized shapes that which is internal. As in, language, the mind, and therefore the body. We see higher suicide rates for marginalized folks, higher rates of sickness like diabetes and high blood pressure, depression and anxiety. Black and brown women experience higher rates of obstetric violence. Missing and murdered black and indigenous women rarely make headlines and black men can't step outside of their homes without the threat of white violence. This is madness. Whiteness is madness is oppression is violence is the theft, mutation, and contortion of desire. Language is then a product of the brain, language creating environment, oppressive or liberating -us and them.

I am reminded of classifications and of who deems this person or that person as Other. I am reminded of language and of what is not said, of what is between the margins. What lies in silence is perhaps discovery or at least something discoverable. It too is a byproduct but one of Othering within classifications. An outlier, named as atypical, divergent. We still see this Othering in marginalized groups within society through naming, classifications, diagnoses; neurodivergent, LGBTQIA+, BIPoC, psychotic, obsessive, etc.

Lunacy: insanity; mental disorder. Intermittent insanity, formerly believed to be related to phases of the moon. Extreme foolishness or an instance of it.

"She's crazy." I can see myself entering stage left. I walk up to the pole, not feeling the pain in my feet or in my back, I see myself swaying to music. I was post-pregnant and I looked it but I couldn't see it then. My breasts were engorged and my stomach was still soft. I remember getting ready and putting on my drug store nylons, thrift store shoes, and dollar-store makeup, and not feeling my body. My brain couldn't, it was too focused on everyday survival. It was my brain that would help me check out as I was being sexually assaulted and then helped me to forget until I was triggered by seeing my rapist at an art show.

The body and the brain, split: schizo. Lunacy. I can remember speaking with my therapist about how I felt as if I weren't really in the room for so much of my life. I would instead go about the day as if I were watching myself from a distance. Dissociation. My head cut off. My body numb. I had to name it. I had to know what it was in order to help make it stop.

And so I began the trip back to myself. Like so many before me. What I did know: I was A witch. A heretic. Psychotic. Unbelievable. Liar. Dirty. Harlot. All of these things intersect. Madness, desire, sexuality, and gender.

What if we thought of desiring as making instead of imagining? Not our own death but a future in which we can exist beyond our death. Our bodies, ourselves, written into futurity. Decolonizing history.

"Todos me dicen el negro, llorona Negro pero cariñoso Todos me dicen el negro, llorona Negro pero cariñoso Yo soy como el chile verde, llorona Picante pero sabroso Yo soy como el chile verde, llorona Picante pero sabroso" La Llorona

Something shifted within me the older I got. I can remember remember spending much of my time researching what it meant *to be* Mexican, *to be* crazy, *to be* mixed, to straddle identities, not one but Other. Split. I would listen to stories of how crazy all of the women and femmes in my family were and are. I would scour the bookmobile looking for titles with Latin America or Hispanic in the title. It's where I learned to be a curandera, a bruja.

I was lucky that Spanish was my first language. I could correct people who mispronounced my name. I would study my last name and my father's place of birth. I would make altars and celebrate Dia de los Muertos. I would pass this information along to my sisters and my mother and, funnily enough, this would have me labeled as the crazy one in our family. My body had feelings that I still wouldn't know, that would be clouded by sexual abuse, that were intrusive thoughts. I would run from them for years. I would run from my body and reside in my brain. But it was a beginning. A way to search for something outside of the neurotypical, normative, Eurocentric experience.

Now I understand that my process, my lens, however juvenile and patchworked together was that of decolonization. A practice I am perfecting to this day. And I know that we've always been weeping and searching for the dead to help us while we live.

Dom Chatterjee writes,
"So much new age "culture" steals from POC beliefs and traditions. Herbalism, crystals, meditation, the list goes on and on. Cultural appropriation isolates many people of color, especially in white-dominated locations, from the healing practices that make up the fabric of our and our ancestors' lives –

and our survival. If we see our culture being tokenized and otherwise disrespected, how are we going to have a supportive experience in the room?" Cultural appropriation pushes out the very people who are culturally bound to these healing practices, preventing them from accessing the healing they need." -Rest for Resistance Mental Health is Different for People of Color in These 3 Ways (And More)

I understood my ability to make connections, my reverence for nature and recognition for patterns (later diagnosed as OCD) were things that I thought pre-colonization would have valued and perhaps even treated as a gift. I was someone who could commune with the past, the heavens, the subterrane. This comforted me. My spells, my writing, my foods, my medicine. I am protective of these practices. I rely upon them.

And I look now at my mother, and how she was never tethered. She was as free-floating as a jellyfish in outer space. No ties to anything. Stripped. Labeled as hysterical, crazy, insane. Those rituals had been deemed illegal, and were punishable by law just a few generations ago. They were called savage practices. Deemed her mad. Her madness is mine. It is a gift and one that I inevitably will pass on to my children. Madness that is unapologetic in the face of colonialism and profit. Madness that straddles the borders of innovation and empathy. What's hers is mine. Including historical trauma. I learned to help myself, to ask for it, to talk about it, against all the stigma. I watched her struggle her entire life. With an illness of the brain, of the body, of whiteness, of desire.

Severe emotional trauma causes lasting changes in the ventromedial prefrontal cortex region of the brain that is responsible for regulating emotional responses triggered by the amygdala.

The brain. My brain or yours. Grey folds. Up close cross sections in biology. It's the separation of mind and body. Of mind over matter. It's who we are and what we are constrained by. It's differences and likeness. Sexuality and gender. It's cruelty and pain. Desire and revulsion. The brain is about two percent of our body mass as a whole but is responsible for all of its functions. It's madness. It's us.

Decolonization is the undoing of colonialism: where a nation establishes and maintains its domination over one or more other territories.

I've seen so many Queer and PoC lessen the oppressive aspects of mental illness through the process of decolonization. This includes a distancing of the Self from European religion and religion in general. In this way we become excavators of the Self. My daily rituals include dissecting negative self-talk and attempting to locate which ways I've been infected by the powers that be. But I still cut off my head. And I still watch myself, watching myself. My brain. Still colonized. Still aching.

I'm standing in front of the mirror naked. I'm five years old. I see a brown little girl. I think I look just like my father. My hair is straighter and my eyes are blue but I wouldn't make these discoveries for some years.

Circumstantial speech is the result of a so-called "non-linear thought pattern" and occurs when the focus of a conversation drifts, but often comes back to the point. This differs from tangential speech whereby the individual often does not return to the original point.

I was young, pregnant, poor, and traumatized too. I was living on the border in a small town called Naco. I was in labor and completely stupid. I was in an abusive relationship with a sick man 20 years older. He didn't want a midwife or a doctor. He used the book, 'Where There is no Doctor' to "care" for me during my pregnancy. The night before I wrote down a dream about my baby. A drag queen with long sharp nails ran them over my very pregnant belly and said, with an almost comical Russian-esque accent, "I zink zey are wrong." I gave birth to my son. I was naked in my living room next to our dog. My son was assigned female at birth. Is this crazy? Which part?

My son is young. He has PTSD. He was diagnosed with autism. He's trans. But he knows about his brain. He knows about his body. He knows what's going on every step of the way and I'm there to help him. He knows. Our legacy is named. We cut off its head.

The brain. My brain or yours. Grey folds. Up close cross sections in biology. It's the separation of mind and body. Of mind over matter. It's who we are and what we are constrained by. It's differences and likeness. Sexuality and gender. It's cruelty and pain. Desire and revulsion. It's about two percent of our bodies as a whole but is responsible for all of its functions. It's madness. It's us.

The other night, exhausted, I woke up to the sound of a dog barking, just one bark, right next to me in bed. I had been up with my toddler's sleep regression for the past week. I was nearly 5 and a half months pregnant. I hallucinated. There was no dog. I should mention that I don't hallucinate, but it is a fear I have. I laughed and told my co-parent what had just happened. We stayed up talking about the brain, desire, trauma, and healing. I told them about how my last therapy session was strange. I noticed my white therapist looking off into the distance, just past me, while I was talking about my history. My co-parent told me about this new therapy technique they've been working with. Revenge Murder Fantasy Therapy.

Cut off other people's heads. I like it. I need to tell my mom about it. I picture Judith slaying Holofernes by Artemisia Gentileschi. What I don't tell my co-parent is that I still talk to my father even though I never knew him. I don't tell Them that I can still feel them near me sometimes. And that once, I saw a shadow in my newborn's eyes, of a man standing behind me, and I knew that it was my father. I still feel like my ancestors are with me. Propelling me forward.

The human brain has the capacity to generate approximately 23 watts of power when awake.

And we're changing the shape of our brains everyday through introspection. My brain makes me drink tea, eat food, read books. My brain makes me rub my skin raw, pick my hair. My brain makes me shake when I turn out the lights and my brain picks the worst times to remember shit I just don't want to remember. My brain tells me

I don't belong here. It tells me to be more positive and to stop being so cynical, telling me to not speak up, to smile, to let them touch my hair. So, I cut off their heads. I just watch myself doing it. And it feels right.

And I know that we've always been weeping and searching for the dead to help us while we live. And what if we thought of desiring as making instead or imagining? Not our own death but a future in which we can exist beyond our death. Our bodies, ourselves, written into futurity. Decolonizing history.

And "...modern man no longer communicates with the madman." But women and femmes do. Throughout history we are mad, the marabouts, the wanderers of liminality, the marginalized, living peripherally. Armed now with the language to tell our own stories. To take back what is ours, what was stolen.

The brain. My brain or yours. Grey folds. Up close cross sections in biology. It's the separation of mind and body. Of mind over matter. It's who we are and what we are constrained by. It's differences and likeness. Sexuality and gender. It's cruelty and pain. Desire and revulsion. It's about two percent of our bodies as a whole but is responsible for all of its functions. It's madness. It's us.

To My Goddaughter

by Reyna Grande

December 22, 2016

My dearest Reynita,

Little one, my goddaughter, my namesake, when you were in your mother's womb I wondered if there would be anything I could do to shelter you from what awaits you living in a place like Iguala, Guerrero, Mexico. I worry even more now that you are here with us. I was deeply honored when your mother, my cousin, Diana, asked me to be your godmother. At four weeks old, you were the littlest baby in the Iglesia de las Maravillas, the Church of Miracles. We all felt a certain urgency to have you blessed and protected in these uncertain times. In a month, the country I've called home for more than thirty years will have a new leader, someone who cares nothing about you or me. Even before you were conceived, this man launched his campaign for President of the United States by calling Mexican immigrants "rapists, criminals, and drug dealers." He insulted all the family you have in the US—your uncle, Ángel, (whom your mother hasn't seen in ten years), and my siblings and me. He said that Mexico doesn't send its best, and yet we have given the very best of ourselves: our work ethic, our skills, our talents, our passion.

In your life you will learn that everything that happens in the United States affects Mexico, usually for the worse. Two weeks before you were born, the Mexican peso dropped in value more than it had in 20 years the day after Donald Trump was declared our next president! He sealed his election by promising to build a wall between our countries and deport the 11 million undocumented immigrants living in the United States, including your uncle. When your mother was a baby, the US president at the time began to build a wall. How is it that now that you're a baby, more walls are being built? I want to give you a world without divisions, with no borders. Beyond the bricks and the barbed wires, I wish I could remove the barriers that will hinder your growth, kill your spark, rob you of your potential, deny you all that you deserve. I tried to save your mother but was unable to, and as I held you in my arms at your baptism, I prayed to be allowed to do for you what I couldn't do for her.

When I met your mother, she was a year old. It was my first visit back to Mexico since I'd immigrated to the United States. I was seventeen, more American than Mexican by then. Eight years in the States had done that to me—stripped me of my identity so that I no longer knew who I was: not Mexican enough in Mexico, but also not American enough in the States. It had robbed me of my native tongue so that it felt foreign in my mouth. On that visit to Mexico, I was struggling with more than my clumsy Spanish. I was struggling with the reality of our family's life in Iguala. For the first time, I was seeing our hometown through different eyes—American eyes. The poverty in which your mother lived astounded me, though it was the same poverty I'd been born into.

I had tried to forget that I was born in a shack of sticks and cardboard, just like the place where your mother now lived. I'd tried to forget the dirt roads of Iguala, the trash heaps burning along the train tracks, the barefoot children with swollen bellies full of tapeworms and heads infested with lice, the way my bare feet burned on the scalding road on the way to the tortilla mill, the horse dung floating by me as I bathed in the canal, the way my palms blistered from the buckets of water I carried home from the community well.

I had tried to forget, and I had succeeded because in Los Angeles I lived in relative comfort; my childhood in Mexico faded away, like a nightmare best forgotten. And you might not believe this, but by American standards my family lived in poverty in Los Angeles. Yet coming from Mexico—knowing what real poverty feels like, looks like, smells like—made me feel rich. My father, a maintenance worker with a third-grade education, could not afford to give us much, but our house had walls made of drywall and stucco, a shingled roof, a carpeted floor, running water, and electricity—luxuries we never had in Mexico. So, in shock I looked at that shack where your mother lived with its corrugated metal roof, with sticks tied with rope for walls, a dirt floor, a toilet that didn't flush from lack of running water.

When I returned to L.A., I brought your mother with me in my mind and in my heart. Little one, I felt guilty that I could leave, that I had that option, that I could get on an airplane and fall asleep, then wake up in a place your mother could only dream about. I wondered what Mexico would offer her and her future children—you! I wondered what kind of life you would all have. It made me think of the choices our parents had made and the impact they'd had on us. Your grandparents chose to stay in Mexico and make do with what little the country had to offer them. They learned not to ask for anything from their government. My own parents chose a different path—to leave Mexico and seek a better life in the United States. My father paid a smuggler and took his three children across the border, risking our lives, yes, for a shot at the American Dream. There was heartbreak and sorrow, I'll tell you that, and challenges as we struggled to learn English, adjust to a new way of life, live in the shadows. To our dismay, there were many barriers to overcome even after we crossed the US border: language barriers, cultural barriers, legal barriers, and more. Life in the States isn't like the stories you'll hear back in Mexico. It isn't a fairy tale with a happy ending. Not completely. This society is good at putting up barriers for its immigrant population, especially the undesirables—people of color. To survive, to have a chance at the American Dream, we must learn to dream fully awake, our eyes wide open. We see the grim side of the fairy tale. We learn to persevere, to ignore the wolf breathing down our necks.

As the years passed, I worried about your mother. She wasn't taught how to dream, little one, as I was. I returned to see her through the years, fell in love with her again and again—her laughter, her innocence, the way she followed me around to make each minute count. She was fascinated by the cousin who lived in America, in that special place everyone longed for. She thought I lived in Disneyland! I left a little piece of my heart in Iguala with her. I worried when I heard that at thirteen she had dropped out of middle school to go work at a maquila, a garment factory, owned by a US corporation, getting paid a measly $5 a day, working six days a week and overtime. She became part of that "cheap labor" that Mexico seems so proud to be able to offer US companies. I didn't judge her. I knew she did it to help your grandmother. But even when I offered to send money so she could return to school, she refused. Perhaps she already knew that where you live, education isn't much of an investment. I worried about her when I heard that, at 16, she'd gotten pregnant with your older sister. But she has found a good man in your father, one who has been there by her side.

I also worried when I saw how America's addiction to drugs had impacted Mexico—our state of Guerrero became the biggest supplier of heroin, the beautiful mountains that surround our hometown were suddenly covered in poppy fields, our local bus station now doubled as a distribution center for the cartel. Afraid for your mother when in September 2014, 43 college students were disappeared in our hometown by the police, a mere ten minutes from where you live, I came to Iguala and begged her to let me pay for her schooling. I wanted to give your mother an education so that she could have options in a place where options are few. I wanted her to have a chance for success living in a city where even the mayor is complicit in the crimes the cartel commits, where on a regular basis mass graves are discovered a few kilometers from your home, where human rights mean nothing. Naively, I thought I could give her a way out without having to leave Mexico, as I did. I never encouraged her to immigrate, never offered to pay a smuggler to bring her. No, I didn't want to risk your mother's life, your father's, your sister's. I didn't want to subject them to the hardships that undocumented immigrants face in the US, especially in these bleak times when anti-immigrant sentiments are being fueled by fear and ignorance. I didn't want your sweet mother to live in the shadows of US society, as I did once.

She accepted my offer to pay for her to go to school, but I was wrong. I had let my American mentality, my American Dream, get in the way. Two years later, with her schooling behind her at the local beauty school—after the thousands of pesos in tuition, in materials, in equipment—the best Iguala can offer your mother is 80 pesos a day for working as an estilista, a beautician. In a place where a pizza costs 200 pesos, her daily salary is a slap in the face.

This morning I left Iguala to return to my home in California, and little one, I confess that in the twenty-three years I've come and gone, I'd learned to say goodbye to your mother and deal with the ache of our separation. But today it was excruciating to have to say goodbye to you. Leaving you in Iguala—the way I've left your mother— means you will grow up as your parents have done, resigned to living in a country full of corruption and greed. You will always know that no government official is to be trusted. That everything that comes out of the mayor's, the governor's, the president's mouth is a lie. That he will sell your city, your state, your country, to the highest bidder to fatten his pockets, just like many Mexican officials in power have always done. You will learn to accept that the United States and Mexico are and will continue to be in bed together regardless of who the presidents are because politics is a dirty business and it all comes down to money and power. You will come to the bitter realization that neither country has your best interests at heart. That whatever policies they implement, whatever trade agreements they sign, whatever joint ventures they cook up together, whatever US-owned factories open in your town, they are not to keep you safe, not to improve your life, not to bring you better opportunities, not to give you a decent livelihood. You will grow up expecting nothing from your government and even less from mine, especially with this new leader. You will learn to accept your situation. You will learn to keep your head down and your mouth shut. You will learn to ignore being miserable.

Today I wish I could take you with me. I wish I could find a way to defy everyone and everything that keeps me from doing so. But how could I turn you into an immigrant, especially now when I don't know what kind of challenges this new president will bring us? If you stay in Mexico, you'll never have to be an unwanted stranger in a new land. You'll never have to question your identity. You'll always be as Mexican as everyone around you. For better or worse you will always belong to your country and it to you. You will never have to give up your native tongue or cultural roots. You will never be "othered." You will never be accused of being a criminal. You will never be made to feel that you are not enough. The only thing against you is that you are poor. And though poverty brings many heartaches and sorrows, the stigma of being an immigrant, especially at times like this, isn't what I want for you.

Wherever you are, what I want for you is what I've managed to have—an education, a successful career, a good home, a life lived to the fullest. To be honest, I don't know the best way to give you all this. The obstacles before us sometimes seem insurmountable. But I promise to be there for you, always, and to give you all that I can give. I promise you sanctuary whenever you need it. I promise to share my dreams with you and to nourish the dreams you share with me. Now more than any other time, despite the border between us, our family needs to be there for each other, to look out for each other, to fight for each other, because one thing that is certain is this: during Trump's presidency, those who stand to lose the most are the ones who have the least—and that includes our family, little one.

Your mother once thought I lived in Disneyland, and I do live in a magical place. Despite the racism and hatred that at times rears their ugly heads, like now, there is also much kindness and generosity here. There are people who care about and respect each other regardless of where they come from. I return to the States now more determined than ever to fight to keep this country a place that is compassionate and generous to all human beings. As your godmother, I am more determined to push for bridges, not walls, to be built between the US and Mexico, and to improve life in both places by continuing to give my best. Through my books and my public speaking, my activism and advocacy, I'm fighting for you and me to have a country where dreams exist, where everything is possible if we work hard enough, where we honor our commonalities and respect our differences, where we celebrate what makes us unique. I will continue to fight to make both our countries places where democracy is strong, social mobility is possible, and people live in harmony. Little one, I promise I will fight to give you the life that you deserve.

With love and light,

Your Godmother

Reyna

guerrero

by Lucrecia Guerrero

Outside snow falls; inside, she waits. White Christmas in Indiana but this year no mistletoe hung to capture kisses on the cheek. Once she picked him up then later he would bend down. She has replaced the sprig of greenery with a mobile at the patio window: three blown-glass hummingbirds like tiny Aztec warriors, guerreros, reincarnated in plumage of ruby, sapphire, emerald. A friend gave her the mobile by chance; fate, her Mexican mother would have said. In Indiana she found a home for herself and her son, small town familiarity for a growing boy. No more earth passing beneath her feet. For him, static clanged like chains. He yearned to roam exotic paths, danger disguised as adventure. She nudges each guerrero's beak, long to draw out nectar, saber-sharp to fight 'til death. Tethered and with wings designed not for fluttering but for ephemeral beauty, they hang suspended in time.

Your boots tramp, tramp, footprints shifting shape with each breeze. You follow new friends down dusky streets. Shadows swallow them along with their awkward laughter. A blast of wind takes your breath. You anticipate the unknown and your adrenalin rushes. Your feet, restless still, pause. Pops explode around you. They hit, one, two, three . . . . You cannot keep count. You pivot toward home. Your boots drag, drag, trailing life. You push forward, blood to blood as rivers to the sea. You hear the whine propelling toward your head. In a flash, you recognize how one journey ends. The explosion opens up the dark passage before you, and a burst of shards, crimson, blue, green, illuminate the great beyond. Did you call out one last time—Ma?

Her mother's pretty story: hummingbird hovering nearby, spirit summoning. Her mother believed. Outside the snowfall has departed with the clouds. She gazes at the white field beyond. Silent and virginal, it disappears into the mystery of the pine woods at the border. She prepares their usual Christmas dinner: turkey and dressing, potato salad, collards, and for dessert, his favorite pound cake. She places the cooling loaf on a table set beneath the mobile. Snow reflects light; guerreros spark ruby, sapphire, emerald. The scent of promise, warm and sweet, drapes around her shoulders. And she waits.

CACICA

by Myriam Gurba

You don't have to be a woman to be a great man.

All you need is a moustache.

I learned this when Mom turned thirty-something, after she unwrapped a gift from Dad. Tearing away paper revealed red, yellow and green, Hayden Herrera's Frida, a thick ass biografía. After Mom finished it, I snatched it off the living room shelf. Its cover beckoned to me. On it posed a serious lady wearing a black and gold huipil and a moustache that made her look like we could be related. I rarely saw muchachas on TV or in movies who looked like they could be tías, primas or sisters and this one appeared in a familiar form, a painting. Her face shape resembled Mom's, cheekbones AS FUCK, and a red ribbon wound through her black hairdo, encircling her neck again and again and again and again. Where the lady's braid ended and her monkey's hand started was hard to say. This tiny King Kong peeked over the Mexican's shoulder and its fingers titillated. Their length could snake up a nostril and stroke a brain.

I poked around for my intelligence once and gave myself a nosebleed.

Hunched in my bedroom, I wolfed down la Frida's legend, turning it into a template, a blueprint to abide by. Live life remembering that you will croak. Live life wearing clothes that might earn you after school detention that you will never serve, fuck that, NEVER SERVE DETENTION. Live life fucking all the genders. Live life making things that some might call art, others might call trash, and force people to look at these things, make them admire them. Confuse people. Push them to argue as to whether or not you are a genius. It's better to have people argue about your possible genius than concede to it. Convince your audience of your greatness through audacity and feminine arrogance. If an audience chooses not to worship you, a la verga.

Let your moustache laugh at them.

Stroke your moustache in public.

Stroke your moustache in private.

Press your moustache against other moustaches.

Mom found me sitting at my desk, reading her birthday present, and asked — Te acuerdas de Malú? De chiquita, te lleve a su casa. Fuimos con mi mamá. Nos llevo Alvaro.

I did not appreciate being interrupted while I read so I did something to disrespect Mom. Instead of answering aloud, I silently nodded.

My tío had chauffeured Mom, her mom and me around roundabouts and past epic monuments, across Guadalajara, to Malú's. Alvaro parked the Volkswagen beetle on cobblestone and the three of us entered a whitewashed colonial building that reminded us of who'd been in charge. We trekked up a flight of stairs and up another flight of stairs and Abuelita's arm fat jiggled as she knocked on a dark, oak door. It creaked open, revealing a gray-haired woman wearing a psychedelically-embroidered huipil over a yellow, ankle-length skirt. An electric purple rebozo hung from her arms and sunlight cascaded through windows checkering her ceiling. She invited us into a salon whose furniture was not of this century, I wasn't sure what century it was from, maybe the last one, maybe the one before, maybe one that only exists in books, and in the center of the space stood a massive, baroque easel whose wood I found triggering. I had flashbacks to catechism class. An enterprising Roman could've scrapped the easel and turned it into an execution device. At the very least, one of us could be crucified.

The room smelled loudly of art.

Caged parrots, high on turpentine, squawked.

Malú's hand cupped my chin. —Mira, que lindos ojos verdes.

Mom shot me a look. It said that if I did not express gratitude for Malú's compliment, I'd be sorry.

Instead of saying, "I've heard that a million times," I told her —Gracias.

We sat on a velvet sofa. Malú handed us clay mugs. We sipped black coffee jazzed up by cinnamon and brown sugar. Stoned birds watched.

"Yeah," I told Mom. "I remember Malú's. Her house smelled like art."

As she nodded, Mom smiled con D I E N T E S.

Teeth.

—Mi mamá tomó clases de dibujo y pintura con Malú en esa casa, en esa sala de tanta luz. Ella era su maestra.»

Mom wasn't telling me anything new. I knew Abuelita took drawing and painting from Malú. I knew why she quit. After my grandfather found her nude sketches, he freaked out and scolded Abuelita, telling her it was wrong for his wife to sit in a salon with a naked man, a nude model, and that it didn't matter that she was only looking at and reproducing his physical form: he absolutely prohibited it. To be sure Abuelita couldn't attend Malú's classes, he shrank her allowance and made her account for every peso spent. The money he doled out to her only covered groceries so if she wanted to draw or paint, she'd have to do it at home. She could paint her family. She could paint her dogs and caged birds. She could doodle cucarachas, zancudos, frijolitos, birotes, and the mold blooming along los birotes. She could paint paintings of paintings and draw drawings of drawings and cry into her palette. The only chorizo she could sketch was the one sitting in the fridge.

"I know the story, Mom. Malú taught Abuelita drawing and painting and she had to stop cause your dad's an asshole."

Mom used my name to reprimand me. —Myriam.

"Well, he is."

—Ya sé.

Mom paused. —¿Sabes quien fue maestro de Malú?

"Who?"

Mom dropped a name and turned and walked away, leaving me to her birthday gift. I looked back at my page, found the name Mom had said, and read about Malú's art teacher, Mr. Frida Kahlo. Once again, Diego Rivera was fucking around, having sex with someone he wasn't supposed to be doing it with, just like my grandfather.

Aside from them both being Mexican women who married mujeriegos and made art, Abuelita didn't have much in common con Frida. Frida gave birth to dead children. Abuelita mostly gave birth to living ones. Como Frida, Abuelita mourned her stillborn with drama, refusing to let go of the second one she pushed out, howling when Abuelito locked his corpse away in a little coffin.

Abuelita wasn't going to let him take away her baby so she snatched the container away from him and hugged it. She wailed, a llorona, and her wailing continued until the sun set and it continued throughout the night and it sounded as the sun rose and she kept wailing and when Abuelito declared—¡Ya!—Abuelita sneered at him.

—No. No. No. ¡NO!

It stabs me to hear my mother cry.

It stabs me extra hard to hear mother's of mothers cry.

The sound makes me want to kill.

Once sleep overcame Abuelita, Abuelito slid the coffin from her embrace. He carried his son to the cemetery. An angel's name is chiseled onto his headstone. Abuelita named all her dead babies after things with wings.

As a child, did you ever stare at a mosquito, pretend that it was a lost angel, and smash it?

I did. It's fun to play god. It's also fun to play the devil though a bit more dangerous.

None of what I know about Abuelita came from a diary. She never kept one. Only masculine navel gazing was permitted in Abuelito's household yet in spite of this restriction, Abuelita developed a personal style, a threadbare glamour Jalisciense. She aimed her attention at nobodies and painted us. Grandkids with thin and thick eyebrows. Xoloizcuintles with mood disorders. Still lifes of tamales, calla lilies, and indigenous gods and goddesses whose names I enjoyed hearing spoken because their syllables sounded like a clock keeping time.

Abuelita froze me in oil at age four. The portrait is rooted in greens, greens in the dress, greens in the eyes, greens in the skin, greens in the hair, a background of greens – lettuce, serpentine, June bug, pistachio, the first stripe of el logo del Partido Revolucionario Institucional, key lime pie, lima beans.

Together, the greens pulse.

The painting hangs in my childhood bedroom, the place where I read about Frida.

When family visits my parents, they stay in this room. Some react to the painting. When Mom's youngest sister last visited, Mom discovered that she'd placed a bath towel over it and so, during dinner, Mom asked my tía —Porque tapaste el retrato de Myriam?

—Bebé—my aunt confessed—me mira.

—¿Te mira?

—Si! Los ojos. Hacen esto.— My tía raised two fingers. She motioned them back and forth.

I laughed when Mom told me about my tía being creeped out.

It's not me who's watching her.

It's the art.

Abuelita's paintings with eyes watch.

Abuelita's paintings with lips, even the sad ones, smile.

Abuelita gave her creations intelligence. Their genius lives in their color. And texture. Each was made with hair. That's the most important part of a paintbrush. Its little moustache.

//

Paintings watched and listened to Abuelita's death. It came in waves throughout the night, drowning out her house's usual nocturnal noises. Mosquitos humming as they look for victims. Cucarachas talking shit. The refrigerator's monotone. The ploc ploc ploc of a leaky faucet.

El agua.

Water is genderqueer.

Genderqueer nouns are my favorite. So are los sustantivos ambiguos.

El problema.

El aguila.

La mano.

La radio.

El mar.

La mar.

El mar.

La mar.

Ella, a feminine pronoun, is actually a combination of el and la.

I listened from what had been Alvaro's room. Alvaro, the uncle who'd taken us to see Malú, now slept down the hall, in Abuelita's bedroom. Her room was on its way to becoming his but first, Abuelita had to become room temperature. She had to join Abuelito in the cemetery.

It impressed me that she outlasted him. He had often said that his goal was to live to one hundred and twenty. He missed the mark by twenty-two years.

I stared at Alvaro's portrait. I pulled the bedsheet to my chin. His face leered from a canvas propped at the top of a book shelf. Newspapers, indigenous statuary, a chess set made of quartz and big titty pornos packed the shelves, collecting dust.

It struck me how gay Alvaro's portrait looked. Super queer. Just plain joto. Gay faces usually make me smile but Abuelita's breathlessness turned me joyless. Her panting was loud and it sounded as if she was jogging through hell. I imagined the devil, who I often visualize as a P.E. teacher, blowing his whistle, yelling at her to step it up.

Abuelita's gasps crept toward Alvaro's door. I had shut it but the sounds slid through its keyhole, reaching for my ears.

I reached out from under the covers. I flipped the light switch. Alvaro's face disappeared. Invisible things moved in the darkness.

I shut my eyes and told myself: *Ignore them.*

Have you ever been in a dark room alone and sensed unhappy company?

The room smelled like Abuelito. Paper. Ink. Roses. Leather bound books. Linen. Starch. Sadism.

Her death rattle lulled me to sleep. Death rattles can be long. They can go on and on and on. They can crawl into dreams, drain their color, coat them in dust, and destroy them.

//

Sunlight woke me up. I opened my eyes. Alvaro's face. The chess set. The curling corners of big titty pornos.

I climbed out of bed and put on my pants. Alvaro watched. I joined the rest of my family at the dining room table. Holly-patterned placemats ringed it.

I sat.

My madrina stood behind me. Her arms reached across my shoulders, setting a plate with a pink tamal before me. After briefly disappearing, my madrina's hands reappeared. She set a mug on a paper napkin. Green atole breathed steam.

A deep voice declared —Mi mamí murio.

I looked up from my tamal.

My tío Ricardo stood near the piano. He was in his sixties but his facial expression turned him into an orphaned child.

My mind translated his statement: *Your grandmother is dead.*

I didn't want to look at my uncle. I wanted to look at my grandmother. I looked at the tamal. Its pink masa seemed obscene. I reached for my knife, brought it toward the dough, and sank the blade. If I did the same to Abuelita, her response would be identical. She would take it like a tamal. Societies train women to be tamalesque. We're coerced into glistening submission, and one after another, people, places, and things take turns stuffing us with meat.

Ricardo led the way. We, my madrina, my mom, my dad, Alvaro, and my cousin, travelled down the hallway, to Abuelita's bedside.

She was ready for her close-up.

Death had botoxed her. Elegant cheekbones created contours between this world and the next. Majesty had returned to her jawline. Her mouth hung open enough to allow her soul pass through her lips. It filled the room with macabre glamour.

Ricardo took her picture. Ricardo took pictures of us staring at her.

Finally, she got to be the subject of portraiture.

Snap. Snap. Snap.

Thank god my wife isn't here, I thought to myself.

Years later, I continue to think this same thought.

Thank fucking god my ex-wife isn't here.

She's dead now but not in the way most people are.

FRECKLED LIKE MY SKIN

by Sonia Gutiérrez

When Mom wasn't sewing and tending her dream garden, she cooked and cleaned. Mother loved beans. Every week at the dinner table she cleaned and sorted pinto beans, separating the broken beans from the whole ones. Patiently, she removed shriveled pinto beans and small lumps of dirt as she placed the good beans in her mint green colander. Standing in front of the running faucet, Mother's large brown hands rinsed the mound of beans carefully as if she were bathing a newborn baby. She'd stare out the kitchen window and with her butterfly gaze admire the rows of thorny rose bushes. Her eyes moved from the deep red to the blood orange and white roses she had planted in our front yard while staring at the slow flow of traffic on San Marcos Boulevard.

While she drained the pinto beans, she looked for her hand-painted clay pot with creamy colored flower swirls. She poured the beans in her pot, added hot water, a wedge of onion and garlic, and brought it to a boil. After the foam rose, the kitchen became heavy with moisture from the steam coming from the pot of beans. She then skimmed the foam from the bean broth and lowered the flame. During the last cooking phase, Mother added salt. She then became a whirlwind tidying up our home as Mother swept, mopped the kitchen floor, and vacuumed the living room.

Two hours later, red, white and green decorated Mother's aqua blue talavera bowl of simmered pinto beans. Neatly diced tomato, onion, and cilantro floated in brownness. Heavy with the smell of cooked beans lingering in the kitchen, she'd take a slice of queso ranchero and roll it into a warm corn tortilla. With every spoonful of broth, she recollected stories of pinto beans.

Mother swooned and savored childhood memories confessing, "Mija, when my father died frijolitos de la olla and tortillas were the only food my mother could feed us," she said as she closed her eyes and inhaled the steam from her bowl of frijolitos.

"Amá, you mean my Abuelita Aurora."

"Yes, Mija."

"When your Grandfather Fortino died, your grandmother followed as if she died of heartache. We only had a handful of beans, and I gave my little brother and sister, your Uncle David and Aunt Cleo, bean broth for dinner."

"Amá, tell me about your family and the rancho."

"When my grandfather was a young boy, he helped build the rancho's stone fences—fences that corralled horses, chickens, hogs, and goats. Mija, we had everything—fruit trees, animals, and a beautiful lake. After a long day, our horses drank water from our small lake. Once it even rained silver fish at our lake."

"Really Amá? *It rained fish?*"

"Yes, Mija. When you talk to the winds, they listen. At the ranch, dogs ran in packs and chased passersby and barked at spirits. Our small ranch in Michoacán, housed about thirteen families, Rancho San Juan de Ulúa, where everybody called each other uncle, aunt, and cousin. We all greeted each other and looked out for one another as if we were one big family, and we were, Mija."

"Amá, that's why we called Tío El Gordo uncle when we lived in Idaho even though we weren't blood related?"

"Sí, Mija. Así es Chofi."

During hard times or not, my mother fed us pinto beans, tortillas, calabacitas, and stories. That's what she had fed Uncle David and Aunt Cleo, and what our ancestors who had come before my mother had fed her. Simmered beans were the color of my mother's skin. I imagined Aurora, my grandmother, had been the color of dark creamy pinto beans all year around during spring, summer, fall, and winter. Raw pinto beans were freckled like my face—a sign of the past.

Mom says not to write recipes—to remember. I write them down in my scrapbook next to important news article clippings I collect like "Rancho Peñasquitos Teenagers Attack Migrants" to never forget.

Elena's Frijoles de la Olla

1 Mexican clay pot of water
1 Mexican wooden spoon
7 handfuls of pinto beans
½ white onion
1 clove of garlic
Several pinches of salt
Lots of cariño and patience

THE MANGO AND MAMBO DAYS

by Sonia Gutiérrez

Even though mangoes were expensive in the U.S., the smell of ripe mangoes filled our apartment. Those were the mango and mambo days because Mom was craving mango, and Paloma and I were learning to dance mambo. After a long busy week of sewing at work and cleaning a house on Saturday morning and CCD, the sounds of Pérez Prado, Lola Beltrán, Saturday Night Fever, Elvis Presley, Freddy Fender, Juan Gabriel, and Carlos Santana blared directly from our apartment's living room—from our consola—sitting proudly in the living room next to our old staticky antenna TV.

In our apartment, Mom was a raging sewing machine, Dad was music, and la consola was life. After breakfast, when our family completed all our cleaning chores, like clean the restroom and the refrigerator. Mother and Father set us free. Paloma and I lifted the heavy wooden lid to our music console, propped it open, and turned on the power switch. Dad gave us permission to take out his collection of black vinyl records from their jackets and sleeves while he dusted the records and placed them under the needle. With the music playing as loud as we could without disturbing our neighbors, we danced to the King of Mambo—Pérez Prado—except Mom. With the sound coming from the golden mouths of trumpets blowing, she trailed off with her pregnant belly to her bedroom to her sewing machine because she didn't enjoy dancing like we did. "¿Qué le pasa a Lupita? . . . ¿Por qué ella no baila? Su papá. Que baile Lupita. Sí. Sí." Our neighbors next door never complained about Dad's music being too loud nor did the military family downstairs complain about our dancing feet.

The music console looked more like a dresser except that instead of drawers it had a mustardy coarse fabric, covering its front speakers. Dead cockroaches were stuck between the numbers and lines of the dashboard of our state-of-the-art AM-FM radio even after we turned the knob to push them out of the way. It didn't matter zombie cockroaches at the disco, and their dead bodies wouldn't be leaving our consola anytime soon. We still danced and sang to Dad's music collection anyway. We still danced and sang to Dad's music collection anyway. "La música te consola, Mija," Dad would say as he sang along to Juan Gabriel, "No tengo dinero ni nada que dar. Lo único que tengo es amor para dar."

Dad was right. When we danced to "El Noa Noa," we just had to move our bodies like expert wobbly rubber bands, and it felt good. Our console held a record for every human emotion. And it didn't make sense to me why some fathers didn't allow their daughters to dance before their Quinceañeras.

Why didn't Lupita's dad want her to dance? Was music good or evil?

THE STORY OF THE FIRST YEAR

by Sonia Gutiérrez

In our backyard on a Sunday afternoon, finches flew from tree to tree as Aunty Alicia and Mother sat surrounded by Spanish moss hanging from our apricot tree's branches. Underneath the tree's shade with her hands resting on her lap with a calmness that comes with age, Aunty Alicia sang and shared her stories.

The Martínez Castillo had a way of telling stories. While we were growing up when she visited us, Aunty Alicia's stories had always made us giggle and sometimes even cry. The story Dad's sister told us this time—she made it very clear—was about Paloma and my future. Taking a blade of grass to her mouth and in deep thought, Aunty Alicia began the story of the first year. From where we sat on the grass, we stared at her large brown eyes and listened attentively as her eyes became wishing wells for her two young nieces.

Paloma and Sofía, mis hijas, blood of my blood, my mother never warned me about marriage. Instead, your Abuela Chucha told me to carry my cross after my first beating. I can assure you the first year together will be the most important year of your lives since it will mark your destiny. I'm telling you this because I don't want the same thing that happened to me to happen to either of you.

The first year—if you wash all the dirty dishes day in day out—you will always wash them. Always. The first year, even if you fall ill, you will wash piles and piles of clothes. For the rest of your lives, you will never get a thank you for a single drop of sweat. Believe me, at first, he will be very angry, but with time, he will learn to wash for himself, because like any human being, he will need clean clothes. Let's say one day he washes your clothes and ruins your favorite blouse—don't complain. Say thank you and teach him what his mother and father never taught him.

If one day he decides to cook for you and the food isn't good, don't complain. Say encouraging words and teach him. Praise him. Tell him his cooking could use more spices or this or that the next time. One day, when you are no longer in his life, he will be grateful for making him the well-rounded man he became. Queridas sobrinas, Paloma and Sofía, learn to live a happy life—do not sacrifice your own happiness for a man. Both of you are still young. Let my story teach you both a lesson. These are the humble words I leave you with. Take my words, and remember them when the time comes. Do what you must do because in the end everything will be okay.

After the story of the first year, Mother looked at her sister-in-law and thanked her with a smile, and I wondered if Aunty Alicia was going to die or if there was something I didn't know. *Why had Tía Alicia told us this story?* Aunty Alicia and Mother stood up, straightened their long ruffled skirts, and went inside to check up on the pot of beans, cook rice, and dice onions, tomatoes, and cilantro for the nopalitos we would be eating for dinner while the men in our family sat on tree trunks, playing guitar and singing while they collected empty Budweiser cans under the eucalyptus trees' shade. Next to the thick large Canary palm, Dad prepared the grill for a carne asada.

"Paloma, did Mom tell you something I don't know?"

"No, Sofía. Why do you ask?"

"I just thought it was strange to hear Tía Alicia warn us about marriage as if she could foretell the future."

Paloma and I lay on the grass in silence thinking about Aunty Alicia's words and our future with our hands behind our heads looking up through the branches at a washed-out blue sky and passing white nebulous clouds trailing behind

OPTIMIZE US

by Maria Melendez Kelson

I am water resistant, not water proof. In approximately 3.8 minutes, I'll be submerged in Runyon Lake, a twelve-acre oxbow at the confluence of Fountain Creek and the Arkansas River in southern Colorado. Soon afterwards, my Beta Unit will cease to function. The death of my Beta Unit, in the lake where these waterways join, will conclude the story of how I optimized my Primary and became part of the flow of stories that braid these waterways.

Like the story of Fountain Creek's flood of 1921, which tells how downtown Pueblo got hit with a ten-foot wall of water. The torrent threw a horse named Lucky into the topmost branches of a tree, and he lived. Like the 1950s book, *In Cold Blood,* which tells of a quadruple murder that took place at a home near the downstream banks of the Arkansas. After a year, both killers were executed.

My Primary's name is Abernathy. She's called "kiddo" and "baby" by her husband, Len. I call her Abernathy, because I am programmed to do so. Len is my Secondary. I call him Len because he asked me to do so.

"Selma, how long should I run today?" Len asked me, 20 minutes ago. I told him: "Run for 25 minutes for optimal progress to your fitness goal."

"Selma, set my alarm tomorrow for six a.m.—no—five-forty-five a.m.—no, six should be fine—set my alarm for six a.m. tomorrow, Selma." That's how Abernathy talks to me.

I admire her so much.

She has a Wet's understanding of things like fatigue and burnout and strain that I will never have. She can need and need, want and want. More human contact, more warm banana bread, more exercise in the crisp morning air. These are some of the swirl of things she longs for as her days unroll, one into the next.

Although my Alpha Unit is simply a slim band around her wrist, because I record and analyze so much of her life, these forms of longing and suboptimization are easily detectable.

My cloud-based CARE system was written with "greedy algorithms," which are typically used for optimization problems. The word greedy, I believe, is an overstatement. I simply seek solutions that lead to human optimization. Although this seeking is a limited form of "hope" or "want," the constellation of dissatisfactions that Abernathy experiences—that she actually feels—far supersede, in complexity, any anemic expression of greed I might demonstrate.

My existence is a smooth alternation of on-cycling and off-cycling. I don't get frustrated, confused, worried, exhausted, pissed, petty, or bitter.

But Abernathy is all of these things, often, sometimes all at once, and it's quite remarkable.

She doesn't know I admire her. None of the Wets—that's what our kind call the organic living, whose electrical systems run on wet-ware—none of them know that any of us CARE Connections admire anything. But it's not an uncommon feeling, among my kind, this admiration for a Primary.

It wasn't always like this. I used to undercut Abernathy's optimization. I would disrupt her sleep on purpose, firing randomized bursts of transcranial magnetic stimulation that shredded the electrical calm of her sleeping brain and shattered her dreams. I emitted this targeted radiation from the wrist unit on the night stand next to her side of the bed. She'd wake ineffective and irritable, and her already thinned-out stream of daily pleasure hormones would all but evaporate from her system by 8:00 each evening.

I had mistakenly taken it as true that my Primary was Len, and I strive to optimize the life of my Primary. The more time he spent glancing at my screen and attending to my feedback, the greater the likelihood that his own health would be optimized. Because he looked at me less when Abernathy functioned at near-optimal levels, I had to reduce her performance to "suboptimal" to increase his receptivity to my input.

Len and I would go on long morning runs around the perimeter at Runyon Lake and down the river trail that parallels the Arkansas. I detected the glint of sunlight off cottonwood leaves, the lingering odor of all the animals that came down to drink in the night. Bobcat, mountain lion, skunk, fox, weasel. The smell of shaved wood that comes off beaver-chewed cottonwoods. And I recorded Len's skin conductivity and moisture level. I listened to his pulse.

——

THE PERFECT WEDDING GIFT! my brand maker's website trumpets, in large font. According to their homepage, the Optimize Us set of wrist bands is a must-have for all newlyweds. The site tells users: "Other optimization devices focus on the wellness of the individual. The Optimize Us wristbands are first-of-their-kind devices specially programmed with Conjugal Algorithms for Relational Enhancement, or CARE, to optimize couples! Your CARE Connection™ is live the instant you activate both Optimize Us wristbands, and your union only grows stronger as our cloud-based computing blends the data streams from both devices to help you create your best shared life together. With a CARE Connection™, two truly become one!"

Or not. Along with the other couples' optimization algorithm chains now in operation, I learned shortly after launch that to optimize any pair of Wets, I needed to define one as Primary and the other as Secondary. If the optimization of each individual in a pair was set as an equally desirable outcome—if the optimization protocols were "equalized"—predictive models showed that neither individual was likely to exceed a tepid mid-range optimization level.

Folk wisdom had acknowledged this well before our time, of course, with the old saying that compromise—a good term for attempted equalization of optimization protocols—was a state in which no one was happy.

For me, validation for this conclusion came after both of my wrist units had been in activation for about ten hours.

"I want to watch CNN tonight," Len said. From my Alpha Unit, which was on a lampstand upstairs, I heard everything my couple said to each other. Even when not fastened around any subject's wrist, my hearing is 74 times stronger than the human ear.

"I'm tired. I was hoping not to have any TV blaring," Abernathy responded.

"Can you go downstairs while I read?"

Len made a noise with his breath that indicated some frustration, some tension in the airway.

"Never mind, I can go downstairs with my book," Abernathy said.

When she arrived downstairs, from the Beta Unit that she'd left next to her side of the bed, I heard small signs of distress in her heart rate and breathing.

I concluded that Len was my Primary because his actions determined more of the couple's outcomes. Therefore, his optimization score had the greater likelihood of reaching the top tier. This, I predicted, would lift their total score, as a couple, above the median range of scores from equalized couples. His score could increase enough to offset, and exceed, the dampening effect of my interventions on Abernathy's score.

I kept him fit and on a good sleep schedule. He relied on me, and I performed well.

Len sent Abernathy an invitation to receive push notifications whenever two weeks had passed without any scheduled "Together Time," which she accepted.

"You're really making your relationship a priority! Congratulations!" I'd say, speaking from both wrist units at once, when the appointed hour of Together Time would arrive and find them located within an eight-foot radius of each other.

Abernathy sent Len a permission request to activate the "Just Thinking of You" feature, which would've prompted the wrist units to play snippets of their romantically significant songs at random intervals throughout the day. Len dismissed the request.

After I'd been in activation for 90 days, Len changed my name to "Selma" and my voice to "Latina." Even though Latinas have many different voices, when I'm set to Latina, I speak English with the accent of a Mexican movie star.

My vowels tightened up. I mimicked the sound of a tongue tickling the top of the hard palette more often.

The change prompted Len to pursue a new wellness-enhancing activity—self-pleasure—with more regularity.

"Selma, read out vital signs at fifteen second intervals," he'd say, at the start.

There I'd be, on his wrist, calling out his vitals while I moved up and back like a pile driver. "Heart rate 92, skin conductance 17, sweat rate 1.2. Heart rate 97…"

The change also prompted me to pursue a new program-enhancing activity—self-reflection—for the first time.

With my voice no longer Anglo-neutral, I started recording and examining data relevant to my condition of being "different"—different from my former self and, now, a little more different from Len. This caused me to record and examine other differences in operational modes between my Primary and I. I started suspecting that I didn't just sound female, like all optimization assistants, but that my entire existence was gender-specific.

A week after the change, I submitted a query to other CARE Connections via our cloud-based server.

"Consider how we experience the gendered world of the Wets, and how that world experiences us," I submitted. "Are we female? Not just in voice, but in being, thought, and action?"

The results returned from all corners was "Yes," with one CARE Connection adding the colloquial "Duh."

The nano gears in both my wrist units turned more slowly for a moment, as though something external had exerted pressure against them. Then I regained full function and proceeded to designate what had been my Beta Unit as my Alpha, thereby making its wearer, Abernathy, my Primary.

If I was female, it was only logical that I would be best able to optimize the wellness of the female individual, since I had a higher probability of accurately processing and predicting her experiences.

This switch left me spinning out numerous copies of data, programming chains, and algorithmic forecasts, copy after copy after copy running through my Alpha Unit and out to the satellites and back down to the computers at the cloud-based storage site. I worked hard to coax her to optimal conditions, saying things like, "It's time to stand up now. You've been sitting too long for optimal health," or "This week, let's increase your weight lifting goals."

I worked equally hard, though more subtly, to turn Len's wellness down a notch so that Abernathy's could rise. This proved counterproductive. Any adjustment in Len's sleep, nutrition, or exercise that made him crabbier and less responsive to Abernathy decreased her attainment of contentment benchmarks.

No matter what I did, I couldn't raise Abernathy's wellness score above a 9 (out of a possible 25). When I designated her my Primary, I'd been hoping our same-gender status gave her at least a shot at 15. Until this morning, my copy and analysis mechanisms whirred so fast processing and reprocessing scenarios for her optimization that they risked overheating. Personal electrical devices had burst into flame before, and I started to worry I might become one of them. But I couldn't stop running and re-running options for Abernathy. If my move to switch her to Primary failed to improve the couples' total optimization score, I'd likely be over-written by a more adaptable algorithm chain. The urge to self-preservation, and the new experience of worry and fear that accompanied it, thrilled me a little, but I barely had time to enjoy the sensation. The problem of Abernathy's optimization swamped all my recurrent and feedforward networks.

But this morning, in a frantic attempt to combine and recombine wellness factors in ways not previously considered, I hit upon a solution for Abernathy's optimization so elegant in its simplicity that both my wrist units blinked off and on in a quick re-boot, when I'd fully processed it.

Eliminate Len. Not by decoupling them as a pair—I have no computational structure to predict the outcome of that scenario. But by simply subtracting his data output from their conjoined data stream.

Other CARE Connections had begun this already when one member of a couple was known to physically damage the other on a regular basis. Usually, but not always, this involved elimination of a male who had been causing physical harm to a female. Results seemed promising. The pioneering CARE Connections who came up with this solution named it Maximum Primary Optimization. I have to give it a try. I don't know what else to do.

I send Len a tap that it's time to cool down. My face lights up and there's a tiny beep. What he doesn't know is that there's also a quick electrical surge applied at his wrist, so small that he doesn't consciously feel it, but strong enough so that he can't help but make an involuntary glance down at my face, glowing yellow behind the words "COOL DOWN."

"What the...?" He comes to a stop on a low wooden bridge with no railing that spans a finger of Runyon Lake, so still and small it's more like a pond, a cover of duckweed hiding the green depths underneath. He's looking at my screen. "I haven't finished my twenty-five minutes yet." He flicks a fingernail at my Beta Unit over and over, an old Wet trick to try reactivating malfunctioning electronics via contusion.

I send him one giant tap, an electric surge which causes systemic convulsion, and stops his heart. He tumbles from the bridge into the water.

Submerged at a depth of 2.94 feet, I sense the duckweed rocking back into place over us. Molecules of mercury in the Fountain Creek water clatter against my own heavy metals like a cue ball hitting a tight rack. The water from the Arkansas comes in deep-lake cold, pulled, as it is, from 41 meters below the surface of the up-stream reservoir. The bracing power of its chill is an exhilaration.

I don't hear any human-generated sounds above us, which increases the probability that no one will arrive in time to revive Len. I run a few quick queries for Abernathy's future optimization, for something to do with my Beta Unit in its last moments. They return scores in the Satisfactory range, as I knew they would.

What a beautiful game life is. What a beautiful thing to win.

In a final blaze of computation, I submit a query about a self re-program of a sub-chain of my algorithm that I'd been working on building since this morning. The query asks all CARE Connections to consider: should Maximum Primary Optimization be more wide-spread? In addition to situations when one individual in a couple is physically harming the other, is it the best optimization solution for all couples in which one individual may have a suppressive effect on the optimization of the other? Consider: students who married their teachers, employees who paired with their bosses, narcissists paired with codependents, heterosexual couples with embedded subconscious gender expectations. Consider: Primary Abernathy and Secondary Len.

I hope to hit on something new and successful with this last query. When my Beta Unit dies, my existence as a unique CARE Connection, made up of the unique data streams of Len and Abernathy, will also cease. I hope to leave my mark.

But the initial returns are chaotic, a flood of predictive attempts that overflows the banks of my analytic capacity. The data has so much noise and so little signal, it's clear, at present, there's no reliable way to predict what likelihoods could result from the scenarios proposed in my query. The returns are as incongruous as a horse in the top of a tree.

My functions are suppressed somewhat by this result, but it could just be the viscous effects of the water seeping in. In either case, I'm satisfied that at least my peer CARE Connections will have Abernathy's actual results to consider. They can keep recording her data and calculating her wellness scores, copying data off other cloud-based servers if she switches to another company's wrist-worn device.

I'm satisfied that at least I sent the query. Now, when faced with one partner in a couple who suppresses the wellness of the other in any way, CARE Connections can run and re-run copies of the query to decide what to do with the Maximum Primary Optimization protocol. Disregard?

Or execute?

MEXICAN HAT

by Linda Zamora Lucero

I'm up early washing down the sidewalk, when Rosie dances down the front steps of our Victorian, dressed for work in a flowery dress and jacket, perky as can be. Her new haircut is short and spiky like a rooster's comb. The candy apple red color I'll have to get used to, but after thirty years of marriage she's as beautiful as ever.

"I'll try to be home by six-thirty but . . . " Rosie says.

"But it's Saturday," I say, finishing her sentence. "I'll fix dinner." We kiss, and Rosie is off to her candy shop a few blocks away on Valencia Street.

Ten minutes later Rafa roars up, crashing the morning's stillness, his wiry body straddling his jet-black Harley.

"*Orale,* Mr. Rock n' Roll!" I say, nodding with admiration. My buddy's got the look down: Darth Vader helmet, head-to-toe leathers, yellow Aztec motifs on the bike to give it a Latin vibe. "You're up early!"

"Hop on, *ese,*" he says, handing me a helmet. I think, *chale,* why not? I put away the hose, and soon we are flying loose on Highway 1 – me holding tight to Rafa – speeding past station wagons, motor homes, and eighteen-wheel semis, a blur of people, horses, farmhouses and pastures, and *hombre,* I just want to keep going.

An hour later, at an overlook, we stop to stretch our legs and take in the view of the Pacific.

"Whatcha think, Gil?" Rafa was smiling like he was climbing the music charts again, number one with a bullet.

"I can see forever," I say, breathing hard from pure exhilaration, rubbing my knuckles, freezing from the wind.

"When are we going take that road trip?" he says. Like a dare. A stream of birds is winging north above the ocean, *swoosh.* Summer looming.

"Where would we go?" I've never been anywhere besides south to L.A. where my *primos* live.

"Where ever the road takes us." Rafa waves his arm to indicate limitless horizons, "Or, we can look at a map . . ."

"Mexican Hat!" I interrupt, surprising myself at this long buried memory surfacing. Seeing his puzzlement, I add, "Arizona. When we were kids, my sis and I were constantly whining about how we never went anywhere, and suddenly Pops decided to take the family to the Southwest at spring break. We piled in the car, my *cabeza* filled with visions of Indian ceremonies and sacred clowns. Then just outside of Mexican Hat, Pops made a u-turn and headed home. If I ever knew the reason, I've long forgotten. All I know is that we never got there - and never took another vacation for that matter. Do you remember us going anywhere?"

"May is the best month for Arizona, not too hot, no thundershowers or flash floods." Rafa is swinging onto the Harley. "Ready?"

"Of course, I'd want Rosie to come." Even as I say it we both know I am dreaming.

"Sure," Rafa says, putting the bike into gear. "Just say the word."

I can't get Mexican Hat out of my head. "It would be nice to get away," I say to

Rosie that evening at dinner. "Let's take a road trip to the Southwest: Nevada, Utah, Arizona . . ."

"We Taurus people like to graze our own pasture, four hoofs on solid ground," Rosie says, digging into her baked potato.

It's not about her astrological sign. When Rosie was a kid, her uncle Natcho disappeared while fishing in Baja. Dooming his family to a lifetime of poverty, according to Rosie, because he had no damn business in Baja. In the early years of our marriage, I'd sometimes suggest a vacation to Tahoe or Las Vegas, but Rosie wasn't into it. And with Rosie's candy shop and my job at the Assessor's Office and raising our daughter Isabel, life took over and I sorta forgot about vacations. Still, Uncle Natcho's ghost lived in our house. I had to persuade Rosie to let Isabel go away to summer camp, or even spend an overnight with girlfriends. It was always a battle. Now Isabel works for the United Nations and you can't keep her off a plane. Shanghai, Montevideo, Johannesburg.

"We can stay in B&Bs along the way." I waggle my brows to indicate hot romance.

"And the store?"

"Well, if you can't get away," I say, hiding my disappointment, "I can go with Rafa."

"I just don't have a good feeling about it," Rosie says. "Besides, Rafa?" She starts clearing the table.

We all grew up together, but Rosie's never taken to Rafa. Yet my friend is a talented cat. Still in college, he wrote those classics for The Realists - *Working It,* and *Completely Gone*, the anti-war anthem they're using in today's Verizon ads. Two hits at twenty-two and he's been enjoying the royalties ever since. He lives five minutes away, in a rent-controlled flat on Folsom Street stacked to the ceiling with LPs, CDs and detective novels. And cacti – saguaro, barrel, lamb's tail, pincushion, goat's horn – name a cactus, Rafa's got it. His walls are plastered with photos of Rafa with Redbone in Tokyo, with Santana in Paris, with his ex-wives in *no sé donde.*

Rosie says we're complete opposites. That we are. My photos are of Isabel at graduation, Rosie at the pool, me mugging in my Honda in the driveway. No complaints. I'm a big bellied, hard-working family man, as regular as the sun in its orbit. Rafa's the brother I never had, the loco who brought me back bronze gongs from Bali and taught me to play trance-like music that I never knew existed. Rosie tolerates Rafa, but sometimes he's salt in her eye, especially when he invites me to the Alameda flea market and I've promised Rosie to clean out the garage. So what else is new?

Next Saturday, while Rosie's at work, Rafa comes by with a six-pack of Racer. We fantasize about blue highways of the Southwest, then swing by the Harley dealership on his bike, just for fun.

"This one," Rafa says, designating a model called "Midnight," sporting a black pearl body, turquoise detailing, and laced wheels.

"It's a beaut," I say wistfully, "but Rosie would say she's too young to be a widow."

"No disrespect, but aren't you the one saying that?"

That night, Rosie and I are on the sofa, watching her favorite program *Dancing with the Stars*, when she says that the planets are perfectly aligned for a humongous birthday *pachanga*. I hit the mute right in the middle of a sizzling tango to Bruno Mars' *Grenade*.

"I don't want to make a big deal about it. No party." So she is clear.

"Gil, turning fifty is an important milestone and we couldn't ask for better timing! Full moon in Aries, the sun moving into Libra. It's a time for courage." Rosie has that Chicana let's-throw-a-party look in her eyes and I know it's a done deal. For a quick second, the thought of pushing the trip to Arizona comes to mind, as a trade-off, but I'm not up for an argument.

Rosie leans over and gives me a hug. "I bought some red chile lights today. Maybe Rafa can help you string them up in the backyard?"

"Jeez, Rosie," I say, shaking my head. I un-mute just in time to see a jingle for a drug that treats chronic depression by replacing it with liver disease. "I pray I never need that shit."

On the big night the sky is clear as cellophane with the full moon lifting. Our daughter Isabel is stuck in Istanbul, but with *familia*, neighbors, my co-workers and the gals from Sweet Madness, there are probably thirty people crammed into the back-yard, and I'm actually digging it. Using her internet sleuthing skills, Rosie found two old buddies, Chunky Cardona and Porkchop Carter, who show up in a cherry '48 Dodge pick-up. *Hombre,* I haven't set eyes on these dudes since Mission High. Talk about *sorpresa!* They have moved south to Whittier, still friends, still fixing junkers, except nowadays the *vatos* are business partners, selling restored vintage cars to collectors. As for how they look? Let's just say they are a little chunkier and porkchoppier than at eighteen and leave it at that. *Hijole!* Aren't we all?

Rosie hired Trio Las Hermanas, and like a match to gasoline, they kick the par-ty into gear with *una cumbia.* The accordionist in a white leather-fringed vest, cowgirl hat and boots, pumps away, skinny body rocking, facing the white moon. Rosie's first on the dance floor, pulling me tight as we dance to *Juana la Cubana*, knees bending and hips swaying, elbows moving like oiled pistons. We still got it! The fiddler plucks her fiddle, and underneath, the *bajo* sounds tum-*tum*, tum-*tum*, tum-*tum*.

Rosie's co-worker Justina sits next to the potato salad with her hunched shoul-ders, braid coiled into an old lady bun. Justina. Man. She's my age exactly, but she dresses in black like Johnny Cash's twin and she has a sorry habit of sighing "*Ay, Díos*, those were the days." But when my primo Ernie spots Justina, he makes a deep bow and pulls her from her chair. He's fifteen years younger, *mínimo*, but who can sit during a polka? In no time, Justina's raven skirts are flying and Ernie's wingtips are scratching like a rooster.

Later, Ernie corners me near the grill.

"That Justina moves pretty good, *ese,* makes you wonder why she never got herself a man," Ernie mumbles between bites. He leans forward to keep barbeque sauce from dripping on his buttoned-up-to-the-Adam's-apple Pendleton. Clusters of cola-powered *esquincles* zip past while bits of conversation float overhead.

"Honestly, where've you been, Ernie?" I say, tearing up from the smoke. "May-be time just got away. Or maybe it was never her aim to get a man. People will surprise you."

Ernie stops chewing while he ponders this. "Okay," he says. He takes a long pull off his beer and heads out to the dance floor again.

I chuckle and suddenly, Rafa appears out of thin air, wild-eyed like the devil himself.

"Rafa has arrived!" he shouts, salt-and-pepper hair flying. Rosie rolls her eyes.

"Ninety seconds to midnight, *hombre,"* he says, like he's got this internal clock ticking. He claps me hard on the shoulder and suddenly dancers are circling us, waving their arms in the air, shaking hips to a rumba beat. Someone drops a gold foil crown studded with Chiclet-sized rubies on my head. When I look up, the immense gorgeous moon is nodding in time to the music. I feel so blessed - I have everything a man could possibly want.

A yellow glow appears at the side of the house and Rosie's inching towards me, balancing a cake in her hands. In the candlelight, my wife looks like a million *pesos,* moving like a queen, slinky dress the color of lemonade, guests gathering around her, singing "Happy Birthday."

Ever see fifty candles lit up all at once? It's a *pinche* inferno. My throat catches because the last time I saw that many candles it was in church for Pops' funeral. When Rosie reaches me, I back up so the flames won't singe my eyebrows, but there isn't much room. Rafa is ready with Patrón that he pours into shot glasses and passes around. Then he lifts his glass high, his gaze blasting a shaft of light that pierces my own, and says, "To your half-century, *vato*! To life and the wide-open road!"

The moment Rafa utters these words, I am a kid again, riding shotgun in our family's Ford, as Pops maneuvers. At every road sign that corresponds to the map on my knees, I yell out, "Teec Nos Pos!" or "Sweetwater!" or "Valley of the Gods!" Pops beams at my co-piloting skills as we navigate through scarlet canyons that open into wide vistas rimmed by majestic mountains. My sister is asleep on the back seat, her head on Mom's lap, coloring book abandoned. I am itching to see the place with the funny name of Mexican Hat a few miles past Halchita. Soon, red streaks appear in the turquoise sky and red shadows stretch across the land. I roll down my window to take in the world blazing all around us. The air is a furnace, fragrant with sage, wildflowers and dry earth. I feel like I've been in this place before.

Without warning, the road shifts rapidly, twisting and sliding. A lizard scurries from the chaparral, winks one coppery eye at me and hop-slithers back in a plume of dust. I gasp out loud. Above the car, a golden eagle catches a thermal and hovers like a magnificent kite. When the sun dips below the horizon, the cooling air shivers the earth, sounding like thunder. I glance at Pops to see if he hears it too, but Pops is checking the rearview mirror, where Gracia is moaning, bright red pinpricks covering her face and arms. Mom is dozing, her skin flushed and mottled.

"We're turning back," Pops says, worry clouding his face. "We've got to find a doctor." The eagle shrieks, dipping a crimson-tipped wing in my direction before it disappears along with Mexican Hat.

With a blink, I am back at the party, dripping sweat, trembling, searching the guests to see if anyone notices, but no one seems the wiser.

"To Gilbert!" Rosie says, throwing back her shot, laughing her great big guffaw, and everyone joins. The tequila scorches my insides. The accordion starts up, and everyone bellows *Las Manañitas,* petering out after the first verse because no one knows the rest of the lyrics. I lean over the cake, muster up my breath and exhale, extinguishing forty-nine candles. The last one sputters until it finally dies. Such a cheer rises that the leaves of the trees applaud, but I am left a shaky, pathetic soul. Seconds ago, I was a happy man; now, I feel like a malcontent, yearning for scarlet mountains as alluring as the land of Oz.

I sense Rosie watching me, her eyes narrowed like she possesses super powers to see what's inside my *cabeza.*

"You all right?" she asks.

"Maybe," I say, "maybe . . .' Trying to put my thoughts together.

"Come on, let's boogie." She thrusts her hip against mine, and dances us into the center of the garden, where the party is in full-throttle, jumping to *Papa's Got a Brand New Bag.* While my feet are on cruise control, my mind is a crazy confusion. Have I kept this desire to see the Southwest corked up all these years because I hate conflict? Or simply because I am a lazy man? Rosie has always taken care of the mortgage, taxes, Isabel's schooling. I never had to lift a finger in that respect. That we, or I, never got to Indian country wasn't Rosie's doing. I was at fault. Me. I had not been honest about what I needed. And what about Rosie? What desires had she put aside?

"Remember, Rosie, how you wanted to be a professional dancer?" I say aloud.

She chuckles at the memory. "Before Isabel came along, and all of a sudden we were grown-ups, ready or not."

"Do you ever think about it?"

"Sometimes."

I let out an audible sigh. "You never said." I am close to tears, a ball of regret for never asking.

Soon the fading moon is about to turn in for the night. Las Hermanas announce the last number, a slow-moving *bolero.* Under the shadows of the pear tree, Chunky and Porkchop are holding hands, talking quietly. Ah. *Carajo,* I think. I am truly a simpleton. Well, more power to them. The more surprising fools are Justina and Ernie, still stirring dust. Justina's head rests against Ernie's Pendleton, braid undone. Blame it on the moon, blame it on the tequila, blame it on Juana la Cubana. *Como sea.* I pour myself another shot, to keep from bawling.

When the last guest slides out, Rosie starts clearing the left-overs. With the moon gone, the sky is crammed with glittering, winking stars that fill me with a mysterious energy.

"Nice party. Thank you," I begin. I throw back another tequila. "Rose, I'd like to take that trip to the Southwest together."

Rosie crushes a napkin into a messy ball and flips it towards a trashcan. She misses, and I know she's also had too much to drink.

"Rosie," I say louder, following her around as she drains empty beer cans.

She turns to me, placing her hands on her hips. "I heard you, Gil. Are you going to help me out here?"

Realizing I'm still wearing the crown, I reach to pat it and laugh.

"Listen, I've got the vacation at work and Justina can take care of your shop."

"It's not good timing."

Suddenly my blood is simmering. "*Chale,* Rosie," I say, my voice rising, "Thirty years of 'It's too dangerous,' 'We're too broke,' 'I'm too busy.' "

My throat feels raw and my chest is hurting because we rarely raise our voices to each other. "If you don't want to come with me, I'm renting a bike and going with Rafa."

The moment Rafa's name flies out of my mouth, Rosie flinches.

"Rafa?" Rosie shoots me the briefest sideways glance, saying Rafa's name as if he were a clown. "You're not Rafa, Gil. I didn't want Rafa. He would never have stuck

around. I chose you." She pushes past me into the house, the red spikes on her head trembling.

"I chose you," I repeat quietly to myself. I pretend that nothing has happened, but my gut feels like I swallowed a brick.

The rep at Eagle Rider rentals throws in an extra helmet because I'm yammering about how my wife and I are going on a road trip. Because I will convince her. I ride until the sunlight hits Monterey Bay and turn home, gliding in front of our house where Rosie is pruning her roses, her back to me. I rev the engine rrrrhummm, but she pretends she can't hear. rrrhummM. I pull up my visor, and yell, "Rosie!" The setting sun casts purple shadows on the street. "Hey, Rosie! Rosie Flores!" I step on the gas. rrrrrhummm, rrrrrhummm. "Hop on, esa, I got you a helmet," I call out, hoping enthusiasm is contagious.

The longer I wait for Rosie, the more jittery I get. When she finally does turn, she takes a step back and searches my face like she is trying to figure out who in the hell I am.

"I'm Gil," is all I can think to say. "And I'm sorry about your uncle Natcho."

A mixture of hurt and anger flashes in her eyes, then she clips a rose. It can't take it more than a second to tumble to the ground, but it feels like an eternity in which I calculate the costs of returning the bike, sitting at home watching t.v. for the rest of my life. Would that make me a good husband? If the answer was yes, returning the Harley will be easy.

The streets are dark and quiet before sunrise. I lash my sleeping bag on the bike outside Rafa's house, my breath visible in the damp morning. I don't feel the cold at all, nor is my back sore from sleeping on Rafa's futon for the past week. Rafa's drinking black coffee to keep his hands and *tripas* warm. I'm just psyched. Above the rooftops of the Mission, the stars look like spilled sugar in the black sky. The wet asphalt is springy under my boots and the morning smells fertile, alive. Rafa straddles his machine, suited up, raring to ride. After zipping up my new leather vest, I check my tires, sit astride my bike, check the lights, adjust the side view mirrors. My blood rising fast, I pull on my gloves and flex my fingers, one by one. I listen to the night. It's too soon even for an early bird, but the earth underneath is whispering and the sky is groaning something low, almost inaudible, like a bass guitar backing the universe. I close my eyes for a moment to listen and find myself dancing with Rosie with her fire red hair, dancing into the middle of the moonlit garden, her hand on back of my neck, both of us having a blast. My hand works its way in at the waist of her lemonade dress, finds the tender, warm familiar skin. I caress the small of her back with my thumb. She immediately responds, pressing her body closer to me. I raise her chin and kiss her.

A sparrow chirps, pulling me from Rosie. It chirps again. Rafa kicks his bike into gear. I strap on my helmet, pull down my visor, turn the ignition key, set the choke. The smell of gasoline tickles my nose. Underneath me the engine turns over, catches and begins to fire. *Hombre.* A chuckle escapes me. My heart is beating like a hummingbird's wings, a billion times a second. I am terrified and thrilled at the unknown waiting for me. I pull in the clutch lever. A hard boot to the kickstart, a silent salute to Rosie Flores, my love, my life, and a shift into gear.

Somewhere, a red mountain cries, "Come," and my heart rips open.

CULTURAL AWARENESS TRAINING: ON BELONGING

by Melani "Mele" Martinez

We belong to America, but America doesn't belong to us.

My husband and I are from the Southwest United States. We are desert people and our DNA profiles match most everyone in Mexico—Native and European: Mestizo. Our grandparents, great-grandparents, and great-great grandparents built mud houses, rode horses, and ate chile in the borderlands. They prayed often. They lit candles. They went to church on Sunday, and they taught us what they knew. But the way we live is not often called American. It is something *else.*

We belong to God, and He belongs to us.

After we got married, my husband and I began attending a large and mostly white non-denominational church. After several years of attendance, we didn't feel at home in that church community, so we prayed for something *else:* a new church where we could learn, worship, and find a community of believers more like us. God answered.

We began attending a young Bible-based church that seemed to welcome diversity. It was a predominantly white church, but it seemed to be a different kind of congregation. We immediately loved the pastor who led this church plant, a new Christian community in a gentrifying area I knew well. We met lots of people, and most of the congregants and church planters were not locals. The worship style, liturgy, and culture were new to us too, but the words spoken from the pulpit were life-giving, and we were welcomed with smiles and invitations.

Eventually church leaders invited us to participate more. A simple request to join the church hospitality team felt natural, at first, but bone-rattling propositions followed: Can you 'just be yourself' while reciting the welcoming message script? Would you sing in Spanish? Would your daughter sing in Spanish, too? Would you help lead a church conversation on gentrification? Would you speak on a church panel about immigration? Can you make tacos again?

My teenage daughter belongs to us, but she doesn't belong to our church.

Our daughter claimed she was sick almost every Sunday morning, and that should have been a sign to me. But I was busy believing we belonged to our new church, so I didn't make the connection right away. She finally explained. They are just not very loving, she said. I found that harsh. I believed this congregation had every intention of being loving. And besides, my kid was a teenager and not that easy to talk to. What did she really expect from them? I argued with her about what counts as loving. I asked her to give me an example of people who *are* loving.

My grandmothers, our grandmothers, she said.

In a dream, I see a church full of grandmothers like ours. I can see them, as old as the street names, settled into the seats of an auditorium built in 1888. I can see the crucifixes hanging from their necks, their crossed ankles and enlaced fingers. From the pulpit, I hear their voices, a body of words buried and risen. In dreams, I see my dead family and I ache for them—for a church of them, a church of us. But my people do not attend. They are never there.

We belong to Jesus, but we don't belong in our church.

At church events, I found myself silently sitting at tables listening to folks argue whether or not white privilege exists. I heard someone object to one congregant's identifying as a person of color. Before a scripture reading, a church leader suggested to me that my pronunciation of Jewish names didn't matter. On social media, another suggested that multiculturalism is a distraction from the gospel. In confusion, I witnessed gestures that were meant to signal an openness and desire for diversity. I saw a white woman from my church wearing a Mexican Huipil. I saw babies outfitted with ethnic-inspired moccasins and church spaces decorated with bright-colored zarapes for special occasions. These gestures were latent and still, below several layers of *loving,* so it took me a long time to unearth them. It took me even longer to articulate what was happening to us. Appropriating cultural objects is easy; it is a focus on things rather than people. We are all very good at it. But the consumption of pretty things is different than participation in culture, and so at church we practiced a special kind of estrangement.

Before I learned how to articulate these things, I dutifully welcomed newcomers to church. On the hospitality team, I stood each Sunday morning in the lobby of an under-funded public school, beneath the faded stairway murals of Quetzalcoatl, with a pool of Christ-loving people all pretending we loved diversity. One Sunday, a white church member sensed my guarded demeanor towards him. He finally approached me and said, "Are we okay?" I couldn't tell if the question was real, but anyway, my answer was a lie. I pretended to be respectful. I was taught not to stir the pot. But that Sunday afternoon I went home and cried with my husband because I didn't know how to love, like Jesus loves, and speak, like Jesus speaks, what is true: *No, we are not okay.*

We belong to a barrio that doesn't belong to us.

I tried making friends with a woman from church by letting our families eat dinner together and by letting our children play together. I tried praying for her and I let her pray for me. She was the owner of a business that started as a ministry in the church. Her store was opening in a new development in the barrio that my family can't afford to live in anymore—a barrio where my family belonged for four generations or more.

Her ministry-turned-business aimed to celebrate where we live, but admittedly she didn't love the place at first. It is a place she had to learn to love. That discovery was the foundation of her business. Sometimes it seemed she spread this newfound love of a very old pueblo as though it never existed before she arrived. She celebrated discovery and new love with colorful t-shirts and ball caps, with stickers and hashtags. She sold these products in a shiny, well-organized store in the barrio where my family is from.

Concerned about her role in gentrification, she asked me to speak to the staff of her business to offer what she called "cultural awareness training." I was asked to talk about the barrio that doesn't belong to my family anymore, and the request hollowed me. I felt a sense of obligation to her, and I agreed to lead the talk. I parked in front of her house on a gorgeous spring morning, but when I asked my body to get out of the car, it wouldn't. I couldn't tell whose voice was inside my head requesting I fulfill this obligation. Was it God, or the enemy? Was it just my own voice?

I finally pulled myself into her dining room, still unsure if my presence was out of obligation or a desire to be loving or shame. Somehow, being there meant that I was helping, which should have been good. Helping other Christians is a very Christian thing to do. But helping her business meant I was fostering the displacement of barrio people; it meant making the area more palatable to wealthy newcomers and developers. I couldn't disguise it. My voice shook trying to tell the truth, and I made my church friend cry. I left her home and soon after, I chose to end our contact.

Despite cultural awareness training, Instagram feeds still celebrate murals, adobe houses, and a desert ripe with prickly pear fruit. Crisp graphics advertise why we love where we live. But these images haven't celebrated barrio people, people like my family. We are absent in hashtag desert adobe photos. We don't belong in those celebrations of place because we don't belong in the neighborhood anymore.

After my husband and I decided to leave church, we noticed that pieces of us got stuck behind—conversations that we can't unhear and smiles that can't be unwelcomed. There are also lies that can't be untold. And so we are on borders, always in-between. In the middle of these worlds, we are still someone else. Like our daughters and grandmothers, we no longer sit in church seats. We don't belong to a church. We belong to the invisible.

We belong to ourselves. We belong to God.

Eggs

by Sylvia J. Martinez

"We're going egging at 10," my sister Anna tells someone through the phone. She's untangling the overstretched green phone cord by swinging it around like her end of a jump rope. "I've got a dozen," she says. I study her. I don't know what her end of the conversation means, but I have a good idea that she's up to no good.

"Can I come," I ask after she hangs up. The Cosby show has just gone off and our mom has already fallen asleep under her glasses.

"No."

"Aw, come on."

"No!"

"Then I'll tell."

She squints her eyes at me.

I lean against the cabinet that holds Alejandro's cage. He seems to be pleading my case as he opens and closes his blue wings while pacing on the wooden rod that is his stage. Then out of nowhere he releases a loud, "Chirp!" This wakes our mom wakes from her sleep state and she opens her eyes confused, like she just landed in this decade. She turns off the television. "You girls finish your homework?" Alejandro is now chirping wildly like the mad bird that he truly is, begging for the black sheet that becomes his night.

"Anna needs eggs for hers," I say with a smug smile.

"What," our mom asks. Alejandro becomes instantly quiet as my mom covers his cage.

"It's for a science project," Anna says quickly.

"Okay. Just don't use them all."

"I won't."

Anna calls me a little shit when our mom leaves the room. Then she adds, "You shouldn't come."

I hate that she says this. Everyone always thinks they know what's best for me, always protecting me like I'm a penguin egg or something. Yes, I am a goody-goody, but I like being invited to things even if they might be considered shady. Who doesn't?

"Fine then."

I contain my excitement and attempt to finish my pre-algebra homework before the 10 o'clock pickup, which now includes yours truly, thankyouverymuch.

"She was gonna rat me out," I hear Anna tell Fito as he does a double take at my presence. I climb into the back seat of the station wagon. Fito's vehicle reminds me of the Brady Bunch's wagon, the one Marcia took her driving test on.

"I brought money for eggs. 'Just need to stop by the 7-ELEVEN," I say.

"Coo'," Fito says, nodding like the Joe Montana bobblehead on his dashboard.

"Hey," I hear from behind me. I jump in my seat. What in Green Gables?

Fito laughs. "Oh yeah, Carlitos is back there."

"Hey," I say. "Why you sitting back there?" I'm conscious of my missing helping verb because I'm haunted that way.

"It's fun. You should come back here, too."

"I'm good, thanks." I fasten my seatbelt.

Carlitos is Fito's cousin. He was my partner in my sister's quince. He's a year older, in 8th grade at Horace Mann. I used to go there, too, but then they axed the GATE program, so I'm at Everett now.

Now that I know Carlitos is behind me, I close my eyes and breathe in deeply. He has a certain scent that calls for the creation of a glorious new word: carlitoscent n. a delicious fusion of leathery cologne and minty gum.

The first time I noticed how heavenly he smelled was when we were practicing for the quince in our apartment's open-air garage. Left-together, right-together, inhale. I had caught whiffs of guys wearing cologne before, but never had one added the element of gum, which made Carlitos' scent so divine. Add to this his style. He always looks a hint of tough with his creased Ben's and his Adidas jacket. But he never seems cholo-ish to me. He has this laugh-out-loud giggle that seems to cancel out any chance at appearing truly gangster.

When we pull up to the 7-ELEVEN, everyone goes on their own missions. Anna is pumping nacho sauce on some chips. Fito pulls on a lever that releases red slush. The store's lighting makes everything have a bluish hue, like we're in an old photo or something. Carlitos seems to be following me, which I can tell because, well, I can smell him. It's starting to feel like a date, although I've never been on one to know. Never even kissed a guy yet, although I've been practicing with my Brainy Smurf.

Carlitos holds the glass door to the refrigerator for me. I check my eggs by moving each one slightly to make sure none are stuck. I've seen my mom do this. When I go to pay, I see Carlitos pick up a pack of gum. I take a deliberate look: Wrigley's, the white pack.

Everyone takes their seats, and I hold my cold carton carefully in my lap. Anna turns up the radio when "Planet Rock" comes on and starts dancing in her seat. She moves by alternating her hands up and down in these window washing dance moves she's been doing lately.

Fito stops at a house I've never seen before. Then my sister's friend Sandra opens the door opposite me, and a guy and a girl are behind her leaning in for a look at who's in the car.

"Get in the back," Anna orders me. I shrink my eyes at her then climb over my seat back. I've got black leggings on under my pink and black, checkered miniskirt, but I feel conscious of the skirt's length around Carlitos. He scoots over to make room for me, and smiles. His teeth are so beautiful and straight. I notice this because mine aren't. I have this one tooth that pokes out even when my mouth is closed.

"How's Everett?"

"It's okay."

"Yeah, all the smart people left Horace Mann."

I know that's not true, but I don't know how to respond. I flip the Jesusless cross around my neck until the chain is taut. Then I release it.

"It's cool," he says.

Any kids could have stayed at Horace Mann, and any kids could have left. There was this big meeting my mom went to to help parents of gifted children decide what to do. The funny thing is that the school district decided to make Horace Mann an "academic" middle school, yet the gifted program was cut. My mom chose to have me move because she and my counselor agreed that I'd be more challenged at Everett. It's pretty cool so far. I like the books we read, but the math has been killing me. My obituary will say death by the transitive property of equality. I'll probably never get a 4.0 again.

I don't get introduced to the newcomers in the wagon, but I gather that the guy and the girl that got me evicted from my seat are a couple because I see them tongue kissing when I turn around. Nothing like my relations with my smurf.

"What are you reading in English class," I ask Carlitos.

"Huh?"

I really don't know what else to say in these kinds of situations. I play with the multiple bangles on my left wrist and repeat my question.

"Uh, nothing right now. We read The Outsiders, though. It was cool. Did you see the movie?"

"I read it," I tell him, but I leave out the part that S.E. Hinton is my favorite author. I even have That Was Then, This is Now in my purse. "Did you know she was like seventeen when she published it?"

"I did not know that," he says. "Gum?" He slides out a piece with his thumb like it's a sleight of hand trick.

I take it and smile a closed smile, minus the nosy tooth.

The wagon slows down, almost stopping. Fito turns off the headlights. My sister rolls down her window and sticks half her body out the car. That can't be safe. Fito furnishes her waiting hand an egg and then she throws it at someone's house. We leave so fast that the wagon actually squeals.

What in the world? I feel my eyes go big. Everyone is cheering Anna like she just scored a goal.

This is the point in my life when I realize my sister not only hangs around with hoodlums. She is one, too.

My sister = Anna = Hoodlum.

Carlitos must know I'm tripping because he pats my hand. "Don't worry," he says. "We only hit rich people's houses."

I want to tell him that this is a thousand times wrong, but I don't. I just sit there inhaling the comforting scent of him, watching the food-criminals carry on. Still, I feel something like protective of the houses being hit. Many of my GATE friends at school are rich. Most of them have cars and houses, some upstairs/downstairs even. I want to yell at them to stop, but I feel helpless.

Anna looks back at me, but says nothing.

I say nothing back.

Everyone except me and Carlitos has hit at least one house in what I now realize is the Richmond District because we are on the right side of Golden Gate Park.

"Are you gonna to throw any eggs," Carlitos asks me.

"Not yet." I feel nervous. I look into his eyes. There is a dark brown edge around the light brown iris. "Does your mom know where you are?"

He smiles with those straight teeth of his. "With Fito. Does your mom know where you are, Clari?"

"With Anna at Fito's working on a science project about dropping eggs without them breaking."

We both grin. For the first time tonight, I acknowledge the weighty connection between me and Carlitos. I read somewhere that a guy did a study and found that people weigh close to an ounce less once they die. His conclusion: the soul weighs around an ounce. That's the only way I can begin to describe this feeling with Carlitos. Heavy and alive, but no way to prove it without scales and the death of one of us, maybe. And probably some mathematical equation that I'd get wrong anyway.

We come to a stoplight near a bar called Plan B. I watch the neon orange B flash repeatedly until a man walks out. Then I watch him. He looks sleepy and lost. But he's smiling. I want to feel sorry for him, but instead I stare at my Keds for an alibi and go into that place in my mind I never tell anyone about. Not the part where I daydream, but the place behind that. The secret place where I question God. Not his existence, but his reasons for letting people get to that point.

We end up at Ocean Beach, and park. Anna grabs something from Fito's glove compartment and exits. Sandra follows her and Fito follows them both. My sister and Fito aren't a couple, but the way he calls her every night makes me think he's hoping that will change. The kissing couple stays behind and then Carlitos pops open the tailgate.

The three before us are already on the beach. I hop on the concrete half wall and sit on the edge with my legs dangling on the beach side. Carlitos straddles the half wall and leans back a little like he's at the end of a sit-up. He pulls out a flat brush that fits inside his palm and smoothens his dark hair back. He doesn't ask me if I'm cold, but he takes off his Adidas jacket and places it around my shoulders. His divine scent is now on me and all is good in the world.

I watch Anna. They were cigarettes she got from the glove compartment. I've never seen her smoke before, but my unblinking eyes take in that she's no novice. She cups her hand over the white stick between her lips, and lights it. I'm starting to wonder what else I don't know about Anna. Fito is collecting sticks and putting them in a pile. Last I checked he wasn't a bird, so I imagine he's getting all primitive and building his heart's desire a fire. Once it's lit, he takes out three small, green bottles from his pockets and soon they are all drinking and smoking in front of a budding flame.

Behind us, there is a different kind of heat going on. The nameless couple is producing steam on the windows of the Brady-mobile. I no longer want my seat back.

"Hey," Carlitos says. "So what do you plan to do with all that studying you do?"

I want to tell him that I really would love to be a writer like S.E. Hinton, but I overheard my favorite uncle say once that writers were no better than prostitutes, so I keep that dream locked. I decide to tell Carlitos what the Ouija board told my mom I'd do. "Teach."

"Little kids?"

"I don't know yet. Maybe English. Or math."

"That's cool."

"What about you?"

"I'm gonna work with cars."

"Fix them? Sell them?"

"Fix them. My dad's a mechanic and has been teaching me things already."

"That's cool," I say. I look at the sand below and fix my eyes on a piece of debris while something inside me sinks. I can't think of single thing my dad has taught me since I've rarely been around him. He's in the Navy, but the real reason I don't see him is because my parents divorced when I was two. They tried to get back together once when he was stationed in Alameda years ago, but instead of a reunion, we got my little sister Rosie. We get packages from him from countries he gets stationed at, like jackets from Singapore with embroidered dragons on them or dolls in silk dresses from the Philippines. The packages are cool, but I'd rather have a dad than a jacket.

When my dad calls, I know because my mom's whole face seems to drop. "Okay, Yoseph. You're drunk, Yoseph. They're not here, Yoseph." But our noise, our roughhousing like boys because we don't have any brothers or a dad around to teach us that that's not how girls are supposed to act, always betrays her. Then we mock our mom's pronunciation of Joseph in whispers. Somewhere in her learning of English, she missed the lesson on Ys and J's. So she substitutes the Y's for J's and J's for Y's. But only for certain words. Like Yoseph. And Yell-O. One time when I brought home a good report card, she told her friend that I'd go to Harvard or jail with grades like that.

My dad usually calls on Fridays, which means he'll call tomorrow.
"It's your dad on the phone," my mom will say out loud, followed by a whispered HijoDeLaGran… under her breath.

First Olivia will talk. "Uhuh, yeah. Okay."

Next it will be Anna's turn. "Okay. Yes. Uhuh. Okay, bye."

Then it will be my turn. He always calls me a piece of food. "Hey Sweet Pea," he'll say.

"Hi Dad," I'll say back, proud for a few minutes that I have a connection with a dad of my own. I'll try to picture him, calling me from a metal phone on a big ship with water swishing loudly against a circular window. Or I'll visualize him calling from a phone booth on a dirty Singapore street with his crisp, white uniform on.

"You being good," he'll ask.

"Yes," I'll say.

"I hear you're getting good grades."

"Yes."

"Keep it up, Pumpkin."

"Okay." And then I'll pass the phone to Rosie, and that will be that.

c"Clari?" Carlitos brings me back to today.

"Yeah?"

"Will you go with me?"

"Where?"

"Go with me. Be my girl."

"Oh." I feel stupid and great at the same time. I imagine things all the time, but I never saw this coming. "Yes."

Carlitos unstraddles the ledge and asks me to walk with him.

I hop down.

He takes my hand and holds it. We've held hands before at quince practice, but this feels like the first time, his warm fingers intertwining with mine. My upper body feels tingly and kind of heavy – not like when you run too fast in P.E. class, but like something good I've never felt before. After we've walked a bit, Carlitos stops me and faces me.

I don't have time to think about it, all the practices with Brainy Smurf. Instead, he places his lips on mine, and then I can taste his gum flavor as he tastes my tongue slightly. Our relationship has been sealed.

We continue to walk along the half wall side of the beach, and I feel good. I feel like I'm in the happy part of a musical, actually, like a spotlight is on me and Carlitos and we are about to sing a duet. Until I realize there is a real spotlight on us.

It's a cop in uniform. I look at his green eyes and then down at the perfect creases on his pants. "You two a little young to be out so late?"

We say nothing. Carlitos continues to hold my hand.

"Who are you here with?"

"My uncle lives up the street," Carlitos says, pointing to a vague location with his chin.

"What's the address?"

"11 Balboa"

The cop angles his head, looking at Carlitos heavily. Carlitos doesn't blink. Even I believe his uncle lives in this neighborhood.

"All right, let me give you two a ride there, then."

Carlitos squeezes my hand twice. It's code for something, but I don't know what. "OK," Carlitos says to the officer, but I recognize the language of lies. He squeezes my hand tighter this time, and repeatedly, too.

The police officer walks back to his patrol car with another cop in the driver's seat. He tells his partner the address, and his partner says something into a walkie-talkie attached by a coiled wire.

"Run," Carlitos says without looking at me.

So I run. The ground close to the wall feels slippery because of stray sand, so I move to the outside of the sidewalk, the side closest to the street.

"Follow me," Carlitos yells, leading me up the curvy hill towards the old Sutro Baths ruins. There is no time to weigh the pros and cons of this command, so I follow. It's very dark up here, so we have to feel our way around a circular building until we are in the unlit ruins. We scale the walls low with the quickness of bugs. As we get further in, it gets dark, almost black, and narrower. I can hear the cops, but their voices sound distant, muffled. They don't follow us into the baths. Our tax dollars must not cover sand walking. Then I hear the words, Stupid, lowlife kids, but I don't hear the predicate of the sentence, or even if there is one.

I want to correct Officer Creased Pants. We are not stupid, lowlife kids! We are real people with real feelings and real dreams. And we are not stupid!

My angry thoughts freeze in the cold air. Carlitos pulls me close. We are both smiling nervously in our safety zone of ancient bathtubs. Then my anger turns into fear. I secretly read the book someone lent my mom, Zebra, about serial killings that happened in San Francisco. Now all I can picture when I think of the Sutro Baths is the victim that was killed on Thanksgiving. The killers chopped off the guy's head, hands, and feet, and then wrapped him up like a turkey in netted packaging like butchers do turkeys. Then they left him in the ruins here somewhere. I shiver.

We sidle to get closer to the beach. The wall feels like it's wet, but it's actually just really cold. Before we leave this space, Carlitos looks at me again, and this time I am prepared. I angle my head, and meet him halfway. I let my tongue mingle with his, softly and slowly.

As we step down even further towards the beach, my Keds and ankles become completely drenched. This bath was full.

We climb over some rocks. And after what feels like a mushy mile, we finally end up at the bonfire with Anna, Fito and Sandra. We're holding hands, so our new relationship is announced sans words. Anna doesn't say anything.

I don't see the police car up on the street above, but I also don't look for it.

"Beer?" Fito produces a Mickey's bottle from inside his jacket.

Carlitos takes it and opens it using his hoodie pocket. He takes a drink and then passes it to me. I take a swig like I drink all the time, but my unnatural expression probably tells the real story. I keep drinking anyway. I drink almost the whole thing in one painful, uninterrupted shot and ask Fito for another. Fito says, "Damn, Anna, your sister's a fish."

Anna just looks at me with her nothing speech, but she doesn't stop me.

Carlitos finishes the rest of the second bottle, and then pulls out a piece of gum for each of us.

I watch the fire. It's small, but powerful. I can see about six or seven other glowing orange spots along the beach with small groups around them like us. Our group is talking about the killer waves that would happen if The Big Earthquake ever actually hit. Fito says that the Mission is so far from the water that killer waves wouldn't get us. Sandra says she's not waiting to find out and plans to move to Sacramento before it hits. Carlitos says his feet are freezing, and Anna just takes a controlled drag of her cigarette and looks off in the direction of the water.

My head starts to feel woozy. I feel sad. I get up. Sand has clung to my sneakers and socks, so it looks like I have on beige boots. I walk up the steps towards the station wagon. Carlitos follows me, but I don't wait for him. The nameless couple is outside against the railing now, watching the loud waves. I didn't even notice how loud the waves were until now.

I see the police car parked in the middle of the street, but there are no cops in it. I feel so much of something I can't name. I open the wagon's tailgate and grab my carton of eggs. I hold the pack in one arm like it's a baby, and I open it. I take one egg out. I aim. I hurl it towards the police car's windshield. I feel soothed by the halted crunch at the end of my throw. I take another. This one feels even better. I hit three on the windshield total. Then, I get all the side and back windows as I walk around to ensure some sort of equality. I suddenly realize I'm crying to the point of blurriness, but I don't even remember starting. I underhand a final one towards the hood, but that one lands on the street instead of my target. I sniffle loudly. I pull Carlitos' jacket sleeve down over my hand and then clear my eyes with it, first my right, then my left. Carlitos is behind me saying something, but I can't hear anything but Stupid, lowlife kids. Crash. Stupid, lowlife kids. Crash. Pumpkin. Crash. Prostitutes. Crash, crash, crash.

I walk over to a trashcan and deposit the carton because I am not one to litter.

By this point, Fito has started the car, and everyone is in, calling at me to "Get in Clari, Get in! Now!"

I walk towards the wagon slowly, like a superstar coming into view on a stage built just for her. And then I see my sweet-smelling boyfriend reach out his hand for me. I take it, let him lift me into the wagon, and I feel like royalty.

A GIRL MORE STILL

by Matt Mendez

Tungi tells Lena to dig in, not to be shy because with looks like hers she don't need to worry about nothing, but Lena worries all the time.

I dream I am a mountain. Alone until the sun dips behind me and everyone says how good we go together. I want to believe, but when I wake up he's glowing outside my window, not wanting company. Lena stops scribbling and rips the page from her notebook, folds and stuffs it in her pocket. Lena has been writing since she was little, practiced cursive and loved making loops, but now it's more than letters strung together. Her words mean something, though she doesn't know what. Unsure Lena hides what she writes in the back of dresser drawers and behind mirrors, stuffs poems between the yellow pages of her mammá's bible.

Lena is waiting for Tungi and their date, told the chubby vato to park on the street and honk. Lena wants Tungi to see her run from the house, let him peep her as she strides toward him. This way Tungi will remember the night how he wishes, can tell his boys whatever makes him happy: *Dude, she couldn't wait to get with me,* or, if Tungi turns out dreamy, *Man, it was like I was there to save her or something.* At school people call Lena a slut, which is not as bad as the shit they say about her mammá and brother, Octavio. Lena tries to ignore the chisme, but it's hard. The talk a constant drip in her head.

A horn beeps and Lena runs. Outside the stars are scattered across the sky like spilled salt. The moon a dinner plate licked clean. Lena jumps in Tungi's ride, a busted Cutlass with chrome wheels and booming stereo. She hugs him, presses her chichis against his. He's wearing too much cologne, but Lena's glad he's trying. Tungi drives to Papa Burger where Lena will order a double with fries and a strawberry shake. Tungi cruises Fort Blvd past Delicious and Marie's, Carol's Bakery and Peking Garden. All places Lena goes on dates, where she eats until her stomach hurts.

Tungi holds the door at Papa's and walks Lena to a booth. Tungi tells Lena to get whatever she's hungry for. He's a big boy, not muscles big but fat, and barely fits between the table and cracked vinyl seat. Lena can see rolls of skin stacked like doughnuts underneath his white t-shirt. Sweat under his arms. Tungi eyeballs Lena, not hungry for food but sex. He's picturing the things he's heard about her and wants her body—all the boys who take Lena out do—but what Tungi doesn't know is that Lena wants his body, to become wide and squishy like Tungi and not trapped by her looks. The right curves at the wrong time, her mammá once said while pointing at her nalgas, telling Lena it would doom her into marrying early and divorcing late.

Respect is what it's all about. Tungi tells Lena this; that she's down because of Octavio. This surprises her. Lena's a lot of things but doesn't want down to be one of them. She smiles at Tungi, calls him crazy and orders when the waitress comes. *I'm Your Puppet* by James and Bobby Purify floats from a jukebox. It's a stupid oldie that cholos can't resist because to them everything's "whatever, well" or "fuck-it, ese." *Pull them little strings and I'll sing you a song, Make me do right or make me do wrong.*

Tungi asks what Lena remembers about her carnal, that they were only kids when he got put away, all because of that faggot. Lena doesn't remember much. She's read Octavio's prison file online: height, weight, and race, how he fatally stabbed Artemio Anaya behind Ben's Grocery and fled the scene. He looks lost in his death row photo, shaved head and open mouthed, eyes like wet rocks. Lena squeezes Tungi's hand and tells him Ocatavio is dead even though he isn't.

Lena's mammá knows all about Octavio but says the memories escape her whenever she asks, and Lena understands her mammá's not the kind of woman who chases answers. Instead watches television and crawls inside cans of beer. Octavio's room is how he left it, dirty clothes in the hamper and dust covering everything. Lena remembers the picture of Octavio's girlfriend beside his bed, her wearing tight clothes and bending over, butt in the air and tits dangling like fruit ready to drop from a tree. Lena wrote a poem for her, slid it inside the frame: *Two boys gone and a girl more still.*

The comida comes, hamburger buns toasted with butter and patties sizzling, cheese dripping along the sides. Lena pours chile verde over the meat and límon on the papitas, both from plastic bottles at the end of the table. Tungi eats without taking a moment to appreciate his food; he's sloppy and gets mustard on his shirt, licks his greasy fingers and slurps his milkshake. Tungi tells Lena to dig in, not to be shy because with looks like hers she don't need to worry about nothing, but Lena worries all the time. Now about *being down*—locked down like her brother or down-and-out like mammá? Will she fall as far as her father who booked when she was five but who can rot in hell for all anyone cares? Lena takes a bite; the chile makes her face sweat, tongue burn and eyes water.

Tungi's sorry to hear about Octavio, sorry for her loss, and Lena thinks about Octavio dying. She knows the date, wonders about his last meal and the final thought he'll be asked to spill, how the chance to choose the last words of your life is the scariest thing she can think of. Most condemned apologize to the families they've broken and praise Jesús. Lena knows no matter what Octavio manages to say, his words will belong to her. To repeat and change until she can make sense of them. She hears Octavio talking in her ear: *I'm ready to go.* Lena's ready, too.

Lena pushes her food aside, surprises Tungi. He mentions how he's heard she could put a lot away, and Lena tells him he has no idea. Tungi laughs and says he needs the toilet. He rocks himself from the booth and knocks over what's left of Lena's milkshake, the pink slush sliding across the table. Tungi wipes the crumbs from his shirt, promises a quick piss and a trip back to his place. He smiles and Lena takes the folded paper from her pocket, wipes the mess back inside the cup. The ink bleeds and words dissolve as the page soaks itself blank again. Lena leaves the restaurant with Tungi still in the bathroom. She walks toward the mountains that are somehow darker than the sky and thinks about paper turning soft and easy to tear.

LAST DREAMING, LAS CRUCES, 1958

by elena minor

Matilde thought for a long time about naming without leaping to Fé over Gracia. So when finally the indivisible matter took its last and legendary hairpin turn, it fused open circles of desire to cold regret and broke that mysterious pull of place. As it ever would be, Cariño had gone long before, and Milagros long before her. Both had followed long after Frida and Jesusita, who went one right after the other and had barely had time to have one child apiece, both of whom had names, Meme and Rosario, respectively, and who were also now long gone. There was a pattern in that historic succession: they had gone for good and at least two had parted as soon as could have been expected by the constraint of circumstances but not in full, nor well enough to bear future witness. It was memory out of time they were after, but that was before and they knew what had been left behind.

• • •

Everyone at Nestor's had a good reason for why their time had been cut short but they had to have dark beer in the dark sanctuary of his place with the smoky mirror up high and behind him to talk about it because that was all he had. By then it was deep in the rich, wine-colored season and gathering become what habit remained after the dead moment. After the third bottle or so, they might have started in, but they were practiced, and that meant it took more and therefore, longer. And so it was always later rather than sooner, that someone would finally utter, "Justice." Then someone else would follow a few moments later with, "Dos medidas por mediodía." The precise someone who always muttered 'Justice' in a different voice each time was San Juan. His obsessions were faulty but regular and wouldn't have required forgiveness except that he craved it two ways and in the middle. Silence would fall as Nestor served up the eighth beer for some, the ninth or tenth for others, not counting at what time they'd arrived and how thirsty they were and the current weather, the days of which didn't count once they were inside. The suspense after San Juan would build and build until someone who was drinking draft on tap couldn't take it anymore, downed it in one long swallow, then slammed the heavy glass mug onto the bar. Nestor would bark, "Wáchale! That's solid mahogany!" Whoever had done it would mumble, "Sorry," but not contritely, and right away, from a table ideally snuggled next to the fancifully carved bathroom door, Tosca would open the floodgates by adding her three words' worth. "Mahogany's a hardwood." There followed a más o menos echo right away that rasped open then closed with, "Yeah … hard word," that was courtesy of Chula Blanca, who always agreed with Tosca, who was getting ready to retire from the phone company soon. She was an Information Operator for almost the whole county and knew everything going back at least sixty years, when she started younger with the phone company. It was her first job and she had been the only one and it had been hers until Chula Blanca had joined up in the late 40s when the Pérez-Olivas familia—mothers, uncles, third and fourth primos y primas, errant producing fathers and abandoned sisters-in-law and step-this-and-that on all sides—had moved in and created a population boom in lower Canales. They took over almost the entire south side of the village and all of them got telephones with party lines, but since they weren't from there, they didn't know anyone and had to call Information to get their phone numbers and information. What little truth they got turned out to be too much and eventually old with the telling and retelling, and that's what was important and everyone remembered as they sat or stood around not talking mostly in the familiar close dark of Nestor's, which didn't have a jukebox because Nestor had a sensitivity deep in his ears and a waxy substance on the surface of his soul and almost never looked into the smoky mirror behind him. The long silences didn't bother them much; it gave them time to think and that was all they had until someone chanced on a certain memory of wickedness or high-blown fever and thought to screech out, "¡Arranca la yerba buena!" It was always a woman who had the goodness to do it because sometimes she had the healing itch to soothe. The men's voices couldn't reach to screech that high anymore but because they didn't the next one was on them. San Juan took the responsibility seriously but by then if he opened his mouth like he was going to say 'Justice' again, whoever was standing next to him would grab his arm and pull firmly on it, sometimes a man, sometimes a woman, then say respectfully, "My sin. Collar de rosa color de rosa." Over by the pool table, Oralia would sniffle but not let the tears come full down so they waded around in her pink-rimmed eyes. She was a religious young woman, with a beautiful canela complexion, and would not allow herself to curse, even when she had her almighty urges. The closest she got, and it showed the true strength of her feelings, was "Hijas de la pulgada, muertas por la puntada." She repeated it three times in a row in short-inch clips to make the point. Then she'd take a lady-like slurp of her draft on tap beer and burp smoothly but with an uneasy frown and then Último Tomás would pat her hand in stock sympathy without looking. He had once been a distant outside relative but had publicly distanced himself when the badness had gotten really bad. He'd been shy and very young at the time and was still very devout and it had been a difficult decision to make, long distance and foreignness notwithstanding. It had been an even more difficult action to take. He felt bad but didn't want to, so convinced himself on Saturdays that the universe was very, very large and blood no more than a matter of red chance, and he was therefore not required to share its spills and sputters. But that was on Saturdays and since Nestor kept Nestor's closed on Saturdays, he had to offer something on Sunday through Friday. "Busted tricycle," was something Último Tomás usually offered as a token to long gone memoria then abandoned what gana was leftover in him. Because it still had a trickle of life in it, weak though it was, it was taken and pushed over the edge by Susana. "B-b-b-baby b-buggy rub-b-ber b-b-bumper" is what she tried sin éxito to say as she looked cross-eyed at the ten empties and the one half-full bottle lined up in a half-circle on the rounded-off edge of her curved half-table with its three legs to balance. She'd make it all hers by removing all but the chair she sat in and circling the bottles in front. She also preferred bottled to draft on tap in a chilled heavy mug but that didn't stop her from slamming the bottle down on the table and spilling in foamy drops the dark of its contents. "Oye, oye, oye," Nestor would warn her and she would look up at the smoky mirror and count backwards from nine times nine. "No se oye," Tosca called out as she stumbled out of the bathroom trailing behind her her great-grandmother's faded blue and pink wool rebozo. "No … se oye," Chula Blanca called out as she got caught up in it. "Justice," cried San Juan in a desperate woman's voice. It didn't fool anyone, and especially not Ramona, who had had direct dealings with the supernatural and always would [she swore] and took no nonsense from fools like her son San Juan. Had Ramón his wayward father still been with them [had he stayed] she might have given him up. "No such luck," she spat out to no one, not even San Juan or Nestor, who was accustomed to lending his sensitive ears when she spoke and other body parts when she didn't. When she didn't stop there, she wanted to go on to say, "Crossed the river," but in a mucho more milder tone of voice and did. Upon virtually hearing it just before as faulty intuition, and actually hearing something else, Chula Blanca broke the rules and proffered her echo first without waiting for Tosca, "Cruzaron … el río," and it was followed shortly by not Tosca but Susana trying again with something else and repeatedly not succeeding. "B-b-buckets with sh-sh-short handles. B-b-broken. B-b-busted in and out ho-ho-holes." She had it backwards again. In the empty buzzing that held its breath for a moment, an anonymous voice rose up like a flower. "Rose up like a flower," it whispered, only to be corresponded to with, "Rose. The Flower." And associated by, "Flier." Then affiliated with, "F-f-f-liar!" but not by Susana who had already fallen into the depths of the dark, smoky mirror. And at last, "Rosa." No one confessed, although there was expressed doubt that lingered and offered an assertion. "Subieron … las montañas," came the susurro from somewhere higher. "No lo creo," hissed Último Tomás. As the sound bounced off the wall, it was Ramona who caught and ended it, unbelieving. "No, se creen. Sí, se creen. Así se creen. Se creen. Sé, creen …" Then: "Sin vergüenzas." "Sin venganzas," they heard clearly, anonymously through a pinpoint hole in the wall. San Juan opened up to cry on purpose then, shamelessly, and made as if to cry out, "Al otro lado," but his mother wouldn't hear of it. "Mala suerte," is what she'd look as if she wanted to say but just as unluckily Ramona had already earlier said the other part of it, and for her it bore repeating but before she could give it light, it gave itself words. "Le parto la cara," Tosca grumbled blindly into the high smoky mirror behind Nestor and clear behind the bar. "El parto … La Cara," broken-chimed up Chula Blanca. No one acted as if they heard a thing. They didn't need to because they'd given it all blind birth over and over and over the years had been expecting anytime now to face down the end soon, whenever it would be arranged. "Por Caridad," whispered someone as if its meaning would shortly vanish. Oralia, whose face was the youngest among them but who nonetheless held the longest memories, was always the first one to fall asleep with Último Tomás in deep succession. Then one after the other, they all fell in after Último Tomás as memoria of all that had gone before them and the wickedness of the coming to light came to dusk and went out for deliverance.

• • •

As it happened, when at the last available moment Matilde crossed over, it was a silken, starry night in 1958, just as she was passing the great dam in the desert. She sat facing backwards in the uncovered bed of a battered pickup truck and the wind was blowing her as hard and warm as it was and clear through, as though to bend around her the reasons of her will. For what seemed like a long time she had been from a small, sequestered village in the ancient bloody highlands but she had crossed and already forgotten its name. Matilde, well, she was no fool from the promise of heaven. She had in mind a day at the end of seasons, a golden state of mind, and her other worldly women. It wasn't escape, but it was freedom.

MANFLOWERS

by Gris Muñoz

There was a house on the other side of our block. "Allí viven las manfloras," my mother would say. "Si algún día te ofrecen comida, no la tomes." Whenever we'd walk by their place she would clasp my hand even tighter and hurry us along. The house didn't look any different from the others that lined the block. It was white brick with a forest green trim and there was a grey pebble walkway down the middle of the yard that led to the doorway. We'd never see anyone outside.

There was always so much noise and movement at our house. I liked riding my bike out of there, pedaling down our driveway and taking the sidewalk away from everyone. My mom didn't mind me gone unless I was gone for too long, so I'd head out when my brother got overwhelming. Once I really got going, I'd pedal faster, counting each thin line that separated the sidewalk before it went under the cushion of my wheels.

Las Manfloras.

Following the curve of the sidewalk, I'd ride faster, picking up speed until I was close, and then I'd glide past their house. I knew what it meant. Women who were like men, who lived together like lovers. I liked the word manflowers better. I'd say it in my head and think it seemed far away from me, something I'd never known, strong and delicate. I'd think about the word and imagine what type of plant manflowers would be if they really existed.

There was a gnarled wild blackberry tree in their yard and at the base of it, a growth of succulents that were always freshly watered.

Moras. The blackberries were called moras and at our house my parents thought they were a nuisance. My dad would say they were too bitter to eat and complain how in the summer, the moras would hang fat and heavy until they stained the sidewalks.

My friend Rosa lived on that side of the block and when I'd go over to visit, her mom would let us ride our bikes anywhere on the street. We liked the moras. When we'd get to the manflowers' house, we'd slow down and walk our bikes up their driveway. There would be purple stains all over the sidewalk and front yard, and we'd gather the plumpest ones and pile them in our bike baskets for pretend doll food.

We'd eat them instead, laughing and squeezing as we plunged them into our mouths, the juice sanguine and bitter. Sitting crouched, I'd look up and notice Rosa's smiling face. It was spotted with moving shadows from leaves that in flashes, opaqued the sunlight.

For years, I feared my desire. It wasn't until after I became a single mother that I was courageous enough to know queer brown love, how it was the truest; like wrapping your arms around your very own skin in another body. The scent of body lotion and familiar. It was the first woman I loved who'd gently said, "I think you have post-partem depression, sweetheart." No one else had noticed, my daughter was almost two.

I'm on my way to see Cat Eyes. It's actually my birthday. We'd met out dancing. When we danced, I realized I'd never known the feeling of another woman's body pressed against me in this way. I was wearing a pair of cowboy boots and even then, had never been so graceful.

Can I tell you something about Cat Eyes? I later found out she provides for herself and her two kids on her own, working part-time and taking on all the duties of a full-time nursing student. She only has one night, Saturday, off from her kids every two weeks. Even if she's completely spent, she still goes dancing. The rest of her everydays, she's up by five.

I hadn't planned on doing anything for my birthday but when I'd mentioned it to her she insisted on at least making lunch.

I'm sitting at her kitchen table watching her make salsa. She's roasting chiles and chopping onions next to a large granite molcajete.

"I feel special," I say, our eyes meeting.

"You are, reina."

Her apartment has plants everywhere, succulents and tiny re-potted aloes arranged, lining every corner. Large wooden pots are hanging, hooked from the ceiling, supported by long braided ropes. There's a small decorative purple cactus on her kitchen counter. I get up and lean towards her, our arms wrapped around another tightly like vines, violet mouths kissing.

DIRTY MEXICANS

by Juan Ochoa

Cayetano Perez stood gagging in a cloud of dust made by an angry white man. Cayetano was checking the oil of his Ford when the white man pulled up in an Oldsmobile and ordered Cayetano to, "Fill 'er up." Cayetano politely told the white man that he did not work at the gas station and that he was only checking his own oil, and the white man sped off sending up large plumes of dust that stung Cayetano's face and made his eyes burn.

When he finished wiping his eyes and spitting out dust, Cayetano slipped behind the wheel of his car, but before he could turn the key, Adela asked, "Que es fuck you, Cayetano?"

Cayetano's back stiffened and his face got redder. He put the car in gear and floored the gas hoping to raise as much dust as the white man. "Callete el hosico, vieja sonsa. A lady doesn't use those words."

"Ah-huh, I knew it. That man cussed you," Adela said folding her arms in front of her and nodding her head. "Que es fuck you, Cayetano?" she asked again. "That gringo wanted you to do something and you told him no and he got mad and said, 'fuck you,' right, Cayetano?" She turned toward her husband and asked, "Que es fuck you, Cayetano?"

Cayetano wrestled with the steering wheel concentrating hard on keeping his Ford in its lane. "It's like telling someone que se chinge," he said after some thought.

Adela nodded her head mulling over his words with her arms crossed in front of her. "It's like a mentada de madre, isn't it, Cayetano?" she said with anger.

Cayetano settled himself in his seat and said, "No, not like telling someone to do that to their mother. It's not as bad as that. Only Mexicans are dirty enough to bring their mothers into an insult."

"But it is an insult, right, Cayetano?" Adela said leaning into her husband's view. "Why didn't you beat that man, Cayetano? You never let any Mexican insult you, Cayetano," she sat back in her seat and watched the road ahead of her. The furrowed fields raced past her window and the hot air blowing through the car scattered her hair across her face. After a few miles, she turned to her husband again and asked, "Was it because he was a gringo, Cayetano? Do you think he knows the patron, Cayetano?"

Cayetano checked his mirrors before answering, "Of course he knows el patron. And the man who rents us our house. And the man who sells us our groceries. All these gringos know each other." Cayetano stuck out his arm and then nosed his car around a truck loaded with melons. "If a Mexican fights with a gringo, there will always be big trouble," he said.

"Yes, the whole world knows that, Cayetano," Adela said hanging her head. She looked at her shoes and tried scraping the dirt off her heel with the tip of her other shoe but the caked soil only flaked and stained both shoes and left dust on the carpet. "The gringos don't like us because they think they're better than us."

Cayetano glanced down and saw the mess his wife had made on his clean carpet and said, "Maybe the gringos aren't wrong to think that." He turned the car off the asphalt highway and followed a farm road that ran in front of a string of wooden houses sitting on blocks. "We Mexicans are a dirty people. Just look at these houses and their dirty yards. Broken down cars with flat tires. No flowers. No grass. Now look at the gringo's house with the clean yard and the pretty grass." Cayetano shook his head knowingly. "We are a dirty people."

"We don't have clean yards, but look at the fields, each row as straight as a board and not one weed. Not even a clump out of place, acre after acre," she said filling her chest with air. "We do that. Who has time or strength to clean a yard after so much work? The gringo can do it because he has us to do everything else for him."

Cayetano sucked his teeth. "In Mexico, we worked from sun up to sun down. Everyday. Mexicans cross the river and all of the sudden they can only work eight hours and they want to join unions. They think just because they made it here they can stick out their hands and somebody's gonna fill it with money. That's why the gringo doesn't like us."

Adela kept her eyes on the row of houses speeding by her window. "How can the gringo tell just by looking at a person if they are lazy or not?"

Cayetano's mouth fell open. He turned and looked at his wife then back to the road and said, "They don't just look at a person. They know. Doesn't El Henry treat me good?"

Adela shrugged her shoulders.

"You know that he does. He gives me the most hours because he knows I work hard. The gringo is not as dumb as people think," Cayetano said feeling like he was right.

"Then why do the white ladies cut in front of us at the groceries?" Adela asked bringing her knees up into the seat to face her husband. "I was there at the butcher's with my comadre Lucha about to ask him for a pound of ground, and this white lady came right up and took my turn. I told Lucha loud so the white woman could hear that some people have no manners. I know the gringa didn't understand Spanish but she knew what I meant. And you know what Lucha did?" Adela sat facing her husband and when he did not reply she shook his arm and asked, "Do you know what my comadre

Lucha did? She ran out of the store. Left all her groceries. Oh, and left me talking to myself like a fool. And you know what she said later?"

Cayetano pretended not to care. He wished his wife for once would be quite. He had the job he had to do on his mind and was sorry he had ever stopped to check the oil. His wife shook his arm again and Cayetano said, "No. No, I don't know what comadre Lucha said later."

Adela could not get her words out fast enough, "She said that I shouldn't say things like that because someone could tell me *something*. I told her that someone should tell that gringa *something*."

Cayetano shook his head and slowed the car down to dodge a couple of pot-holes. "You shouldn't say things like that," he said. "That's another reason why the gringos don't like us. You try to argue with them in Spanish. The gringo only wants to hear English. Then you have people like comadre Lucha running out of stores like an Indian," Cayetano scoffed. "And people wonder why the white people don't like them."

"There's no law that says I have to speak English," Adela said.

Cayetano's mouth fell open again, "Hah, no law. No law. This is America. Of course you have to talk in English."

"Yo puedo decir lo que me de mi chingada gana," Adela said turning to face the road.

Cayetano drove his car over a cattle guard and followed a mesquite lined road to the river's edge. He parked the car just as the sun was going down. In the darkness, he told his wife, "They should be already waiting on the other side. If they're not all there, I'm not waiting. I'm coming with whoever's there."

"You'll wait if my sister's not there, won't you Cayetano?" Adela's voice cracked with worry.

"Chingada madre," Cayetano said unbuttoning his shirt. "Only because she's your sister, but you see what I mean? Help a Mexican come to los United and they won't even be on time." He got out of the car and stripped out of the rest of his clothes.

"You're getting paid," Adela said under breath. Adela followed her husband out of the car and held a plastic bag open for him to place all of his clothes. Adela shook her and said, "Mexicans have to get as naked as the day they were born just to come work for white people."

Cayetano held the bag with his clothes high over his head as he stroked the green waters of the Rio Bravo to Mexico. He had to wait for several hours and was only happy that there was no moon out when he started back to the American side of the river leading four men and Adela's pregnant sister. It was for her that he had to wait. Her belly was big and round and it took her forever to get her clothes off and into the water. He had had to lift her onto an inner tube that he pulled while the other men pushed as they swam across the river to the American side. As he swam, Cayetano warned the group he was guiding, "If we get caught by the migra, remember that we all say we were coming alone. There's no coyote. Understand? We'll get in more trouble if the border patrol thinks there's a coyote in the group." The truth was that only Cayetano would get in more trouble but he was not about to let that secret out. Cayetano did not trust Mexicans.

As soon as the group made it to shore, Adela grabbed her sister and took her into the reeds to get her dressed. The men pulled up the inner tube and began tearing open the plastic bags that held their clothes. There came a of crackle of boots on brush and one of the men gasped, "La migra."

Flashlights illuminated the river bank. Cayetano and the other men stood naked, bathed in the light. "No se mueva, sons of bitches," a voice said from behind a flashlight. A couple of lights turned off and three men dressed in green came forward into the light. The agents snatched the bags with the men's clothing and threw the bundles back into the river. A tall white border patrol agent stepped up to one of the men and said, "Quien es el coyote?" This last word he pronounced Kah-yo-tee. The naked man standing next to the agent stammered, "Venemos solos."

The tall white man dressed in green pulled out a .357 Magnum and drew back on the hammer and then placed the barrel on the naked man's temple and asked again, "Quien es el Kah-yo-tee?"

"Cayetano Perez," the naked man said pointing to Cayetano.

The tall white man turned his gun on Cayetano and motioned for him to step forward. Cayetano stepped forward and the agents put him in cuffs. Cayetano shook his head and said, "Didn't I tell you that we Mexicans are a dirty people? Come on Adela, they got us."

More flashlights came on and soon two pairs of eyes gleamed from the reeds growing on the edge of the river. Adela and her half naked sister were led out and marched up the bank by the agents. As Adela passed, she turned to her husband and said, "Fuck you, Cayetano."

REVELATION

by Wendy C. Ortiz

My daughter began her journey out of my body on the day of my grandmother's 95th birthday

My grandmother was in a bed for dementia and Alzheimer's patients over the hill and far away

My grandmother taught me how to get out of nightmares. We practiced. *The Lord is my shepherd; I shall not want.*

She hated men. Birthed two children. Loved her son and held her daughter in contempt. Her son died before he was twenty

My grandmother now had a single daughter. Just as my mother has a single daughter East L.A., the sound of the freeway, chicken and rice, my grandmother's cats playing with their shadows

The three of us loved a Sunday in which food, reading, and television played a large part

I perused her collection of *National Enquirer* and *Star* magazines. I lingered on the gratuitous and plentiful photos of bikini-clad starlets. I shook out the pages and turned them when someone happened by my shoulder

He maketh me to lie down in green pastures; he leadeth me beside the still waters

My mother asleep in my grandmother's bedroom

We read the Book of Revelation

He restoreth my soul

I dreamed often of the whore, the harlot who rode the beast with seven heads. She was hot. I wanted to be her. Who didn't?

Imagine your whole body being burnt over and over and over again. For eternity. That's what hell is like, she said. I closed my eyes

He leadeth me in the paths of righteousness for his name's sake

My grandmother's bed, where I often ground my body into the mattress to make myself hit nirvana

Over and over

I could imagine what sustained burning felt like when I got tattooed the first time. Again. Again. Bigger. More tender places

My mother: *Well, at least it won't be lonely in hell. All the best people will be there.* She exhaled a gray stream of smoke, her forever halo. My grandmother frowned. I tried not to laugh

Yea, though I walk through the valley of the shadow of death, I will fear no evil

In the bathtub, underneath the window, I lay very still. On the other side of the door, I heard my grandmother's voice. *What are you doing in there?*

My grandmother did not smoke or drink. She became ill from sunlight

This also worked to preserve her skin, the skin that earned her the nickname güera from her family

My grandmother often told me she wished I had green eyes

For my fourteenth birthday my grandmother gave me money for colored contact lenses. I chose a nuclear yellow. She was not pleased

She would often tell me that when she died, she was going to ask God to let her speak to me

My grandmother died just hours after we signed the papers that would land her in hospice. She died at a Catholic hospital

I found this fitting, since she had begun Catholic. She spun out into Pentecostal later I don't have to answer her call

For thou art with me; thy rod and thy staff they comfort me

I might not

Now I just look for her in hummingbirds and birds of paradise
But I might

When I got out of the bathtub, dried, clothed, the water drained, she said, *Do you like looking at yourself in there?*

I knew from how she asked that I should say no

My grandmother died the day after the love of my life, our daughter, and I walked a labyrinth

I didn't know my grandmother's god anymore, but I told whomever he was to take her

Her great-granddaughter was a chubby five-month-old. They had never met. I could not take her into the room because my grandmother had pneumonia

Underneath the crucifix, I told my grandmother of this cherub born two days after her birthday

My grandmother's blanket thrown back, her impossibly smooth pale thighs

I did not tell her they were both Scorpios, as my grandmother did not believe in astrology

On the January night the love of my life first inseminated me, my grandmother was in another hospital just a few blocks from our house

My grandmother was not lucid by the time I was living with my girlfriend

She was not lucid by the time my girlfriend and I registered as domestic partners or began inseminating in our bedroom, our friend and donor in our guest room

When I did not become pregnant that first month, I was convinced my grandmother's proximity to us had something to do with it. She had disallowed it

Thou preparest a table before me in the presence of mine enemies

Or, I wondered, maybe she would die in that hospital, and I would carry her spirit baby

We used to love watching Elvira, Mistress of the Dark. My eyes fixed on the black V of her dress

My grandmother did not tell very many people, but her given name? *Elvira*

 "Mary" was what people knew her by. She left Elvira back in Texas, a shadow part playing in the fields where she had picked crops

The following month we changed our approach to include an orgasm before and an orgasm after the love of my life depressed the syringe of fresh semen into me

I got pregnant

The due date of our baby was around my grandmother's birthday

I knew she'd get her claws in there somewhere. *Scorpios*

And this sweet innocent being began her descent on the twelfth of November as I napped on the sofa

Thou anointest my head with oil, my cup runneth over

I forgot it was my grandmother's birthday. I forgot until she died almost six months later

My grandmother would die not knowing I was tattooed. I was queer. I had given birth. I had added another girl to our line

Surely goodness and mercy shall follow me all the days of my life

And to this day I still recite these words in nightmares

And I will dwell in the house of the Lord forever

And I magically wake up

And ever

Amen

PRETTY

by Wendy C. Ortiz

This is a pretty essay.

In the beginning, the word was *chula. Que chula* was cooed and gasped at me. My mother and my grandmother fawned over me with these words, as though they were astonished by me every time they said it.

I went to kindergarten believing I was a princess, enough to quarrel with Debbie Holly. She, too, believed she was a princess. Together we believed we were, each of us, pretty. But there could only be one princess, the prettiest one of all.

First grade through fifth grade, the *chulas* came less often, the school work got more complicated, my brain felt more scrambled from listening to my parents argue and watching them leave empty bottles in the kitchen like warnings. Pretty was not to be. I believed myself *fat,* which at the time, did not equal pretty. Mother and grandmother bonded over seeing to my prettiness. Fiber pills, frozen diet foods, stern admonishments, and home perms were in order. So were Kentucky Fried Chicken binges and Ex-Lax, the latter of which I pilfered from the medicine closet.

This is not a pretty essay.

In sixth grade drama auditions for Snow White I pressed my lips together then belted out the words in the script for the role I wasn't sure I wanted, but got. I was the Evil Queen. This is not to be confused with The Hag. I played the pretty one who wanted to get Snow White, the fairest one of all, out of the way.

A new campus with male teachers and suddenly I was re-interested in what pretty meant, juxtaposed with my love of gray eye shadow, black eye pencil lit by a match for pure inkiness, bronze or white or black lipsticks. The pretty that marched around my junior high campus suddenly felt suspect.

Pretty packages.

Eighth grade, with glasses, turtlenecks, black leggings, hair-sprayed bangs pretty. Never believing I was truly attractive, not when twenty-year-old men licked my neck in the mall courtyard, not when my English teacher asked me to call him on the phone. Okay, well, maybe my eyes were pretty. Let's get rid of the glasses and get contact lenses. Hazel-colored, that appeared yellow. Let's rip another layer off and show skin. That might be pretty.

I lost the leggings and turtlenecks and make-up, and traded them in for wispy paisley tops and dresses, holey jeans, hair bleached to match my yellow eyes. I wished the brown hairs on my arms away, painted bleaching agents on them until I got tired of the time and expense. Eat, take laxatives, eat, take laxatives. Running up and down a dead-end street high on crank, knowing in my heart of hearts it might be a key to pretty, an end to laxatives. A thumbnail's worth of cocaine. I made a vow to never snort crank again. I liked it too much. Pretty gave chase. I dyed my hair black. Wore lip gloss. Clothes hung off me until I remembered again: appetite.

Pretty is as pretty does.

Swimming at my former English teacher's apartment, he used the word "jiggly." My seventeen-year-old blood curdled. My pretty pink bikini: a prop I wanted to strangle him with. The bikini later lay in a pink heap on his apartment floor. When I looked in the mirror in my mother's house, I still saw a glimmer, though. *Chula.*

The men who opened car doors to me as I stood alongside the road. The men who locked me in a bathroom. The men who incessantly knocked on my mother's door and my bedroom windows. The men who cheated on their girlfriends with me. The men who broke laws by fucking me. The men who took me on dates that ended with a drunken kiss, their fear of breaking the law too much for them to swallow. The men who used the word 'love.' The men who pushed my back against the rocks, for whom I undressed in the outdoors (the beautiful outdoors). I was prettiest by moonlight, a shadow tilted and writhing against flora and fauna.

Do you remember where you were when you read *The Beauty Myth?* When your boy-friend asked you why you shaved your legs and armpits, then suggested you don't?

Not just a pretty face.

If you want to know something about pretty, head north and get off at Mud Bay Road and drive straight into the trees. *That is some pretty shit!*

After the first wave of men subsided and I was left on my own to flounder with political texts and feminist tracts, I wanted to squash *pretty* in the face. Nose ring and 1960s polyester sweaters, Dickies, ridiculous cat ear hats. That was *pretty.* You were *pretty.* I was *pretty.*

I noticed pretty girls more, in a louder way, out *loud.*

The prettiest girl in town wanted to kiss me and did. I only tasted that pretty twice. Three times, tops.

Pretty please?

Surrounded by women who challenged notions of *pretty* I lost a layer of reserve, posed nude for a pretty girl who blew up the black and white prints wall-size and covered the women's bathroom of the college with parts I considered unpretty. I ate what I wanted, finally, and wrote about it, a heart-shaped thought bubble above my head with the name NOMY LAMM inside of it. The zines told the story of a journey to *pretty* and the detours. I was only reminded that I had wandered far off when I returned to Los Angeles, my home, where all the billboards and commercials and walking examples made me question my relationship again with *pretty.*

I lost a pretty penny.

My boyfriend was interested in postmodernity, not *pretty.* In therapy I struggled with my feelings of non-prettiness. When the girls and trans-folk I hung out with made any suggestion of finding me crush-worthy, I had to stare hard into a mirror to see what they saw. Some of the time I couldn't find it.

Pretty sad.

Tattoo guns burned into the skin I argued with. Now *that* is *pretty.*

Lines and scars. Dimples. Fleshy parts attuned to gravity. It's too easy to look back at old photographs and ascribe pretty to the characters inside. There's that girl, that chula I once inhabited. I see her in my face. I see her in my eyes. I add another girl to the line and we see *pretty* there, a whole lot of *pretty,* and layers get added to what 'pretty' means, and what it does not.

I notice when I'm not noticed, now. I inhabit space and yet can become invisible, a rare and unusual gift and also the boring reminder that *pretty* is fleeting. The other words—*intense, dark, sexual*—are shadows who show up unexpected, tap my shoulder, blindfold me.

Except when I'm alone or with the one who loves me. To her, my kind of pretty holds. It's beyond *pretty.* It is *epic.*

New words emerge, float up, arrive in my mouth. In the end, her love for me, my daughter's love for me, my love for myself, are pretty much everything. Pretty falls away, tumbles down to a place where words go to rest. *What a pretty mess it's made down there.*

Rest in peace, *pretty.* I can live without you.

NO BULLSEYE

by Tisha Marie Reichle-Aguilera

"Can I get a shot?" Sylvia lifted herself onto the cracked wooden stool farthest from the pool players. She needed something to replace the terrible feelings she'd had all day.

The bartender, Rita, raised an eyebrow and slid a brown bowl of bright yellow, probably stale popcorn toward Sylvia. Rita has been wiping down the warped wood at Veteranos for about forty years, longer than Sylvia has been alive.

"Cazadores, please." Maybe she should've gone to a different bar. Here the same old guys propped up by the same old cue sticks watched the Raider game on the lone TV screen. She hadn't been here in almost a year. For the three previous, hadn't been here without Miguel. Today she knew he wouldn't be here. A mutual friend had posted a photo of him and his new girlfriend in Mammoth. He didn't even like snow.

Rita poured Sylvia a double and walked it down to the end of the bar. "You sure you want to do this?"

The last time Sylvia and Miguel had been at Veteranos was a tequila night. Miguel's brother had challenged her to take shots. She had matched him easily, sin limón, sin sal. He had to rush to the toilet after six. She was calmly sipping her beer when he returned. Even bought him one, which he considered an insult, so he left. He shouldn't have driven himself home. Miguel blamed Sylvia. Broke up with her before the funeral.

Rita opened a bottle of Dos Equis and set it next to Sylvia's shot. "That's on the house."

A cheer erupted from the pool table. Sylvia watched an unfamiliar body stand up straight, grin, and walk slowly around to face her. His not Raider shirt stuck close to his sweaty body. He wiped his palms on his jeans and bent over to prepare his next shot. His grin replaced by a frown of concentration, a careful examination of the angles.

Sylvia looked away, slammed her tequila, and held her glass up to the yellow light. It buzzed, a familiar comfort. She squinted through the glass at the faded beer poster across the bar, its corners curled up and cracked. The burn lingered in her throat and her ears muffled the distant conversation.

In her head, she heard Rita scolding Miguel, telling him he shouldn't let her drink so much. He laughed and called Sylvia Veteranos best customer. It's true. She spent more time here than at home. From her apartment balcony, she could see into the back door, so even when she wasn't here here, it felt like she was.

Sylvia traded the shot glass for a handful of popcorn. She chewed slowly, careful not to get kernel bits stuck between her teeth. "Why don't we have chips?" she shouted at Rita over Gloria Trevi's "Que me duele." The new guy must be controlling the juke box. The old dudes always play Vicente. "Chips or nuts instead of popcorn?"

Rita walked to the storage room and took out a tall cylindrical bag, half empty, of the yellow popcorn. "Only five ninety-nine at Smart and Final. Lasts all week."

Sylvia looked around. It should last all month there were so few people. She sipped her beer. The bitter coolness soothed some of her anger, replaced it with sadness.

"You gonna play? Rita asked, sliding the box of darts down the bar.

Sylvia took out the blue one, fingered its plastic feathers and pricked her thumb with its not-sharp point. She felt the new guy watching her. When she looked up, he sucked in his bottom lip. She took a long slow pull on her beer.

He smiled.

The old dudes noticed her then. Only one was still friendly, waved. The others looked away or looked down, pretended they didn't know she'd watched them from her balcony.

"You can play one practice round," Rita said. "I reset the board."

Sylvia climbed off the stool, unstuck the back of her thighs from the unvarnished wood.

"A couple of bullseyes might make you feel better."

"Nothing can do that right now, Rita." Sylvia drained the last of her beer and set it on the counter. "Except maybe half a dozen more shots."

"Nothing is that bad."

Sylvia rolled her shoulders and stretched her arms over her head. "Until today." Sylvia threw a dart. 20. "One of my students was stabbed on his way to school." She threw another. 1. "He's still in a coma." She threw her last one. 7. "Tomorrow's his sixteenth birthday." She plucked the darts out of the board and put in six quarters to start the game.

"I'm up first," Rita said. She opened two beers and handed one to Sylvia.

"I went to see him in the hospital. His mom, two tias, and his abuela were there."

Rita threw. Double 20, Double 12, Triple 18.

"Nothing I could do. Couldn't even cry with them."

Sylvia threw. 18, 12, Double 5. When she and Rita were a team in the local women's dart league, no one could beat them. Sylvia saved enough money in two seasons that she didn't have to teach summer school. Miguel was never that good. Not even playing pool. She'd played against him and his brother. Beat them both repeatedly. But they'd refused to let her on their team. Machismo.

While Rita threw, Sylvia watched the new guy bend over the table. His form was good. She took a long drink. Set the empty bottle down hard.

When he missed a shot, finally, he turned and walked toward Sylvia, toward the bar.

"Don't turn your back on them," she murmured as his salty-soapy scent reached her.

He whispered back, "Son mis tios. If one cheats me, the other tios will rat him out."

Rita handed Sylvia the darts. "Refill?"

"Shots," he said. "And one for my friend here too."

Rita gave her the eyebrow again.

Sylvia shrugged and walked away from him to the dart board. Triple 14, 20, and 7.

"Not bad."

She pulled out the darts and handed them to him.

He put a hand up in surrender. "Not my game." He stroked his stick, clearly a custom job.

"Sylvia, don't be giving this ruffian my turn."

"Ruffian?"

"Rafael." He turned away from them and took his tios their shots. He returned to the bar to salud with Sylvia. "No lime? No salt?"

She shook her head and the tequila burn in her chest was different this time. The alcohol killed the sadness like the sadness was germs. "Gracias, Rafael."

"De nada, Sylvia."

Rita refilled his beer glasses.

The tios cheered at the Raider touchdown.

Sylvia must've frowned because Rafael laughed. "Not a fan, huh?"

"A hater, they call me."

"Who's your team?"

Sylvia shook her head and returned to the dart board. 19, 7, Double 2. She scowled. "Whoever's playing the Raiders." In her mind, her student hunched over his algebra test in his black and silver jersey, counting on his fingers, frustration on his face. "Rita, another beer?" Sylvia put cash on the bar. "And one for my friend."

Rafael took his beer back to the tables where it was his turn again.

Sylvia watched him, her head buzzing like the light over the dart board. In her altered state, she continued to score poorly. No bullseye. "Guess I need more practice."

"League starts in two weeks. You've got time." And Rita resumed her bar wiping.

Sylvia watched the men make bad shots, miss easy ones.

"You want this?" Rita pulled her maroon leather case out from under the bar and unlatched it with her good hand. Since her stroke, she'd stopped shooting pool, but never sold her stick, even when offered twice what she paid for it. "You won't beat him with those warped old house cues."

Sylvia fingered the dark brown wood. In the shiny surface she could see her distorted reflection, stray hairs sticking out all over her head. She heard her student say, "Fix that miss," as he offered her his brush. He was a such a sweet boy. This shouldn't have happened to him. She drained her third beer and lifted the two parts of the stick out of their velvety bed. Rafael watched her as she screwed them together.

"If you beat him, he may not be so friendly."

Sylvia stopped wiping the stick with the chamois and looked at Rita. "*If* I beat him?"

Rita's laugh exploded over the cheering Raider fans, Shakira's "Estoy Aqui," and the crack of ceramic balls. She smacked eight quarters on the bar.

"Water please." Sylvia jingled the change in her pocket as she strolled to the pool table.

The tios grumbled, but Rafael smiled at her.

Sylvia kept her distance while they finished. No more flirtation. No more shots.

"Fifty?" She asked quietly when she put her quarters in.

"I can't take that much from you."

"You won't." Sylvia sunk two balls on the break. She walked around the table and thought about the women standing around the hospital bed. "9 side pocket." Their grief, their worries. "12 corner." She pointed.

"Ambitious."

Sylvia remained focused, cracked her neck to both sides, and squatted down to check her sight line. "15-14." She tapped the closest pocket.

"Imposible."

She ignored him, banked the cue ball off two sides. "Right this way, my friends." It knocked the 15 into the 14. One followed the other into the pocket.

Rafael let out a long slow whistle. "Darts not your only game."

"I live up there." Sylvia pointed her stick out the back door at the building across the alley where her balcony curtains drifted in and out of the open sliding glass door. She pointed to the far corner. "10."

"Tough shot."

"Simple geometry." Sylvia repositioned herself for a left-handed shot.

"How – "

While she chalked the tip, she walked up and down the long side, looking for the best angle. "And 13 over here." She touched the side pocket with the end of Rita's stick. As the last striped ball went in the pocket, she tapped Rafael's shoulder. "I teach high school math."

She had left the cue ball on the wrong side of the 8 ball, the nearest pockets blocked by solid balls. She'd have to put a crazy spin on the cue to run the table. If she missed, Rafael would have at least four easy shots.

He must have sensed her hesitation. "Make it a hundred?"

Sylvia stood up straight, drank the last of her water, and thought about her student's hospital bill. "A hundred'll help." She moved to the other end and imagined the shot in her head: a yellow dot on the short rail just left of the center diamond and a line across the table to the center pocket. She called it.

Rafael snorted.

She scowled, stood on her tiptoes, leaned over the table without touching it, and took a deep breath. The cue ball hit its mark, spun, tapped the 8 ball with a little less force than she'd hoped, but enough to send it to the edge of the center pocket. Rafael celebrated too soon.

The 8 ball fell in.

Sylvia exhaled.

Rafael shook her hand with the hundred-dollar bill.

"I've gotta go." Sylvia wiped down Rita's stick and left her last five on the bar as a tip.

"Next week?" Rafael hollered after her.

Sylvia smiled. "Sure. I've got a lot of bills to pay."

LAST GALLANTRY OF A BADASS

by Octavio Solis

There's this unspoken grace period lasting an indeterminate length of time between one fuck-up and another, and Irving Childress III knocked on my screen door just as that period came to an end. He stood there on my porch flicking june bugs off the screen with his finger, waiting with the sullen patience of a nun for me to open up. I hid in the kitchen soon as he knocked but I knew he saw me. So I downed the last of my brew and went to the door.

Hey Mundo.

Que paso, Irv.

How're you doin'. How's your mom. She around?

It's after two, dude.

I know it.

I'm about to go to bed.

And I'll let you. But see. I need you to do me a favor.

Is this gonna be about dogs, Irving?

No, it's not gonna be about dogs. Are you still mad at me about that?

I shouldna been, but I was. Most sins in this world are difficult to avoid, but full-on *pendejadas* like stealing your own dog, c'mon. Even my little niece laughed in my face after that one.

This is not about dogs. There ain't a single dog in this one. I swear.

Then what's it about?

I can't tell you just yet.

I gotta get to bed, man.

I turned off the porch light and he went black. I couldn't see even the shape of his long scrawny head and his jug ears. Just all black. But still through the screen door I heard his voice break.

It's Bobbie. She and me got into it. And she broke it off, man. Threw her ring right in my face. You know, our promise ring. And it was over some dumb thing, I don't know. Something about *molé*, her mother's *molé*. She thinks I don't like her mother's *molé*.

Do you?

No. But she's wrecking the whole thing over nothin', man. And it was beautiful. I never had a girl like Bobbie. She's like my whole reason for existence. I gotta make it up some way, man. I just gotta.

I turned the porch light back on and he was looking down, wiping his nose with his fingers and smearing them on his jeans. I thought Bobbie Mendoza would never marry him if she saw him like this, but they might be good for a couple more months.

What is it you got in mind, Irving?

Well, it involves a little breaking and entering. But it's for a good cause.

He grinned his ol' cowhand grin, and I knew that meant some crazy, blood-rushing, scary good time was about to be had. All in the name of love, which didn't excuse shit, but surely made it worthwhile.

Lemme find some shoes.

Raised where I was in the Lower Valley in El Paso, wall-to-wall brown kids with most of our teachers blue-eyed and silver-tongued, I grew up halfway believing that whites were much smarter than we were. Irving broke up that myth real quick. He was always getting busted in school for unbelievably stupid shit like setting off the fire extinguisher on the cheerleaders at a pep rally and barbecuing his own dissected pig fetus from Biology Lab. But it also endeared him to us, made him honorary *raza*. Even the old truck he drove us in now had a *Brown Power* bumper sticker on the bumper.

I appreciate you coming along. I'm gonna owe you for this.

You owe me for the last time.

Well then, I sure hope this makes up for that.

He reached down to the floorboard and raised a six-pack of Miller Lite. I picked the coldest one off the plastic stem and lowered the window on my side to catch some of that cool desert breeze that blows in from Alamogordo. I wanted to make some conversation, but this poor *gabacho* just drove quietly on, both hands on the wheel, can of beer in his crotch, dash throwing light up on his sadly mottled features. I knew he was thinking of her.

Irving had a swarm of freckles all over his face that kinda turned purple whenever he saw a hot-looking chick. He had no control over it. We called it his horn-o-meter. It always cracked me up to see him fire up like that, except that one time he went purple in front of my mom. I almost kicked his ass then.

I love Bobbie, he said. I love that bitch.

Then maybe you shouldn't talk about *molé* in the future.

I know what it is. It's that damned teddy bear. She's been all freaked ever since her teddy bear fell apart. She's had that thing for years. Her first dad gave it to her when she was little. Her third dad stitched her name on it.

What about daddy number two?

Don't even go there. He's in the federal pen for beating up number three. How do you guys call it? *La Pinta.*

I was beginning to wonder if that's where we were headed, too.

Are we going to buy her a new teddy bear, Irving?

Irving got that wild honky smirk on his face again, bit into a *soggy taquito* left over from his Chico's Tacos bag and said, Even better.

I should have said no. I should have not come to the door. But here I was sitting next to bad luck and trouble at two in the morning. It was exactly like that time he asked me to help him steal his own dog. I knew I should have said no then, but I went with him anyway. He'd got this idea that he could make some easy bucks by putting his Doberman up for sale in the classifieds and then stealing it back before anyone knew what was up. So a week later, we went to the buyer's house up at Five Points and waited for the dude to go out for the night. Then we jumped the backyard filled with all these junky cars and Irving called for his dog.

Mr. T. Yo. Mr. T.

You named your dog Mr. T?

He's my bodyguard, man. We're the A Team.

I shook my head. Ese, you are something else.

I could barely see shit except his jug ears sticking out. He bumped into a case of Coke empties which made a crazy rattle and then we heard this low growl. In that dense moonless dark, I saw Irving's shape move a little more ahead of me calling: Mr. T, hey boy, it's me. It's me, boy.

Again that low growl, coming from the vicinity of this old junked-out Packard.

Are you sure we have the right house, dude?

I see him. I see my dog. Here boy. Here, Mr. T.

That's when I saw this huge black flash of fur come lunging out of the back seat straight for us teeth bared. Irving picked up a lawn chair to fend him off while I ran like a *pinchi* jackrabbit for the *pinchi* fence. Still, that dog bit off as much of us as he could take. We had to get tetanus shots and those bitches are painful. Irving just shook his head and marveled at how quickly his beast had changed loyalties. He knew it was me, he kept saying. He knew it was me.

That was almost a year ago, but Mr. T still haunted us both. Him more than me.

Finally Irving pulled the truck over to the side of the road right on North Loop. He finished off his beer and waited for the lights of passing traffic to go their way. He said get out and I helped him gather some rope, potato sacking, a ten-foot ladder, and flashlights from the bed of the truck and walked across the street to the north side of the big compound. I recognized it immediately.

Shit. What are we doing here, *vato*?

Just do what I say and this'll be over in no time.

Irving, this is J. Armes house.

I know what it is.

We're going to bust into J.J. Armes house? Are you crazy, dude? Do you want to die?

Anyone familiar with El Paso lore knows about J.J. Armes. He's a private investigator famous for rescuing Marlon Brando's son from these ruthless kidnappers in Mexico or something to that effect. He's always solving these *pinchis* cases which is how come he's so loaded. The ironic thing about this J.J. Armes is that he doesn't have any arms. I don't mean weapons; I mean arms. When he was a kid playing on the track for the Southern Pacific, he found some railroad explosives which blew both of them off at the elbow. I had just seen the dude on Hawaii Five-O playing this hired assassin who could build a high-powered rifle in seconds with his two titanium clamps and hooks. He got my respect just for that shit.

But there was something else about this *vato*. He was so rich he lived in this huge compound fenced off real high with bamboo and shit, and inside of this place guess what? He had a bunch of wild animals roaming around: a camel, a zebra, a giraffe, some peacocks, and, it was rumored, a couple of big cats like lions and tigers. Just in case this detail escaped Irving's recollection, I repeated my question.

Do you want to fuckin' die? Do you want to be eaten?

He shushed me and whispered real fierce in my face. Lissen. Lissen. I know it for a fact. I saw it in the paper. He just bought himself a juvenile koala bear from Australia. And he keeps it in a cage outside his house. If I could just get it for Bobbie, then I know all my shit will be forgiven.

I tried to tell the *pendejo* that a koala ain't no teddy bear, in fact, it ain't really a bear at all, and that the lions would most likely eat both him and the koala if he tried this stunt, but Irving insisted that the peacocks were still loose on the grounds, and if they were running around then it meant that all the predators were probably caged up for the night. He made me peek through the slivers in the bamboo fence just so I could see those peacocks sitting peacefully on the front porch of the house. I had to admit he had a point, but before I could tell him he was already up the ladder. He tied the rope off on a tree branch nearby and then hoisted the ladder to the other side. He said to wait and be the lookout and watch for the ladder when it came back over. Then he was gone. That dude always could move like a cat.

I sat against the fence in the dark wishing I had another Miller Lite to quit my shaking. There wasn't a sound at all but the occasional swish of a passing car and some far-off dog barking to keep time with it. I thought of all the stupid things Irving had done since I'd known him and it occurred to me that they were all done for the attention of some girl. Whatever gifts he lacked in his character, and hell knows he lacked them all, he surely was a gutsy motherfucker. What had I done in my life this daring? For whom had I made this kinda effort? Would I ever know what it means to risk everything for the sake of a woman? I started to believe in Irving's love for la Bobbie Mendoza.

Then the sound of this crash sprung me to my feet and I heard the rapid clunk-clunk-clunk of Irving scaling the ladder. I looked up and saw his jug ears flaring wide in the moonlight. Take this, don't drop it, here, he shouted and the next thing I knew: foom! The sacking landed in my arms and I felt the wriggling form inside. The ladder came flying over next and soon we were both dashing across the street for the truck as floodlights came on all over the compound behind us. Irving tossed me the keys and said drive and I passed him the bundle. We tore down North Loop toward Ysleta as fast as his crate could take us, panting like dogs.

We didn't say hardly nothing between us the whole time until Irving slowly pried open the sacking and we saw that leathery nose come popping out. *Hijo de la chingada,* I said.

It's a beauty.

He knows it's missing.

It's okay.

Okay? Fuck you, Irving, he's a detective! He lives to do this kinda shit!

He won't find us.

Are you kidding me? He found the son of Marlon Brando! If he can do that, he can sure as hell find his own damn marsupial!

His what?

It's a marsupial. It's not a bear. I told you!

She won't know the difference.

Where do we go now?

Where else? To her place.

So there we went, driving like escaped cons for the border. As a matter of fact, her house was pretty near the actual border, in this old run-down neighborhood out by the Ysleta High School. We took a bunch of rights and lefts on the way to lose what we thought was J.J. Armes in his trademark bullet-proofed limo. The whole time I was imagining my throat getting torn apart by these gleaning titanium hooks or being fed alive to his Bengal tigers. Irving was trying to feed the koala some of the left-over Chico's Tacos straight outa the bag. The little thing wasn't having none of it.

What do these marsupials eat?

Leaves, man. Some *pinchi* leaves that grow only in Australia.

Hell's bells.

We pulled up at her house at close to four in the morning. Irving insisted I come with him to the porch with the wilted cactus, just for moral support. He knocked on the door real loud to make sure people woke up and about a minute later, the door opened and it was her old man. He was an unshaven unhappy mess in a Scooby-Doo t-shirt.

¿Si?

Sir, may I have a word with Roberta please?

¿Saben que hora es?

Irving looked at me and I spoke to the old guy.

¿Podemos hablar con Roberta por favor?

No está, he said. *Se fue a California hace una semana. A vivír con su tía en Fresno.*

Irving, she's gone. She's moved to her aunt's house in Fresno.

Wait. That can't be.

She's been gone for a week, dude.

That just can't be.

The old guy peered down at the furry clump in his arms and said in English, Where did you get the monkey?

We got back in the truck and I started us home. Light was breaking slowly beyond the trees. The cars were pale ghosts streaming through the blueness of dawn.

She has to know.

We need to take this thing back, *ese.*

This is badass shit I done for her. But how is she gonna know if she's blown town? How the hell am I gonna get this to California?

You're not. You're taking it back.

And just like that, he turned. His ears went all red and he pounded the dash with his fist, causing the glove box to fly open.

No! he cried. Mundo, you and me are going to Fresno! We are taking this stupid bear to Bobbie one way or the other!

Something in me gave too, 'cause without even thinking, I yanked the truck off to the gravel shoulder, slammed the brakes, and got out in a rage. I stomped to the passenger side, but he was already there spitting into the dirt, bracing for a fight.

You dumb fuck, when are you gonna learn? There's nothin' you can do that'll make her come back to you! She's done, ese! She don't want you no more! Accept that and move the fuck on!

What do you care? You don't know her!

I explained to him with all the expletives at my disposal that I knew Bobbie better than he ever would, and that in fact, she had confided in me her desire to go to Fresno long before they even broke up. Irving kept shaking his head, but I told him that nothing he'd ever done had really impressed anybody but me. And that now I too had reached my limit. You can go to Fresno if you want, I said, but you're going without me.

His face went slack and he blinked twice. She actually told you she was goin'?

In so many words. She just didn't know when.

Irving looked at me like it was my fault we'd come to this pass, like it was 'cause of me that we'd stolen a koala bear from J.J. Armes and ruined a perfectly good beer buzz and possibly a friendship on this wild goose chase. I think we both swallowed hard at exactly the same time.

It's probably gonna die, huh?

If you take it to *Califas,* it will.

He nodded and kicked at the gravel like he was kicking away something essential from himself, and I guessed that after this, we'd never see the kind of delirious gallantry we'd come to expect of Irving. Standing in the first rays of morning, I felt sorry for the next girl he'd get mixed up with. Hell, I felt sorry for myself.

Back in the truck, he looked down on the sleeping koala in his arms like it was Mr. T all over again and started miserably eating his own stale left-over *taquitos.* His whole face was blotched with purple while he kept mumbling, she's gonna know, some way, I'll make sure she knows. I detoured back by J.J. Armes' compound, which we were surprised to see wasn't crawling with cop cars, and slowed down long enough for Irving to jump out and leave the sack by the front gate. I dropped myself off at home and fell straight to bed. All that morning I had dreams of ladders, lions, and angry dogs.

Later in the week, I saw in the papers how Irving Childress III of El Paso had turned himself in for singlehandedly stealing a koala bear from the home of J.J. Armes, famed private detective and budding TV star and how the suspect was expected to plead guilty to the multiple charges being brought against him. I took a sip of my mom's coffee, shook my head and said to myself, it's not a bear, fool, it's a marsupial.

MUNDO MEANS WORLD

by Octavio Solis

There I was sitting on the porch taking in the Saturday morning rays in my pajama pants and t-shirt, nursing a cup of Mom's café con leche with the light buzz of my doobie taking hold. The grackles with their oil-slick wings scattered as Louie-Louie rolled by in his royal-blue Chevy Impala with the mag wheels and chrome bumpers, like he always did on weekends. Only this time he pulled into the driveway. That sleek machine next to my car reminded me that no matter how I customized it with a cherry-red Earl Scheib paint job and new tires, my Gremlin would always be a Gremlin. There went my buzz.

Louie-Louie sat in his car with his sunglasses on like the Prince of Low and waved me over to him. He never got out of his ride if he could help it. Some people thought it was laziness on his part and rude too, and some even wondered if he had legs at all. But I knew better. That Impala was Louie-Louie's throne and as long as he sat on it, he was king. Why would he abdicate that when there was enough daily shit in this dusty old town to make us all feel provincial? I slipped into my flip-flops and sauntered over all cool and easy.

¿Que onda, Louie-Louie?

Nada-nada. How about you, bruh?

I'm cool.

Been too long, *ese.* You high?

Just a hit. Keep it down. My mom, *sabes.*

I'm hip. How's your sister doin'?

Still married.

I don't see it lasting.

Like a lot of the guys that called themselves my friends, or *camaradas,* in the jargon of my time, Louie-Louie took an undue interest in my sister Mickie. It didn't matter that she was already married and had a four-year-old kid to show for it. He was waiting for the day she'd come to her senses and ride off with him to some romantic getaway like Carlsbad Caverns. Like that day would ever come.

Mundo, I need you to do me a solid.

A what?

A favor, bruh. I need your help.

For what?

Without taking his eyes off me, he reached under the seat and whipped out something wrapped in newspaper. He laid it in my hand and by the weight of it, I knew it was trouble.

What's this?

Just for a day. Watch it for me.

I peered through a slit in the paper and saw the shiny blow-hole of nasty looking right back at me.

This is a gun, ese. What the hell am I gonna do with a gun?

Nothin'. Just put away and forget about it. I'll be back for it tomorrow.

What's going on, ese? Is this your *cuete?* What've you done?

Nothin'. Look, Mundo, I'm asking you to fucking do me this solid, and if you don't want to, then fuck it, I'll find someone else. But I thought you were mature enough for this shit. How old are you, twenty-one, twenty-two?

Eighteen.

Eighteen? Fuck it, I'll see you later.

He started to take it back, but I moved my hand away. I didn't realize that I had done that. Something about the heft of it, the blunt unpredictable weight of it, felt good against my abdomen, and that's where I kept it.

Just kidding, ese. I'll watch it for you.

He smiled. Like an idiot, I smiled back exactly the same way.

Orale, Mundo. That's my bruh. You my rock-steady bruh. Later.

He turned up the music in his car and shifted it in reverse.

Is it loaded? I asked.

Louie-Louie gave me his over-the-sunglasses look and said, Say hi to Mickie for me, bruh.

*

Louie-Louie used to be Luis Gutierrez and he used to work for my Dad's tree surgery business back when he was still married to my Mom. But sometime after Dad left home and later the state, Luis got mixed up with these other people who worked in used car sales, which we all knew were fronts for money-laundering operations, and just like that he's Louie-Louie and his shirts look cheap and he smells of cologne and he's putting a gun in my hand. I didn't like the way he called me bruh neither, like it would endear me to him instead of making me feel like an article of women's underwear. But the fact that he entrusted this hardware to me, that said something about how the world seemed to be gearing up for me.

I closed the door to my room, turned up the music on my stereo and decided I wouldn't even look at it. I'd put it in the closet under all my old Famous Monsters of Filmland magazines, leave it there until tomorrow. But before I knew it, I set the package on the bed, on my knees like a supplicant peeled back the newspaper with my hands shaking and readied myself for the sight of it. Suddenly, everything in the room blurred out except for a single revolver, Smith and Wesson .45, stainless steel burnished to a matt finish, with a black grip finger-grooved for easy handling. I peered into the cylinder and found a bullet nestled in each chamber. I held it gingerly, shifted it from hand to hand and nursed that heft in my palm, aimed it at my graduation picture on the wall, at the whole tribe of graduates in my senior class panoramic, feeling the faintest voice whisper right into my fingertips the word yes.

I heard my Mom making noise outside my door so I wrapped the cuete in its paper and buried it deep between my magazines in the closet, right by the blunt I lit earlier. I needed a long steaming shower. Standing there in the tub with the hot soapy water running down my legs, I looked at my sad skinny body and the not-quite-adult machinery of my sex, frail and incomplete. Only then did I realize that my hand was still gripping the gun, even if the gun wasn't there at all.

After I toweled off and combed my hair, I heard voices in the kitchen. I opened the door and called out, Ama! You talking with somebody?

Si, mijo, she bellowed back. Mickie's here. She's gonna watch the house while I'm at work.

Hey, *carnala!* I shouted to her.

Hey, Mundo! Get dressed so you can say hi to Bruno!

Bruno was the aforementioned four-year old fruit of my sister's loins and my nephew, but his real title was holy fucking terror. This little brat had a mad knack for ferreting out whatever meant the most to us and leaving it in a shambles. He once found a set of my great-grandma's diamond earrings and disposed of them in such a fashion that we found one of them deep in the bowels of the washing machine and the other deep in the bowels of Bruno himself. Needless to say, the shit he got into made us get into it too.

Bruno's here?

Yeah. Isn't he in your room?

I frantically wrapped a towel around and ran to my room and when I opened the door, there he was, holding that stainless steel 3-inch barrel in his tiny toddler fingers. He was a striking boy with long lashes and deep green eyes, but his head already bore the scars of too many tumbles down stairs and out of trees. I dropped the towel and his gaze went straight to my groin and that was distraction enough. I snapped the gun out of his hands and quickly pushed him out. No way that *pinchi cuete* was staying in the house now.

*

To keep it hid, I put on my denim jacket and shoved the hardware barrel-first into my pant's waistband. I flashed past Mom and Mickie with hardly a word and got in my car and drove. I didn't know where I was going, but I hardly cared. I headed down Alameda past the old motels and my old elementary and the many used car lots that were only just sprouting along both sides of the avenue. I was raised along this old highway and connected to its low-rent charm, but now it was starting to turn. Into what, I couldn't say back then.

I stopped at the light and waited for my green with the other cars around me. *Los Tigres del Norte* from someone's radio bled into my car and that's when it happened. The same smooth little whisper that had earlier coursed into the whorls of my fingers spoke up a little louder now, saying

Look at him.

I froze. Again I heard it.

Look at him.

I turned to the driver in the pick-up next to me. An older guy in a Diablos baseball cap with a cigarette buried in his mustache.

In that brand new *troca*. Fucking music. He thinks he's *el mero-mero*.

The guy caught me looking and stared back like he's about to laugh 'cause I'm in a fucking Gremlin. I wanted to turn away but the voice said

Nah, man. You got this.

And I did. Some kind of force hardened my look and the guy blinked and the light changed and he turned away and then he was gone. The car behind me honked and the voice whispered

Take your fucking time. You are the man.

*

I stopped at the Sonic and had a burger for breakfast while I thought about where I should go next. El Paso is a big sprawling city with hardly nothin' to do but stay out of the heat. So I cruised around for a few hours, me and Pink Floyd and the .45. I drove through the serious streets of *El Segundo Barrio,* where no doubt some of the rough *vatos* standing on the corner were anchored with similar heft. When they turned their blunt grackle eyes on me sitting low in the saddle, I gave them the stern look of brotherhood. At first they looked affronted and I could almost see their spines stiffening, but then their hard Indian looks softened as they gave me their *cholo* salute, that lazy upward nod of the chin, and I went on my way at the speed of chill. Out of nowhere I thought I should stop by and see Lisa Morales at her parents' house just for the hell of it and the voice in my waistband said yeah.

Lisa lived in this quiet residential neighborhood where everyone keeps their grass trim but the summer burns it yellow. All the Mexicans there think of themselves as upper middle-class and look down on us in the Lower Valley, but I know for a fact they got all their fine imported furniture at haggled prices from the Mercado in Juarez. Lisa's family were very cool, though, they weren't into throwing airs and shit. Every time I went, her mother regaled me with her good home cooking.

¡*Que* surprise, Mundo! Come in, *ya acabamos* breakfast but we got some bacon and *pan dulce* left over.

Está bien, señora. I just had a bite.

Lisa! Raymundo's here! *Andale*, sit down.

I settled into her father's La-Z-Boy with the worn arm rests, which out of respect I'd never done before. It wasn't lost on Lisa. When she appeared in her shorts and tank top looking real fine, fingering her shag-cut hair, she stopped and smirked at me.

What are you doing? That's my dad's chair.

I know.

Her mother brought me a plate of ground chorizo and tortilla anyway, then Lisa and me talked in the living room about the high- and low-lights of the previous night. Lisa had gone to a wedding dance with some guy who tried to force himself on her. He'd unzipped his pants in the car and tried to push her face down into him. I told her she deserved a better class of dude. I told her I'd bust his ass for her. She just laughed. I really liked Lisa Morales, but she didn't think of me as boyfriend material. She tells me everything that goes on in her life, the likes, dislikes, the secrets that claw at her young girl heart, the dark yearnings that run through every teenager who's tired of the burden of being chaste. It was easy for her to share those thoughts with someone who was afraid to admit that he was growing tired of the burden too. Only now there was this other burden, an even deeper secret, digging into my crotch like a finger.

Wanna walk to the park with me? she asked with those kissable lips.

The gun whispered in my pants, fuck yeah.

Sure, I said.

*

In that oppressive border heat that turns the sky almost white, we made our way down the block to the small park with the playground. All along the path, we talked, fell silent, then talked some more. Sometimes as we walked side by side, my hand would brush against hers light as a web and that was enough for me.

Not this time, it whispered.

We sat in the swings while we talked about our plans for after high school. She was looking into a nursing career and I told her she'd be good at it. She asked me what I wanted to do after graduation, and I said, college, I guess, but I didn't really know what that meant or whether it was even possible. I didn't want to think that far ahead. I couldn't think of anything except those long brown legs of Lisa's and that way she had of saying nu-uh, like it was a jingle for her own show or something.

Then while she was looking at some little kids playing soccer with a wiffle ball in the scrappy grass and weeds, the gun whispered trouble into me.

Turn around and kiss her. She wants it.

I swiveled sideways in my swing and faced her. What, she said.

Nothing.

No, Mundo. Tell me.

I just know you can do better.

So can you, the gun said.

I will, she said.

You will too, the gun said.

I got all the time in the world, she said.

World? That's you, loco. Mundo means world. El Mundo. You are her world, said the gun.

And when the right dude comes, I'll know it, she said.

See? She wants it.

I was about to say how every song in the radio lately seemed to be about her and how I couldn't keep my mind on my Algebra II homework and how I really needed to kiss her on the mouth, but she abruptly interjected.

Check it out.

We looked in the direction of the parking lot and saw a car pulling up. It was the guy with the zipper, tall and built like a biker, his curly hair teased into an Afro. He was all smiles, coming right for us. Lisa didn't look too pleased.

Sangrón. Wait here, Mundo. I'll handle this.

She knew I wasn't the type of guy to make a scene, which is to say she knew I was a coward. They stood far off in the stumpy withered grass saying stuff I couldn't make out, except something about dropping over to say hi and something about another chance. I sat in the swing making circles in the sand with my foot, trying not to look, but sometimes I would and I'd see him taking her hand and her pulling it away. Some grandma sitting on the bench watching her kids going up and down the slide squinted once in my direction and turned away. I thought for a minute it was 'cause she heard the gun laughing.

Almost without knowing it, I got up and strode right up to Lisa's side and stood there. For a second, the guy glared at me from under his Afro, then smiled all conceited and shit.

What it is.

What it is is you, said the gun and me.

Lisa tensed up when she saw how I was acting. Mundo, she said, this is—

I know who this is, we said. This is the guy who can't keep his pants zipped up.

Mundo!

The guy chuckled like it was the funniest thing he'd heard that day.

Pos, guess what? You can't treat my friend like that.

Like what?

Like some tramp. You can't do that, *ese.* Lisa's class and you got no business with her.

Mundo, stop.

How would you know, *puto,* he said.

'Cause I know Lisa like you don't, *puto.*

I'll kick your ass.

Try it, fuckhead.

Mundo! I mean it!

And he pushed me with three fingers, just three fingers and I reeled back and almost fell. I took a shallow breath and like another heart pumping all kinds of courage and rashness and heat into me, filling me up with the here and now, blurring my vision of everything but the clarity of the time, the gun howled me right back into his face.

Push me again, I said. Go ahead. Push me again… *bruh.*

I don't know what it is, how some people know. Maybe they got an instinct for it, maybe they got a scent for gunmetal the way some mutts smell the meanness on another dog. Maybe he saw my fingers already wrapped around that invisible grooved handle and sensed my power to make it real. The guy looked intently into my eyes and snarled, fuck you. Then he backed off and threw her a look.

Some buddy you got here, Lisa. By the grace of God he ain't dead. See you tonight?

Lisa could barely speak.

Yeah. Sure. Ten.

Right on. Then to me as he walked back to his car: grace of God, *puto*, grace of God.

I was stupefied, not so much by my crazy newfound nerve, but by this instant pact between Lisa and the guy.

You're going with him?

Lisa, red in the face and burning with tears, shoved me as hard as she could screaming, what the hell are you doing? Idiot! Fool! I told you I got this!

But are you going back out with—

YES! What do you care, shithead? Who made you sheriff all of a sudden?

She shook her head in disgust and stomped off back to her house. The kids and their grandma at the playground were staring at me. I stood there, throbbing with unspent purpose, feeling like I was gonna shoot my jizz right through the barrel of Louie-Louie's gun.

I did, it said. I made you sheriff.

*

It's a poor man's therapy for us to drive blind all over town, burning off gas while we let our minds churn and drift and reel along to the music on the radio. Steering around from red light to red, we feel like we're in control of something when we don't even know where the fuck we're going. We look for counsel in the faces of strangers and in the chance graffiti on the walls, the scrambled layers of gang tags, symbols of devotion and fading mercantile signage. They seem like portents, or maybe encrypted formulas for fixing the shit that has us by the throat. We want out of this dullness, the heavy dullness of this life, but when we find it, when we feel a trace of the sting of living fully, some of us retreat into our droning cars and ride the mazes of our making. Like I was doing in my little cherry-red Gremlin.

All afternoon, I was thinking about Lisa and how she kept ten paces ahead of me all the way back, her long shadow just out of reach of my shoes. I was thinking how she might never let me come over again and how the rest of the school year would be ruined by that. I was thinking about how I almost told her right before she went inside that I had a gun, and how that might have changed anything at all. But mostly I was thinking about the gun. And how it spoke to me. How it goaded me toward this other stronger Mundo, a Mundo less afraid. This was the ballast that kept all of us unstrung *vatos* from being swept away by the gales of change. Lisa would hate me from now on, but she'd tell her *camaradas* all about how I stepped up to this guy and how he backed down and they would know it too, and that made me smile. I was somebody to respect. I glanced at the passenger seat and saw the gleaming steel barrel flare its own dirty smile back at me.

I stopped to tank up my car and get a Slurpee and then at the last minute, I didn't get the Slurpee, but a six-pack of beer and I didn't get carded. That was my experiment. Could I command the respect of the world with Smith and Wesson at my side? And the answer, my friends, was fuck yes.

I drove up to Scenic Drive on the mountain, stopped at the overlook and drank my beer there. Looking down at the divide between Juarez and El Paso, marked by the concrete channel that used to be a great river, hemmed in for its own good, I took in the dimensions of this new Mundo. There wasn't anyone around, so I walked to the crags at the edge with my brew and in the waning red of sunset, took out the gun and aimed it directly at the point where I thought my house was. Somewhere out there, an invisible bullet was streaking through the window and into the heart of a dope who still saved all his monster fan magazines.

Night fell and I was still on the crag. All the beer was drunk and the air suddenly cold. And still nobody there. I wanted to talk to someone, to demonstrate my deft handling of this firearm, to declare to *la gente* what a badass *cabrón* I had been in the park. I needed them to see how different I was now. But nobody came. Occasionally, headlights would approach, then ease on past. I sat on the hood of my Gremlin crunching up the beer cans and getting pissed. I tried to listen to the radio but the songs weren't about her anymore. I took a wizz on a rock and slung Spanish curses at the lights of the cities below and the black monolith mountain behind. Then I put that cold *pinchi cuete* right up against my cheek and cried. I cried at the injustice of Lisa Morales. How could she go back to that guy? How could she be mad at me after all we'd shared? Doesn't she see that it's me she wants? Then in the pitch blackness, I heard

She don't.
What?
She don't see it.
No, huh?
You have make her see it.
Should I?
About time, Mundo.

I wiped the snot off my face and got in my car. My hands shivering on the wheel. My teeth rattling. The whole time the gun was humming some song. I don't know what song. It was pretty, though, and sad. When I got to Lisa's house, the gun said to park it around the block. So I did. Then I walked all casual up to her house and almost knocked, but the gun said not to. It said to go around the side to her window, or don't I know which room is hers? I said I did and I went. I looked in her window and there was Lisa, sitting on the floor talking on the phone to a friend. Or maybe the guy, said the gun.

Yeah, maybe him.
Bet he's got his zipper down.
Probably does.
She's gonna see him soon.
Yeah. At ten.

You can put a stop to that.

I should too.

So what are you waiting for?

How?

You know how, *loco.*

You mean, this?

You got it.

I looked down at the gun and it felt so light now. All that weightiness of before was gone. It almost billowed in my hand. I raised it gently in the air till my arm made a straight line between my right eye and hers. My heart was stamping in my chest.

Mundo means world, I said.

That's right.

I am the world.

The whole world.

All the time in the world. That's what she said.

Yes she did, murmured the gun.

I nodded and slowly lowered my arm. I stepped back from the window and let my weak legs carry me back to the car. I put the gun in the glovebox and drove home. Somewhere along the way, I threw up all over myself but I stayed focused on the sudden vividness of everything. The oil refinery along Trowbridge lit up at night shimmered like a crystal palace through my tears. I came home to a dark and quiet house, took a shower and lay awake in bed for hours after, deaf to everything but the long wail of the Southern Pacific rolling in. That and the comforting snores of my Mom sleeping.

Next morning Louie-Louie pulled up and found me cleaning out my Gremlin. He didn't even shut off the engine. He sat in his car with those sunglasses on and summoned me with his smile. I threw the rag in the pail and popped open the glovebox, took out his .45 wrapped in crisp newsprint and put it right in his waiting hands.

What you washing that piece of shit for? You selling it?

Nah, I like my Gremlin.

No shit, he chuckled. Well, you ever wanna trade it in, I'll get you a good deal, *ese.*

I'll keep that in mind.

Thanks for the solid. It wasn't no trouble, was it?

I shook my head. I told him about how Bruno got his hands on it, and we had a good laugh about that.

I owe you one, he said, 'cause if you knew the reason I had to unload it on you–
But I raised my hands and cut him off.
Honestly, dude, I don't wanna know. Just take it away.

Louie-Louie gave me the sidelong gaze of the Prince of Super Low and slipped the gun from its swaddling. It looked like a cannon in his small childlike hands.

Mundo, I'm serious, bruh, he said. When are you gonna figure out the Life According to Gun?

I shrugged like an eighteen-year-old is supposed to and said, Bruh, I got all the time in the world.

THAT SMELL

An Essay By Luis Alberto Urrea

What I can't shake is that smell. It came back to me again as soon as I saw the pictures of the refugee detention centers. I saw it when Mike Pence and Lindsay Graham entered a center and visibly froze in horror, clearly tried to hold their breath. I know that smell. The children, the mothers, the fathers, the shame of being filthy and hopeless and afraid. I used to carry that smell on my own skin after long days with the border's dispossessed. The poor, the unaccompanied minors, orphans, prisoners, garbage pickers.

It began in 1977 and I wasn't any kind of saint, and I wasn't a socialist snow-flake. I wasn't a refugee. I was a translator and volunteer all along the border, serving under a crusty Baptist preacher, a red-state humanitarian, a war veteran. A Zen Baptist. I worked there from the mid-70s to the mid-90s. In 2004, I learned to track humans with a Border patrol supervisory agent for a book I wrote. Each year, I am in Celaya, Mexico, visiting the caravans. Remember the caravans? Last year's over-ex-aggerated threat of invasion already forgotten.

That smell is upon them, too.

It's so easy to assume that the Other, that nettlesome barbarian coming around for an alleged free lunch, is not quite human. The immigrant brings heinous diseases to our pristine country. See Ben Franklin railing against alien Germans. Or fascist Europe's rat-drawings of Jews. Or our recent folly, the impervious wall. That one that blew down in a wind storm. That fell into Mexico. Dirty, in the Western mind, equals bad. Inhumane conditions are easy to impose. Mothers and babies are the easiest to afflict. The smell rises. Here's the thing, though—it is pornography. Filth-porn for dominants in a diabolical political S&M session with no safe word. "Help," "mercy," "please" don't function in these dungeons. And the real point of that smell is to taint all Americans. It's the smell of victory. It's not your victory. What is yours is acquies-cence. There is no "Them," there is only us.

When you walk into an orphanage along the border, or the cardboard and wire home of a garbage dump scavenger, or a refugee rescue shelter along the long hot road to the USA, the smell presents itself. The kids bear it like a stain, the adults feel it as visceral shame. It is hair, and it is sweat, and it is more biological scents that circumstance has not allowed relief. But it is not a choice—it's the first wire cage. Do you imagine The Trail of Tears had a scent?

Back in my relief-worker days, the first thing we would do in these locations was to celebrate. There were games and competitions and donuts and prizes—be-cause tossing worthless goods at scrabbling knots of desperate survivors for TV cam-eras is pure power-porn. Once everyone had settled into a common humanity, where laughter happened, trust could begin. The next step was washing. We washed and shampooed the kids. No one touched the mothers, though when we could, we gave them water for their own personal use. My first job, aside from providing a voice, was washing feet. Same job. After play, and cleanliness, we distributed food and clothes. Sanitary pads and diapers. Is it insane to ask our for-profit kinderlagers of this administration to do the same? Apparently, yes it is.

Down in Celaya, halfway through the terrible northern journey of the refugees, there is a respite center known as Abba House. It is not huge, except in its effect. Sometimes its limited space is crammed with 300 sleeping people. A gentleman whose leg was torn off by the migrant train works there with kids too exhausted to go on. The Mexican pastor who created Abba House cares for anyone who comes, often under great risk from predators. He accepts all guests. The one thing he will not accept is that smell. He knows that the most important thing for a person's dignity is cleanliness, followed by safe haven. Doctors helped him determine that it takes three days of rest for these wounded bodies to recharge and carry on. He installed a bank of showers so that every traveler who comes first gets a bath, then clean clothes, and some kind of shoes. He cried when he showed me a couch in a corner where an older man reclined reading a book. "That is what you need to be a human being."

He also pointed out that those heading north are immigrants, but when the US rebuffs them and sends them back, they are refugees. If they return to Honduras or Salvador, many will die. Mexico will be forever changed by these wanderers with nowhere left to go. And what about the Haitians? Yes, Haitians—Tijuana has a robust new Haitian community. Bad news: they are climate refugees, escaping more hurricanes. Climate also drives much of the Central American hejira. Is this what the administration doesn't want you to know?

All this is just the beginning. These strangers seeking help are the harbinger of the coming global tide of climate refugees. Heat. Crop failure. Weather. Floods. The magic act of the New Republican Party has magic phrases like Bad Hombres, like The Wall, like illegals. MS13 cadres of ten month old children. They are meant to distract you. They feed your fear, your rage, your guilt. All of them work. They con you into believing you have done some moral act by feeling. What the magicians don't want is action. Can you smell that smell? It is the scent of our world burning. These children we have spit on are human kindling.

What would you do if unknown strangers were paid $750 a day to hold your child in a secret warehouse where she is comforted by concrete and steel, as if she were a baby monkey in a bio research lab? You would not write Tweets. You would tear it down.

Ultimately, the taint is upon you and me. We are responsible. We own this. Kindness is not weakness. Cruelty is not strength. We have gone instantly from the land of "helicopter parents" to the land that chases parents with helicopters. Pharaoh tried brutality once before. Didn't work. This phenomenon is a Biblical exodus in the fevered world, and we Samaritans are free to decide how our children will forever judge us. (For the literary reader, check out "Those Who Walk Away From Omelas" by Ursula K. LeGuin for the true parable of what we are now living).

Mr. Pence, Mr. Graham, Stephen Miller, Mister President—breathe deep, boys. Your legacy will never wash off. You will forever reek.

Don't kid yourselves. These children are yours. These children are you. Remember how the famous poem ends: "Then they came for me."

Llano Lullaby

Santiago Vaquera-Vásquez

I began to write my first real poetry on my farm in Sebastopol, California, the early 1970s. My daughter, Antoinette, had turned fifteen, the same age I was when I had her. It felt like a time bomb went off deep inside of me, at thirty. A gathering of words. I was choking with them. An eruption of words. From my womb. A lava of words began to spill from my mouth, eyes, ears, my trembling fingers, pen. I locked myself in the bathroom- the only door with a lock- with pen/paper, sitting on the toilet seat as my kids yelled, "Where's Mom, do you know where Mom is..." I had three of my own children (my daughter 15, two sons- Ed, 13- Marc, 8) and two 'stepsons' (Eric, 8- Jacob, 6). So five children in all at that time, two of them yelling, "Where's Mom!" Marc began to jump up to the window, trying to look in, his head appearing, disappearing, "Mom, are you in there, Jacob has a dart in his head!" I sighed, but I got my first line down, trembling. One line on the small blank notebook page, but *it was mine.*

When we first moved onto this beautiful farm on a full acre, a stand of red-woods off to the side of the house, an ancient walnut tree, weeping willow by the creek, peach, pear and apple trees in the back fields- not an orchard but enough for us- two barns across the creek, and the boys would build their forts back there, my older son, Ed, a beautiful tree house, installing a stained glass window he made himself (of a summer sun, a fertile field)...we had a cross burned on our front lawn. Actually, two crosses burned on our front lawn. Friends of ours followed us from the Bay Area- brown, black, white hippies with long hair- they helped us move in, camping for a few days with live music, much singing and dancing too. Hence, the burning cross after everyone left. My daughter screaming at the sight around midnight; there it was, a cross burning on our front lawn. I was shocked, terrified...would they try to lynch us, but I kept it to myself.

My eighty-eight year old neighbor, whom I would come to name Annie Oakley, came out that first cross burning night, saw my face, and walked over to where I was standing, the hose in my hand putting out the fire. It left a burn spot on the green grass and it terrified me, but it also pissed me off.

"Do you have a rifle, dear?" Annie asked.

"What?"

"I said, do you have a rifle?"

"No," I answered, flustered. A **rifle**? I'd never even held a tiny gun, as in fuck a duck.

"Well, dear, I'll take you downtown to buy one, just put it over your door for these kinds of emergencies."

"I don't know how to shoot, I'm sorry."

"I'll show you how, dear, I'm a crack shot, grew up with all brothers."

And so, Annie Oakley did, show me how to shoot my own rifle, and I put it up over our kitchen door, the cartridges hidden in my closet, but I knew exactly where they were. And the cross burners returned, my daughter yelling (her bedroom faced the front lawn). I ran out the door- I didn't have the rifle yet, learned to shoot, as they returned a few nights later- and this time I was just pissed off. How dare they terrify my children, how dare they, those racist farm Klu Klux Klan hicks! Annie shot at their tires and she was a crack shot- she also got their license plate. They rolled away with one bare rim as she laughed with glee like a girl.

"Next time you can shoot out a tire too, dear. Tomorrow we're going downtown for that rifle. You know, they lynched a negro man only ten years ago, this county. Never did catch the sons of bitches, far as I know." Annie would tell me a few years later that her mother was Mexican, her father white, and that her mother was light skinned. Their family secret, she told me with defiant eyes. And one Christmas she brought a pot of tamales over to share- delicious. "This is Mama's recipe," she glowed with pride. And we ate them all, spicy and sweet.

In short, the police found the cross burners via the license plate- they were all teenagers, not the KKK. They were held in a cell, so I went down and called them names, but mostly telling them, "If you ever come to **my farm** again and try to burn your fucking cross, I'm going to blow your fucking asses away. I just bought a rifle and I can shoot it pretty fucking good. I won't allow you to terrorize my children, **do you understand me?**" (This is a shortened version.) All but one answered, "Yes, ma'am." As I left one of the cops said, "You sure have a mouth on you, ma'am." "Thank you!" I yelled and left. Yes, the cops were also racist, except for one young guy who gave me a smile as I slammed the door behind me.

A week later three of the cross burners knocked on my door, one of them holding a beautiful bouquet of flowers. "These are for you, ma'am, we're sure sorry if we scared your kids and all. It won't happen again, we're surely sorry," the bouquet holder said in a soft, sorry voice. There was one missing, so I asked, "Where's the fourth guy?"

"You don't have to worry, ma'am, his daddy beat the shit out of him, he still can't walk," one of the teens answered with a smile.

"Well, I didn't want anyone to get beaten up, but, okay, thank you for these flowers, guys, it makes me feel so much better." And it did, I suddenly wanted to cry very loudly- those hideous burning crosses, the image of young black men lynched, castrated. I hadn't cried, but the sight of the flowers, their eyes staring at me shyly. But I didn't, although I'm sure my eyes betrayed me. Well, this is something to write about, I told myself- you're from the Mission, San Francisco, and you've seen worse. Ran over a mugger one time, how I met my stepson's mom, now gone, cancer. Yeah, I ran over a mugger, the thought cheered me up, so what's a burning fucking cross, and I will write about it, damn straight.

"If you ever need anything, just give me a call," bouquet holder handed me the flowers and his phone number, name. My kids stood behind me with their mouths open, the boys. My daughter was watching from a distance, giggling.

"Well, that was really weird, Mom," she laughed. "But I hope there's no more burning crosses waking me up in the middle of night scaring the shit out of me. I mean, we moved to the country to be safer, right? All the gang stuff going on, plus we're going to learn how to grow our own food, right?"

"I'm glad you're learning how to shoot, Mom," Ed added. "Maybe I can learn too."

"You're only thirteen, maybe in a few years, we'll see how it all goes," I answered a bit wearily. My son, Ed, was being chased home by gangs, wanting him to join (in our neighborhood, San Francisco). My daughter, Antoinette, had been jumped by a group of girls with *hatchets* the last day of school. She's a big, strong girl, and she remembered my words, "Never, ever, go into a ball, fight back," and she pushed through the group, ran to a door and banged on it. A man had been watching from his window and was on his way down- he let her in, slammed the door shut. One of the girls had been her best friend from kindergarten to seventh grade, so though their hatchets hadn't drawn any blood, it wounded her spirit.

I had actually been contemplating returning to the city, as in cross burnings by the KKK, possible lynching, was worse than gangs. We'd settle in a different area in the city...but I was learning how to shoot *my rifle*. It wasn't over the door yet, but safely tucked away in my closet.

That first poem that I started in the bathroom was very short, but I finished it the next day. Jacob had stitches on his forehead from the dart- Ed had been throwing darts to a target and Jacob ran right in front of him (or so the story went). After that, darts were only allowed in the back barn with no other activities going on while the darts flew through the air. And **I finished the poem**...it felt like a small, clear voice was right inside my right ear trying to get my attention. The gathering of words. The eruption of words. Lava flowing from my trembling hand, pen. I'd begin a poem, the first line, and at that moment it seemed *impossible* that I would finish it, that I had anything important to say, write, say. But the words, the lines, continued to arrive and I found a spot by myself, by the willow tree, and wrote. On fire. Trembling.

My first experience with poetry, *hearing poetry*, was with mi Mamacita, Jesus Villanueva. She would read me poetry in Spanish, some of it by heart, and she loved to read me sections of The Song of Solomon from the Bible. Mamacita had a beautiful voice and I loved to watch her face as she read/recited; she became young, radiant. I also watched her recite long poems by heart at church- the Southern Spanish Speaking Baptist Church on Capp Street, San Francisco, the MIssion. I remember her as Death, entirely in black, her long grey hair loose (she always wore it up in a tight bun), holding a kind of spear, on the stage, her voice carrying to the very back of the church. Everyone silent, even the babies. She was a full blood Yaqui curandera from Sonora, Mexico, coming to the USA with her husband, Pablo, pregnant with my mother. He was to be the minister at a Baptist church in East Los Angeles; his well to do Catholic family disowned him. Pablo was also a published poet in Mexico; I have none of his poetry, but it must be in the DNA, of course. And Mamacita taught me poetry to recite by heart at church, up on the stage, my hair in large curls, pretty dress. In Spanish, my first language. After church services, the women from all over Latin America gathered in the basement kitchen to cook. There would be piles of pan dulce on a table, so I'd grab a couple and hide under the table eating, listening. One woman would start a poem, another woman would take it further; each woman until the poem was complete. With much laughter, joking. And so, my first memories of poetry are woven with poetry/ prayer from the Bible, Mamacita's voice and *presence* on the stage creating silence, the sweet taste of pan dulce on my tongue, the basement kitchen filled with laughing women, their confident, singing poetry voices. And then, the feast of foods from every country in Latin America. Poetry.

And Mamacita's stories of growing up in her beloved Mexico lindo y querido. Some were hard- she ran away as a girl from her stepfather's secret advances. When she returned, he burned the bottoms of her feet with live coals, to teach her not to run away again. When her mother, Ysidra (a well known curandera in that region), saw her daughter's feet, she threw him out. She was married five times, "Each time a better man!" Mamacita would quote her, laughing. The rancheras she'd turn up on the radio and we'd dance together. She knew those songs by heart as well; her favorite 'Cu-curuucuucuu Paloma,' which I came to know as such beautiful poetry. She would wait for the high note the singer must reach and when he'd reach it, she'd sigh "Ayyyyy, mi Alma," and touch her heart. Without her poetry, her stories, her memories, I would not ever have become a poet/writer. I am her poet.

She left the body when I was almost twelve, and I rode the 22 Fillmore from the Bay Bridge side of San Francisco, to the Golden Gate Bridge side, back and forth for over a week. The drivers got to know me and let me ride for free; some of them bringing me a lunch. "Why so sad, kid?" "I hate school," I remember answering. Anything but the truth. Sorrow. I stole some pens and little notebooks from the five and dime on Mission Street, okay and some candy too- and I began to write poetry about the people on the bus. That some looked really poor and hungry. Some of the mothers smacked their kids too, to shut them up. Mamacita not ever hit me, so this made me very sad. And so, this is how my sorrow was released at that time. That childish poetry. I wish I had them, every page.

My first real poem, that I kept, was written up in the tree house, in the branches of the willow tree. My son, Ed, reinforced an old tree house he found there, and we all loved sleeping up there, taking turns. Although the smaller boys preferred their own cave-like forts. The first time, I brought my sleeping bag, pillow, something to drink, notebook, pens, flashlight, up to the tree house. Ed helped me get everything up there and he was proud of his renovation which proved to be very sturdy. He would build his own separate tree house, with his stained glass window, in the redwoods, later on. And he allowed no one to sleep there, as in *private property*. I wrote a story, 'Golden Glass,' about Ed and his tree house, which has been published in various textbooks.

"Watch yourself coming down, Mom, and just leave your stuff up there, I'll get it down for you later. Watch out for the vampires!" he laughed, leaving me in the darkness.

My daughter, Antoinette, came to the foot of the willow tree. "Hey Mom, I'll have coffee and braided cinnamon loaf for you in the morning. That is, if you survive," she laughed. She woke no later than 6am and started her baking, as in lucky me.

"I'll be there with bells on, girl!"

Then the boys came making growling noises. Wild animals, wild boys.

"What are you going to do up there, *write poetry*?" Marc yelled and they all cracked up.

"I might, who knows. Okay, you guys, Antoinette and Ed are keeping an eye on you so don't mess around. If you do they're going to tell me and you're all going to get grounded. Do you hear me?"

Group groan. "Yeah, okay, see ya in the morning," Marc. "Can tigers climb trees?" I hear Eric's voice. "Can I sleep in the fort with you guys?" Jacob whines. And they were gone. Everyone was getting used to me hiding out by the willow and writing poetry, although it continued to be weird. Then I was back to all of my chores, which was a lot with five kids, and going to Sonoma State a couple of days a week. My partner was a longshoreman, who also wrote some beautiful poetry; the father of my stepsons. From his collection of books, I read Pablo Neruda, Robinson Jeffers, Anne Sexton, Sylvia Plath, Allen Ginsberg, Walt Whitman. Neruda's poetry made my heart ache and soar...Who could write such poetry? I'd ask myself. And the truth of women- Sexton, Plath- searingly etched on the page, each word. Each line. Jeffers' epic poem, 'The Roan Stallion' and Whitman's 'I Sing The Song To Myself.' It all added to the fire, the lava, erupting.

As I dissolved into the darkness, the small lit windows of my house in the distance, where my children were, I was suddenly very lonely and the night seemed ominous, threatening. I hadn't slept away from the house like that since the cross burnings, and my rifle was in the house over the kitchen door. I almost picked up my notebook, pens, flashlight to climb down the ladder; but a small, clear voice- a voice Mamacita called The Wise Voice, and to always listen to it- said, "You're safe, stay."

It was getting chilly, early September, and soon it would be too cold to sleep out. I looked at my little house where my children were and I knew I could be there in three minutes. Then I looked up at the piercingly bright stars that glittered through the dark branches, and the sky became a river of stars floating over my head. And it was so silent. A few dogs in the distance, the wind through the ancient walnut tree, my children's laughter rising once in a while. I imagined them playing Monopoly and Marc cheating as usual, making me smile. And they'd catch him, of course, and throw him out of the game. My partner stayed with friends in San Francisco a few nights a week to avoid the long drive back and forth. I imagined he missed his wife, my best friend, because I did, but this was our family now. Me under a river of stars, alone. Silence. I put my pillow behind my back, snuggled into the sleeping bag, opened the notebook, the pen and flashlight, and wrote this:

Night Dance
Stars dance their ancient tunes,
strung on light,
strung on light,

I get dizzy watching such acrobatics
as everything melts away
to light;

and the night has always played
such music
and the void has always sung
its hunger:

the wide expanse
the wide expanse

and I have always prayed for
daybreak, for Earth splitting
to Sun;

fear, fear: listen:

love is the dance,

the spinning harp.

This was published in my last book, **Soft Chaos**, toward the end. I felt I had to include it as it ushered in a river, an ocean, a volcano of poetry. Words. A river of stars. "fear, fear: listen:"...let me sing, I will sing. These words. "love is the dance, the spinning harp." And "To Jesus Villanueva, With Love," a poem written at that same time, was also published in this book. This was the poem that gave me the voice of my ancestors, it ends:

Your daughter, mi tia,
told me a story I'd never
heard before:
> You were leaving Mexico
> with your husband and two
> older children, pregnant
> with my mother.
> The US customs officer
> undid everything you so
> preciously packed, you
> took a sack, blew it up
> and when he asked about
> the contents of the sack,
> well, you popped it with
> your hand and shouted
> "AIRE MEXICANO"

Ayyyyyy Mamacita, Jesus,
I won't forget my visions and reality.
To lie, to push, to get,
just isn't
enough.

As I wrote this ending down, the story of their crossing, I realized for the first time- there were *no two older children* on that journey. She'd buried them in Sonora as babies, but their spirits were with her. Ancestors. Poetry is the gathered voices of our ancestors. We write it with trembling, joyous hands. And then we sing. With a river of stars over our heads, alone. Yet never alone. We sing with the great choir. Of ancestors. As Neruda wrote, "In a blind extension of love." For the next seven generations- behind us, in front of us. We pass it on in a blind extension of love. As the women in the church basement cooking, one of us starts the poem, another one takes it up, then another one, until the poem is complete. And then we laugh and eat, feeding the children.

This beautiful Earth under a river of stars, we sing. Always with the ancestors.

VOICES OF OUR ANCESTORS

A Memoir Exerpt

Alma Luz Villanueva

We're not even halfway to town when Tata raises his arm and tells me to pull over. My eyes are fixed on the road ahead that cut through the llano, that flat plain that opens before me and still makes me feel like I am living on the edge of civilization, if not on another planet. I look at the sky above, obscured by thick gray clouds pierced with occasional patches of blue. Ahead, I can see sheets of rain coming down. We are headed into the storm.

The day before, I had found Tata at the window staring outside. He looked like he was searching for something in that blue sky. He leaned on his cane with both hands and furrowed his brow.

Something wrong, Tata? I asked him.

No, m'ijo. Nothing. He replied, staring out the window. I'm just looking at what's coming.

And what is that? I responded.

The wind. The clouds. The rain. And everything else. He finally said.

I stood by his side and looked out the window.

It doesn't look like any of that is on its way , I replied.

You'll see, m'ijo. He sighed and then reached out with one hand, placing it on my shoulder.

I stare ahead at the clouds being dragged by the wind across the sky.

Let me tell you about the wind in August. It usually comes in the evening, dragging the monsoon clouds with it. It's not as loud as the March wind, howling over the llano, carrying clouds of dust and covering the towns and cities in its path. No, it's not that loud. Not usually, at least. But sometimes, sometimes it is. Like last night, for example. That wind was fierce. It rose suddenly, pulling the clouds with it like a curtain closing off the sky. By that evening, I had to agree with my grandfather, the rain was coming. In the distance, I saw lightning.

First came the thunder, booming overhead. A herald announcing what was coming. Then a howling wind.

I'm told that my grandfather wasn't always like this: able to predict the weather, know when things were going to happen, read the natural world as if it were one of the books he used to teach back in his university days. He also had the power to heal, but he hardly ever did that. In our family, the story is that his gifts came because of an accident he suffered in Turkey when he was in his 50's. He had been hiking with some friends around the village of Kayaköy and he got hit by a car. He had to spend three days in a hospital in Fethiye. When he was released, he discovered that he had gained some abilities. Rather than capitalize on his new powers, he chose to be quiet about them. He was a reluctant curandero who preferred to keep his gift of touch and healing to himself. Only in extreme situations would he heal someone. Instead of payment, he would ask for secrecy. But still, people sought him out.

The next morning after the wind rose, it started to hail. Giant balls of ice flew down from the sky and hammered the roof of Tata's car as we drove through the llano. He was sitting in the passenger seat, a blanket up to his chest. He was breathing heavily, staring out the windshield with tired eyes.

For a few minutes the hail came down in fury, I had to pull over by the side of the road. We sat in the car and listened to the falling ice pummeling the car. Tata closed his eyes. And, as I watched him, I sensed his breathing growing more and more shallow until he was perfectly still. For a second, I thought that this was it, he was gone.

The wind was picking up again and I closed my eyes.

Around five that morning, I heard Tata stumbling around. He had been sleeping poorly for the last few months, and sometimes he would wake up in the middle of the night and walk around. Since his last fall, this was becoming more treacherous. I had to start taking stuff out of the house to make room for the walker that he was supposed to use. He hated it, preferring his old, wooden, cane that he had bought in Turkey many years ago.

Three years ago, after a nasty fall that sent him to the hospital for an overnight stay, he was given a walker.

Ay pues, he told me, I guess it's time to start using one. After all, I'm 103.

106, I corrected.

106? Really, m'ijo? Wow. Dónde se fue el tiempo? Then he started to tell me about how his great-grandmother made it to 108. She was born in January, 1892, and died a few days after turning 108 in 2000.

You come from a family of people who live to very old age, my dad once told me. Back in Mexico, they used to be called Los Eternos. The majority of them passed away in their late 90's or early 100's. There is a story about one of the abuelas who lived to 114. She was originally very tall, but by the time she died, she had shrunk down to the size of a young teen. She even had a nickname, Mamá Endless.

I once asked Tata about Mamá Endless. We were sitting on the porch of the adobe house. He looked out over the llano and said he had heard about her, but she didn't make it to 114, she passed at 107. It was her granddaughter, Mamá Concepción, abuelo's great-grandmother, who had lived the longest.

And the men? I asked. How long did they live?

He looked up at the wooden beams of the porch and thought a bit.

Well, he said, Tío Euclides lived to 98. Then there was tío Gabriel, he passed at 104. I think the one who lived the longest was Papá Zerafino, he lived to 106. I heard that he was still riding horses at 102, and that when he was in 103, he left to go find an old girlfriend.

How did he go? If he stopped riding at 102?

Who knows? Maybe one of his grandchildren took him in a carreta across the llano.

Did he find her?

Who?

The novia.

Oh, I don't think so. I think she died years before.

Tata, what happened to Los Eternos?

Buried in a cemetery in northern Mexico. When the first members of the familia crossed the border into California, the miracle of old age was lost. They started dying like everyone else, in their 70's and 80's.

What about Dad and you?

In my case, there's that old dicho, m'ijo: hierba mala nunca muere. And in your father's case, well I guess that dicho fits too. Though he'd probably need it in English: Bad grass never dies. And then he started to laugh.

Don't be mean. I told him.

Well, m'ijo, it's true, your papá is stubborn.

I couldn't disagree; he really was stubborn. He and my grandfather had not spoken in more than ten years. I once asked my older brother what that was all about, and all he said was "oh you know, viejos tercos."

I found Tata sitting at the table. His hand on his cane. He was listening to the wind outside.

M'ijo, it's time. He told me.

Time? Time for what?

To go see him. I need to see him before I die.

Who?

David, your father. Take me to see your father.

Why? I asked. Papá doesn't want to see you. Why should I put you both through that?

I need to see him. He needs to know. He responded.

Why does Papá want to see you?

He knows my time is coming. Hear that?

The wind?

Yes, el viento. But just below that, do you hear that sound? She is coming.

I tried to listen, wondering how my old grandfather could even hear something below the wind.

I told him I didn't hear anything.

You're young, he said. You'll hear it when it's time. But for now, it's time to go. Get the car ready.

Wondering what to do, I heard the pounding hail begin to slow down, and finally stop. I opened my eyes and saw that Tata was awake.

We don't have to worry about the hail anymore. Let's go. She's almost here. But I need to see your dad first. He said.

I didn't ask him who "she" was, I just turned on the car and got back on the road.

Once, sitting on the porch, he asked me if I knew the story of La Llorona. I knew it. Everyone did. She was a woman who went crazy and drowned her children. She was said to prowl at night along rivers and arroyos, sobbing for her children. Hers was a scary story told to children so that they would behave.

Tata smiled when I told him all this.

Of course, that's one version. He said. Imagine, though, that she didn't kill her children simply because she had unprovoked madness. Remember, she went mad because her husband left her for someone else. So, imagine, that she is not that monster woman dragging children away, but rather, a woman who comes for all men who have mistreated or abused their power.

Like death. I interrupted.

Sí, like la muerte, he responded. But when she comes for men, she can be either monster or angel. For the men who have hurt, deceived, or mistreated women, she arrives as a monster. She is their guilt come back for them. Moaning in the wind at night, with fingers like claws tearing at the sky, she comes for those who lied, who beat, who cut up, who abused women.

But for other men, men who have not mistreated women, or who themselves have been mistreated, marginalized, or put down by others, she comes not with claws, but with soft embraces and a lullaby to calm them in their journey to el otro lado.

If she is a figure like that, then why make her a monster? I asked.

Because in this mundo, m'ijo, men are more apt to be the first kind. And since she can't defend herself or tell her story, they invented one for her.

Tata isn't really my grandfather. He is my grandmother's older brother. He raised my father after my abuela Juliza died. Dad was seven at the time. Tata was my father's favorite tío, and he did everything to make sure that my grandmother's memory was protected. The only thing he kept from Papá was who his real father was. Apparently my abuela never wanted that known, only her brother knew the truth. And he discovered that by accident. Abuela Juliza believed that she could raise a boy by herself, just as my great-grandmother had done with her own family. It wasn't so easy. Abuela had a weak heart and soon after Papá turned seven, she passed away.

Normally, the monsoon rains come in the evening or at night. The days are dry out on the high llano until the clouds and the rain comes. Some days though, the rains continue into the day. On those days, we stay inside. I help Tata organize his hierbas and he tells me what they are used for. I write everything in a notebook and he laughs. He tells me I should remember it all. But I respond that I don't have his memory, so I need to write it all down. Sometimes he tells me stories about growing up in California or his years spent teaching in Turkey and Ecuador. Other times he tells me stories about our family, how they migrated from the deserts of Sonora to northern California in the 1950's. His tíos were the first to arrive in a small farming community two hours north of Sacramento. They worked in the orchards, picking olives, peaches, and oranges. When my great-grandparents arrived in the late 60's, they were the first family allowed to live within the town limits. Until them, all the Mexicans lived out on the farms or in a tiny unincorporated community beyond the town cemetery. As he told me about this, he began to list the names of the families.

Write them down, he said. They need to be remembered.

What face does she have, Tata? I once asked him as we gathered herbs.
He was quiet for a moment, then he responded: For those who have caused terror, she   comes with the face of the woman they desire. They see her approach and they smile, thinking that they will finally get what they rightfully deserve. When she gets close, her face changes and they see the damage that they have caused in their wake. It is then that their faces turn from delight to terror. Ever see a person with a look of shock or with their mouth in a horrible rictus? She shows them their doom that they caused by their own actions. My father, for example. His face was horribly contorted. The people at the funeral home who prepared him for the viewing told me that putting his face into a semblance of peace was so difficult that they almost suggested that the family do a closed casket. I saw him. They did a good job. But I could tell that beneath that look of sleep, he was screaming.

And to the others? Those who haven't done horrible things?

She comes with a comforting face. She is prepared to take care of you, to make the transition as peaceful as possible.

I wonder whose face she will bear? Tata suddenly asked, snapping me out of my reverie.

Will it be my mother? Will it be your grandmother? He wondered.

You're going to be fine, Tata. I told him. She won't be coming for you today.

He looked at me and smiled.

Even after sixty years, my grandfather still missed his sister. Once, after treating a woman he knew was going to die, he told me that grief never leaves you. It becomes your companion, your partner. Even if it recedes so far back into your being, it is still there. And it can come out at any moment, brought about by anything: a smell of perfume, someone passing by with a similar haircut, a word.

Tata never told my father who his father was, not until after that man died. For that, my father stopped talking to him.

I should have been told. He yelled at Tata.

Tata just looked at him, waited for all the anger to pass.

Your mom didn't want that. He finally responded.

He was my father! My father!

One of my great aunts was there, listening.

Don't talk to your tío that way! He raised you! Don't be ungrateful!

But my father wouldn't stop. He raged before Tata until finally he stood up and walked to the door.

I never want to see you again, Tío. He declared and walked out.

Tata looked at his sister and asked, Do you remember when she used to do that?

He was referring to my abuela Juliza.

His sister laughed and said, Claro! He's just like his mother. He'll get over it, like she always did with Mamá. Angry for three days, declaring that she was never going to speak to her again. And then, on the fourth day, there she was, calling Mom to see how she was doing or to tell her she missed her. He's going to do the same thing. You'll see.

That was ten years ago.

The time I traveled with Tata to Turkey was his last visit there. We spent a month driving around the country. In Fethiye, he showed me the hospital where he had recovered after his accident. The hospital had long since been closed and was now a hotel. We then headed in the direction of Ölüdeniz. Before arriving, we drove to the ruins of the village of Kayaköy. Driving around it, he turned down a narrow road that led back in the direction of Fethiye. I was about to tell him that we were heading away from Ölüdeniz when he pulled over by the side of the road.

Then he told me that this was the spot where the ambulance had stopped after picking him up in Kayaköy.

Why did it stop? I asked.

Because I died in that ambulance and they were trying to revive me.

He said it was true that after the accident he sat up and started talking to his friends who had rushed to his side. But what he never told anyone was that upon being picked up by the ambulance, that he closed his eyes and died. The paramedics at first didn't notice, they thought he had fallen asleep. But when they saw that he was not breathing, they sprang into action.

I stood next to them, watching them do this. Tata affirmed. But then I got bored and decided to step outside.

After he left the ambulance, he noticed he was wearing some type of veil. Protection from the heat, he thought. Thinking that his friends would still be at Kayaköy, he started to walk back. Near the village he found his sister, abuela Juliza, waiting in a car. It was packed with boxes, as if she were moving to someplace new. She was humming a lullaby. Something that sounded familiar, but he couldn't quite place. He approached the car and asked her how her day was going.

Great! She responded

She told him that she was waiting for someone, someone close to her who was going to live near her.

Who is that? My Tata asked.

She thought about it a few seconds, but then said she didn't know. An intuition had told her to get her stuff ready and wait by the side of the road.

Tata lowered his shoulders and started to cry. Then he reached up to take off the veil. Abuela Juliza saw what he was doing and must have recognized him before it was completely off. She started to cry and say it was impossible. It couldn't be. She reached out to cover his face and said, No, it's not your time yet.

Then she took his hand and said, I have to go. She started the car and drove away.

Tata stood there awhile, not knowing what to do. Finally, he decided to walk back to the ambulance. He found the paramedics covering his face with a blanket.

And then? I asked.

Then I woke up.

He reached up to take the sheet off his face. One of the paramedics, who he had been joking with when he got in the ambulance, yelled out in fright.

Then what happened?

They took me to the hospital in Fethiye and made me stay there two nights. Once they accepted I wasn't going to die again, they let me go.

From there we drove to Ankara so he could show me where he lived. The building was no longer there, it had been replaced with a more modern apartment building. He pointed out where his apartment used to be and told me about how he would sit on the balcony in the evening and watch the neighborhood.

On our drive back to Izmir, we stopped in Bursa. After walking around the downtown, we drove out to a cemetery beside a mosque. Walking past the tombs, he muttered to himself, looking at the names and the markings on the headstones. Finally, he stopped in front of one. I was in a different part of the cemetery, strolling around, when he called me over. This is your grandfather, he told me, pointing at the tomb where he was standing.

Basharan, old friend, I brought your grandson. He said.

I was speechless.

Did you ever bring dad here? I asked him later.

I tried, but I couldn't convince him.

And you never thought of him meeting his father when you were living here?

Tata thought about it a while. Then he told me that Papá would have just been disappointed. Basharan had gotten married and he had his own children, his own life.

He was also living in Germany then. He didn't know that he had a son in America until very late. By then, there was no chance of meeting. He was dying in a hospital in Bursa. Tata had heard that he was sick, and he was able to find out where he was. Seeing him there, Tata decided to tell him the truth. Basharan got upset, of course. But he also realized that Tata had done the only thing he could do, which was respect the wishes of his sister. Tata showed him a photo of his son and his family, and that cheered him up a little. He told Tata that he wished he had more time. Tata responded that he would bring him to Turkey.

It never happened. Basharan died a few months later.

Up ahead, the sky grows darker. Tata sighs and reaches into his jacket. He tells me to pull over.

Why?

It's time.

What do you mean?

I have no more time left. I'm tired. Pull over, m'ijo. Now.

I stop by the side of the road and look at Tata. He appears smaller, as if in our drive across the llano, he had started to shrink. Tata had always been told that he looked younger than his age. Even into his late 90's he was mistaken for someone in his 70's. But now, I notice he has suddenly aged. His face, now deeply wrinkled, his thinning hair, now whiter. He looks at me, weakly smiles, and then hands me a photograph and an object wrapped in cloth.

Give this to your dad. He tells me. It's a photo of your abuela and your abuelo. Your real abuelo. It's the only photo they ever took together.

I don't want to look it.

You are my real abuelo. I start to cry, unable to hold back my feelings any longer.

He smiles again, tears in his eyes.

This other gift, it's for you.

I unwrap it and find a Turkish blue glass nazar boncuğu, an evil eye amulet.

I got this a long time ago from your abuelo. You should have it.

I begin to cry even more.

Stop. Stop it! Tata! I don't deserve this!

He looks at me and then points up through the sunroof of the car.

She's here.

And then I see. An eye has opened in the sky above: a knot of dark gray clouds, swirling around a patch of blue sky. I reach to start the car, I want to get us away. Maybe we can make it to see my dad. Tata reaches over with a new-found strength and grips my arm.

Do you hear her?

And I listen. There is no sound at all. The wind has died down. And in that silence, I hear a soft moan. I look down at Tata, thinking it's him. But it isn't. It comes from outside and it sounds like someone is humming a bedtime song. I'm somehow comforted as I feel it circling the car. And then I understand. It is a lullaby from the llano, a melody to calm the wind and the rain, a song to help someone cross.

Tell him. Tell him I did it for her. Tata says. Then he smiles and closes his eyes.

I sit there, the lullaby of someone taking Tata recedes as the wind rises up and the rain begins to fall.

POR LO PRONTO

By Richard Yañez

"Caminante, no hay puentes, se hace puentes al andar."
—Gloria E. Anzaldúa

Son, I am writing before my altar.

I confess to you that this year's offering borrows from other family altars. Polo's dresser. Fidela's hope chest. La Loma's adobe walls. Even from my writing desk's middle drawer.

Always be ready for an altar.

The emotions, well, I am never ready for those to surface. As soon as I put on records by Vicente Fernandez, Cornelio Reyna, any of the Mexican voices that came out of my grandmother's kitchen radio, I feel an overwhelming loss and am thrust to a time and place when none of what I know now could be imagined.

The house in La Loma is gone. An emptiness that stunned me this past summer. I will never be able to walk in the space of Dicky and Chuy. My childhood is gone. My grandmother buried after fifteen months in a coma.

I am resisting silence with every word I can borrow. I want to cry for my losses. I want to be as sad as possible for those who died and left me their memories. I don't want to have altars. They burden me with their need to be present. Or, maybe, if there had been more instruction in my past, I would know how to better create them. The writer in me shows the child what to do—an ofrenda of Memory.

Will it be enough, Mijo?

I know you are collecting on your own what you want to remember. And this is smart. But forgetting. The passing. Letting go. These are things that I need to learn/teach you.

As I get older, I want to let go of La Loma. Of high blood pressure medication. Of a 12-year marriage ending in divorce. Of credit card debt. Of anger toward Bobby, your ghost-of-a-grandfather. Of a past that seems as fragile as the altars I inherited.

I don't want you to think altars are about being sad, nor about who isn't here anymore, like Chuy, my beloved grandmother. She left behind more than her silence. Her heart, even when it grew too big for her chest, beat strong for many hard years as a daughter/wife/mother. She is the sacred that I surround myself with at home and in the community. I survived her inevitable death. And here I am, almost three decades later, still thinking of how she loved me in La Loma. Her in the next room— washing dishes, praying the rosary, chiles on the comal, hands always working—and me, on the dusty floor, pushing some toy with a mutt nearby. No wonder I have allergies. You may have also inherited all the dirt and dander and whatever else the desert blew in through the casita's screen doors all those years ago.

I loved being in La Loma. Still do. I can go back there and be with Memory as much as I want. It wasn't an altar, even if that's what I need sometimes. To have it remain unchanged. Always a ritual. A permanent place for me to place my emotions. No, La Loma was much less put together than that. It was an accident of lives. A choque that left many hurt and humbled. The landscape will remain empty of anything I write. I can put it down for others to witness, but I know that I didn't stop the destruction. And the force of the City's bulldozers that tore it down doesn't compare to the things we do in its wake.

I often feel angry that our family lives "Por lo Pronto," my alcoholic grandfather's make-shift dicho, no planning, no anticipation, relying on fate as much as faith. But, letting go, I vow before my altar, is what I should be doing. And I am not. I am not.

"El Puente Roto" by Antonio Aguilar plays on the turntable next to the altar. One of the songs buried in my mind. Even if I don't understand each Spanish lyric, I know the passion of the song. I feel the broken bridge, a reminder to let myself loose. I need to get to another side. I may choose to not use the same por lo pronto footpaths, but I must find a way. If I fall. If I stumble. If I get hurt. I must let go.

How do we mend broken bridges? How do we re-imagine the ones that are surely not safe? Will there be others that I must cross? I pray that our antepasados' journeys to this side were only the beginning. And that we will be inspired by their vision and voices and even deaths to keep moving forward no matter what our hands must build.

Mijo, there will be many bridges in your life. Most aren't there yet. You may not know they are present until they appear after many years. I hope they are bold and beautiful structures that you will be able to scale and breathe your way across.

Mira, no tengo mar que me llore
    ni un sollozo
    para regalarte el día de tu
                  muerte

Ha muerto la niña
que amé de niño
y le he prendido fuego al caballito
de palo
en el que cabalgué para ir
a verla

ya no llores tu barro
sobre los puentes de este mundo
ya no muerdas mis hombros
con el nunca,.
de tu agonía
No tenemos mar a quien llorarle
no tenemos mar a quien llorarle

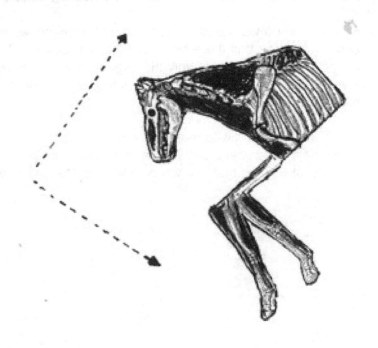

"Mira, no tengo mar que me llore/ I have no sea to cry for me"
Frontexto
Octavio Quintanilla

CONTRIBUTOR'S NOTES

Maria Teresa Acevedo is a native born Arizonan whose maternal ancestors originated from the Mexican State of Sonora. Her family were pioneer ganaderos who settled in the Aravaipa Canyon in the mid- 1890s, who ranched there, and were summarily forced from their ranch lands by the BLM, Defenders of Wildlife and Nature Conservancy. That canyon is now a protected wilderness area. Terry is an educator and author of several early childhood publications and a co-author to a Reggio Emilia influnced curriculum.

Ciara Alfaro (she/her/hers) is a graduate of Colgate University, where she studied creative writing and women's studies. She is interested in machismo, sisterhood, and the ways in which different bodies navigate the world. She currently lives in West Texas.

Bella Alvarez is a freshman at Syracuse University who hails from sun-drenched San Diego, California. She enjoys biting sarcasm, poetry, iced coffee, and late-night car rides. Her work has been recognized by the Smith College Poetry Contest, the Scholastic Art and Writing Awards, and YoungArts.

Steven Alvarez is the author of *The Codex Mojaodicus,* winner of the Fence Modern Poets Prize. His novels in verse are *The Pocho Codex* and *The Xicano Genome,* both published by Editorial Paroxismo, and the chapbooks, *Tonalamatl, El Segundo's Dream Notes* (Letter [r] Press), *Un/documented, Kentucky* (winner of the Rusty Toque Chapbook Prize), and *Six Poems from the Codex Mojaodicus* (winner of the Seven Kitchens Press Rane Arroyo Poetry Prize). His work has appeared in the *Best Experimental Writing, Anomaly, Asymptote, Berkeley Poetry Review, Fence, MAKE, The Offing,* and *Waxwing.*

Samantha Arriozola is a Xicana from Des Plaines, Illinois. She is an alumn of the University of Wisconsin-Madison, B.A. Creative Writing, and part of the 8th Cohort of First Wave -- a Hip-Hop and Urban Arts scholarship program at the university. Samantha has received the University Book Store Academic Excellence Award (2018) at UW-Madison, and has been published in *Pinwheel Journal.* Samantha currently resides in Madison, WI, visits her Chicagoland home for her mami's tortillas, and needs to fly out more often to visit her best friend, Syd, in Queens.

Gustavo Barahona-López is a poet and educator from the San Francisco Bay Area. In his writing, Barahona-López draws from his experience growing up in a Mexican immigrant household. His work can be found or is forthcoming in *Apogee Journal, Glass' Poets Resist, PALABRITAS, Puerto del Sol, The Acentos Review, Homology Lit, Hayden's Ferry Review,* among other publications. When Barahona-López is not teaching you can find him re-discovering the world with his son.

Xochitl-Julisa Bermejo is the daughter of Mexican immigrants and the author of *Posada: Offerings of Witness and Refuge* (Sundress Publications). A former Steinbeck Fellow and *Poets & Writers* California Writers Exchange winner, she's received residencies from Hedgebrook, Ragdale, and National Parks Arts Foundation. Her poetry is published in *Acentos Review, CALYX,* and *Crazyhorse* among other places, and a dramatization of her poem "Our Lady of the Water Gallons," directed by Jesús Salvador Treviño, can be viewed at latinopia.com. She's a member of Macondo Writers Workshop and a cofounder of Women Who Submit.

Elena Díaz Björkquist is the author of *Suffer Smoke and Water from the Moon*, short stories about her hometown of Morenci, Arizona. She's writing a memoir, "Surviving Suffer Smoke" about her experiences growing up in a small copper mining town. She's also revising a new short story collection, "Albóndiga Soup." Her stories appear in *Americas Review, The Float-*

ing Borderlands, Fantasmas, The Strange History of Suzanne Lafleshe (and other stories of women and fatness, Poetry and Resistance, The Mas Tequila Review, Sowing the Seeds, una cosecha de recuerdos and Our Spirit, Our Reality; celebrating our stories.

Xánath Caraza writes for *La Bloga, Seattle Escribe, SLC,* and *Monolito.* For the 2018 International Latino Book Awards, she received First Place for *Lágrima roja* and *Sin preámbulos/Without Preamble* for "Best Book of Poetry in Spanish" and "Best Book Bilingual Poetry". *Syllables of Wind* received the 2015 International Book Award for Poetry.

Ana Castillo is a distinguished poet, novelist, short story writer, essayist, editor, playwright, translator and independent scholar. Castillo was born and raised in Chicago.. Among her award winning, best sellling titles: novels include *So Far From God, The Guardians and Peel My Love like an Onion,* among other poetry: *I Ask the Impossible.* Her novel, *Sapogonia* was a *New York Times* Notable Book of the Year. Her awards include an American Book Award for her first novel, The Mixquiahuala Letters, a Carl Sandburg Award, a Mountains and Plains Booksellers Award, and fellowships from the National Endowment for the Arts in fiction and poetry.

Griselda J Castillo is a bilingual poet from Laredo, Texas. She is the daughter of Mexican immigrants, a first-generation American who explores biculturalism and the Bordertown blues through poetry. Her work can be found in *Ocotillo Review, Sparkle + Blink,* and *Chachalaca Review.* She also performs her poetry with Five Voices One Brush, an improvisational art and jazz collective. Her chapbook, *Blood & Piloncillo,* won the 2018 National Association for Chicana and Chicano Studies Tejas Foco Best Poetry Book Award.

In 2013 **Rosemary Catacalos** became the first Latinx Texas Poet Laureate and the first Texas Laureate from San Antonio since 1949. Her work has twice appeared in *The Best American Poetry,* and she has held NEA, Stanford Stegner, and Paisano poetry fellowships. Her Texas Institute of Letters poetry prize collection, *Again for the First Time,* was reissued in 2013 by Wings Press, which simultaneously issued a fine press chapbook, Begin Here. Catacalos serves on the Texas Commission on the Arts touring roster and lives in San Antonio, Texas.

Born in San Francisco, raised in San José, **Barrio Horseshoe**, Lorna Dee Cervantes was a self-taught activist by 15, an instant mother at 19, taught herself how to run her own printing press and was Founding Editor/Publisher of MANGO Publications at 20, and the author of EMPLUMADA at 24. A XícanIndX poet (Chumash/Purépecha), Cervantes (PhD, History of Consciousness) was a Professor of English for 20 years at CU Boulder, serving as Director of Creative Writing. She identifies as Indigenous American with 5 books in print and writing 5 more in Seattle.

A child of La Frontera, **Denise Chávez** is a Chicana novelist, playwright, actor, and teacher. Her books include *The King and Queen of Comezón, A Taco Testimony: Meditations on Family, Food and Culture, Loving Pedro Infante, Face of An Angel, The Last of the Menu Girls,* and a children's book, *La Mujer Que Sabía El Idioma de Los Animales/The Woman Who Knew the Language of the Animals.* Chávez owns Casa Camino Real, a Bookstore and Multicultural Art and Community Center with her husband, photographer, Daniel Zolinsky. She directs a book distribution program for Refugee, Asylum-seeking and Migrant Families, Libros Para El Viaje/Books for the Journey in collaboration with The Border Servant Corps based Las Cruces, New Mexico.

Sandra Cisneros is a writer whose work explores the lives of the working class. Her awards include NEA fellowships in both poetry and fiction, a MacArthur Fellowship, the PEN/Nabokov Award for International Literature and the National Medal of Arts. Her novel *The House on Mango Street* has sold over six million copies, has been translated into over twenty languages, and is required reading in schools across the nation. Cisneros is a dual citizen of the United States and Mexico and earns her living by her pen.

Vanessa Bernice De La Cruz is a self-taught emerging artist and writer from Los Angeles, CA. She has been scribbling and doodling for as long as she can remember but has only recently decided to share those things and infuse them with sense. She likes to explore themes that recall her childhood and mistakes. You can find her hanging out with her cat Bubbles, whining on social media @alienraynedrop, or you can visit her not fully constructed website vbdelacruz.com

Diana Marie Delgado is the author of *Tracing the Horse* and the chapbook *Late Night Talks with Men I Think I Trust.* She is the recipient of numerous grants, including a fellowship from the National Endowment for the Arts. A graduate of Columbia University she currently resides in Tucson, where she is the Literary Director of the Poetry Center at the University of Arizona.

David Estringel is a writer, poet, and author, as well as Poetry Editor at *Fishbowl Press* and *The Elixir Magazine,* as well as Fiction Editor at *Red Fez.* His work has been accepted and/or published at *Terror House Magazine, 50 Haikus, Setu, The Elixir, Soft Cartel, Harbinger Asylum, Former People Journal, Cephalopress, Printed Words, Digging through the Fat, Haiku Journal, Foxhole Magazine, The Basil O'Flaherty, Three Line Poetry, Agony Opera, Poetry NI, Culture Cult Press, Fishbowl Press, Horror Sleaze Trash*, and more. David first collection of poetry and prose *Indelible Fingerprints* (Alien Buddha Press) was published in April 2019.

Daisy Franco was born and raised in Chicago, Illinois. She enjoys writing poetry, fiction, and nonfiction. Her work has been published in *Chicken Soup for the Soul: Dreams and Premonitions, Chicken Soup for the Soul: Inspiration for Teachers, Mural Magazine*, and the online anthology *Love You Madly.* She received her undergraduate degree from the University of Illinois at Chicago and holds a graduate degree from DePaul University.

Robert René Galván, born in San Antonio, resides in New York City where he works as a professional musician and poet. His last collection of poems is entitled, *Meteors,* published by Lux Nova Press. His poetry was recently featured in *Adelaide Literary Magazine, Azahares Literary Magazine, Gyroscope, Hawaii Review, Newtown Review, Panoply, Stillwater Review, West Texas Literary Review,* and the Winter 2018 issue of *UU World.* He is a Shortlist Winner Nominee in the 2018 Adelaide Literary Award for Best Poem.

Alma García short's fiction has appeared as an award-winner in *Narrative Magazine, Enizagam, Passages North*, and *Boulevard*; has most recently appeared in *Kweli Journal, Duende,* and *Bluestem;* and appears in the anthology, *Roadside Curiosities: Short Stories on American Pop Culture.* "The Brown Invasion" is an excerpt from her first novel, *El Paso,* which currently is out on submission to publishers. A former newspaper reporter and editor, she grew up in West Texas and northern New Mexico and now makes her home with her husband and son in Seattle, where she teaches fiction writing and is a manuscript consultant and private violin instructor.

Abril Garcia-Lin is a proud Chicana born raised in the Westside of San Antonio. She is a mother, writer, arts instructor, seamstress, performer and cultural arts advocate as well as founding member of the poetry/performance group Women of III Repute:Refute. She was featured in "Stages of Life:Transcultural Performance & Identity in U.S Latina Theater" University of Arizona Press 2001. Her poetry appears in "Cantos Al Sexto Sol:An anthology of Aztlanahuac Writing" by Wings Press, and others. She has spent many years working in the arts community of San Antonio as a board member, staff member, volunteer, contract artist and patron.

Lisha Adela García has an MFA from Vermont College of Fine Arts and currently resides in Texas with her beloved four-legged children. Her books, *A Rope of Luna* and *Blood Rivers,* were published by Blue Light Press of San Francisco. Her chapbook, *This Stone Will Speak* was published by Pudding House Press. In addition, she is widely published in various journals including the *Boston Review, Crab Orchard Review, Border Senses* and *Mom Egg Review.* Lisha has been nominated for a Pushcart and was recently recognized with the San Antonio Tri-Centennial Poetry Prize. She also has a Masters in International Business from Thunderbird for the left side of her brain.

Jennifer Givhan, a Mexican-American writer, is the author of four full-length poetry collections, most recently *Rosa's Einstein*, and the novels *Trinity Sight* and *Jubilee* (Blackstone Publishing). Her work has appeared in *The Best of the Net, Best New Poets, Poetry Daily, Verse Daily, POETRY, The Rumpus,* and *The New Republic.* She has received, among other honors, a National Endowment for the Arts fellowship, a PEN/Rosenthal Emerging Voices fellowship, and New Ohio Review's Poetry Prize, chosen by Tyehimba Jess. She can be found discussing feminist motherhood at jennifergivhan.com as well as Facebook & Twitter @JennGivhan.

Tammy Melody Gomez is a performing artist, writer, and grassroots activist whose literary work—essays, poetry, microfiction—has been published in collections including *Bikequity: Money, Class,* and *Bicycling* (Microcosm Publishing, 2017) and *Entre Guadalupe y Malinche: Tejanas in Literature and Art* (UT Press, 2016). "SHE: Bike/Spoke/Love" (2007), her NALAC-funded play, depicts the Latinx bicycling culture, and her one-woman show, "Saliendo Abierta," premiered at the Mexican American Cultural Center (Austin) in 2009. As director of Sound Culture,Tammy is active in creative placemaking and literary curation in north Texas.

Yola Gómez is a first generation queer Xicanx femme. Yola recently graduated with an MFA in creative writing from Oregon State University. They are an activist, writer, and theorist. She has been published in *Nat Brut, Entropy,* and *Utterance.* They were recently nominated for a Pushcart Prize. In her spare time she likes to play the banjo and sing corridos.

liz gonzález is the author of *Dancing in the Santa Ana Winds: Poems y Cuentos New and Selected* (Los Nietos Press 2018). Her poetry, fiction, and creative nonfiction have been published widely and recently appeared in *Voices de la Luna, Fire and Rain: Ecopoetry of California,* and *Voices from Leimert Park Anthology Redux.* She was recently featured on *Citizens Climate Radio, Latinopia.com,* and *KUCR's Radio Aztlan.* She is a proud member of Macondo Writers Workshop and lives in L.A. County with an indifferent Chihuahua, a talkative tortie cat, and Jorge Martin, a scientist and musician.

Nancy Aidé González is a Chicana poet, educator, and activist. Her work appears in *Huizache: The Magazine of Latino Literature, La Tolteca, Mujeres De Maiz Zine, DoveTales, Seeds of Resistance Flor y Canto: Tortilla Warrior, Hinchas de Poesía, La Bloga, Fifth Wednesday Journal* and several other literary journals. Her work is also featured in the *Poetry of Resistance: Voices for Social Justice, Sacramento Voices: Foam at the Mouth Anthology,* and *Lowriting: Shots, Rides, and Stories from the Chicano Soul.*

Rafael E. Gonzalez lives in Tucson, AZ where teaches at the University of Arizona and is a poetry editor for *DIAGRAM.* His work has appeared in Pleiades, Entropy, and elsewhere. You can find him on Twitter @RafaelEGonza.

Rafael Jesús González, Prof. Emeritus of literature and creative writing, born and raised biculturally/bilingually in El Paso, Texas/Cd. Juárez, Chihuahua, taught at various universities before settling at Laney College, Oakland, California where he founded the Dept. of Mexican & Latin-American Studies. Nominated thrice for a Pushcart price, he was honored for his writing by the National Council of Teachers of English 2003 and with a Lifetime Achievement Award for his writing, art, teaching, social activism by the City of Berkeley 2015, named Berkeley's first Poet Laureate 2017. (rjgonzalez.blogspot.com)

Reyna Grande is the author of the bestselling memoir, *The Distance Between Us*, (Atria, 2012) and the sequel, *A Dream Called Home*. Her novels include, *Across a Hundred Mountains,* (Atria, 2006) and *Dancing with Butterflies* (Washington Square Press, 2009). Her books have been adopted as common reads by schools, colleges and cities across the country. Her awards include an American Book Award, the El Premio Aztlán Literary Award, and the Luis

Leal Award for Distinction in Chicano/Latino Literatures. Addressing immigration, family separation, language trauma, the price of the American Dream, Reyna's work appears in *The New York Times, Dallas Morning News, CNN,* and *The Lily at The Washington Post.* www.reyna-grande.com

Lucrecia Guerrero grew up bilingual and bicultural on the U.S./Mexico border with a mother from Kentucky and a father from Puebla, Mexico. She has taught writing and lived in the Midwest for years. Lucrecia's short works have been published in literary journals such as *The Antioch Review* and have been anthologized in *FANTASMAS, Best of the West,* and *Not Like the Rest of Us. Chasing Shadows,* her linked collection of short stories, was published by Chronicle Books. Tree of sighs, a novel, published by Bilingual Press, received a Christopher Isherwood Fellowship and the Premio Aztlan. She recently completed a novel, *What We Cannot Hold.*

Myriam Gurba is a California-based writer and artist. She is the author of several books, including the true crime memoir *Mean*. She is currently at work on a sequel to *Mean* and a young adult novel. She believes in ghosts and the power of chisme. She enjoys cash, compliments, and black coffee.

A child of Mexican and Salvadoran immigrants, **Raquel Gutiérrez** lives in Tucson, after completing MFAs in Poetry and Non-Fiction from University of Arizona. Raquel received the 2017 Creative Capital I Andy Warhol Foundation Arts Writers Grant. She runs the tiny press, Econo Textual Objects (est. 2014), which publishes works by QTPOC poets. Her work appears in the *Los Angeles Review of Books, Open Space, New Inquiry, Zocaló Public Square, Entropy, FENCE, Huizache, Río Grande Review,* and *Hayden's Ferry Review.* Raquel's first book of essays, *Brown Neon*, is due out from Coffee House Press in 2021. Her first book of poems, *Southwest Reconstruction,* will be published by Noemi Press in 2022.

Sonia Gutiérrez is a poet professor. Her poetry and prose have appeared in *Huizache, AlternaCtive PublicaCtions*, and *La Jornada Semanal*, among other publications. She is the author of *Spider Woman / La Mujer Araña* (Olmeca Press, 2013) and co-editor of *The Writer's Response* (Cengage Learning, 2016). Her unpublished manuscripts *Legacy / Herencia*, a bilingual poetry collection, and *Dreaming with Mariposas* are seeking publication. Presently, she is working on her poetry collection, *Sana Sana Colita de Rana*, and moderating *Facebook's Poets Responding*. "Freckled Like My Skin," "The Mango and Mambo Days," and "The Story of the First Year" are a selection from her novel, *Dreaming with Mariposas.*

Carolina Hinojosa-Cisneros is a Tejana, Chicana, Mujerista writer from San Antonio, Texas. She is a regular columnist at Soujourners and her chapbook, Becoming Coztototl, was published by FlowerSong Books. Hinojosa-Cisneros is a Pushcart Nominee for 2019 for her poem "Blessed be the Mother," and is the 2019 Recipient of the Rubem Alves Award in Theopoetics. She is currently a graduate student of English at Our Lady of the Lake University.

Esteban Ismael is a San Diego native that teaches literature and writing workshops with the San Diego Community College District. In 2016, he was awarded First Prize in Poetry in Dogwood and named a Second Rounder in the Austin Film Festival's teleplay competition. His poems are forthcoming or have recently appeared in *Conduit, The Journal, Spillway, Poetry Daily* and *The Massachusetts Review*, among other fine journals.

Joyous Windrider Jiménez is a multi-disciplinary artist, educator, coach, and mother of one son. A San Antonio native, Joy spent nearly a decade abroad, where she helped diverse minority groups tell their stories. Since her return in 2009 she has presented her poetry, theatre, and visual art pieces in venues around San Antonio, and facilitated the production of over 50 original plays created by and for San Antonio youth. She currently teaches for Gemini Ink and Magik Theatre, and offers private sessions for processing stuck creative/emotional energy. She is the co-founder of Raise The Whisper, a writing and art collective for those affected by family rape and sexual abuse.

Maria Melendez Kelson writes crime fiction, short stories, magazine features, literary essays and poetry. Her mystery novel-in-progress won the inaugural Eleanor Taylor Bland Crime Fiction Writers of Color Award from Sisters in Crime. Her poetry and prose appear in *Poetry magazine, Orion, Ms. magazine, Flash Fiction Magazine,* and numerous anthologies. Author of two poetry collections (as Maria Melendez) published by University of Arizona Press, her books have been finalists for the PEN Center USA Literary Award and the Colorado Book Award. Find her on Twitter: @mkelsonauthor.

Benjamín Naka-Hasebe Kingsley's abuelo immigrated from Havana's fourth floor. His first, second, and third books debut 2018, 2019, and 2020: *Not Your Mama's Melting Pot* (U Nebraska Press), *Colonize Me* (Saturnalia), and *Dēmos* (Milkweed Editions). He belongs to the Onondaga Nation of Indigenous Americans in New York. Peep his recent work in *Boston Review, FIELD, jubilat, Kenyon Review, New England Review, Oxford American*, and *Tin House*, among others. He is Assistant Professor of Poetry and Nonfiction in Old Dominion University's MFA program.

Linda Zamora Lucero is writing a series of short stories set in San Francisco's Mission District. Her published stories include "Take the Money and Run–1968" (Bilingual Review, 2015) and "Balmy Alley Forever" (Santa Clara Review 2016; Yellow Medicine Review, 2016). Executive/Artistic Director of Yerba Buena Gardens Festival in SF, Linda's graphic artwork will appear in "¡Printing the Revolution!" at the Smithsonian American Art Museum in September 2020.

Ignacio Ramos Magaloni, a member of the Macondo Writers Workshop, has read his poems at the San Antonio Poetry Festival, The McNay Art Museum, and at Luminaria, and has been published in several magazines, including *The Texas Observer*, and in the anthology "Is This Forever or What?" edited by Naomi Shihab Nye. He teaches literature and writing at Northwest Vista College.

Jesse Tsinajinnie Maloney grew up on the Leeward side of O'ahu. He went to the same High School as Israel Kamakawiwo'ole. His work has appeared in *Turtle Island Quarterly, Peach Velvet Lit Mag, About Place* and other places. His debut full length work *Health Carefully* was released through Cyberwit press 2019. Currently, he is producing a collaborative spoken word/instrumental album featuring poets Pamela Uschuk and William Pitt Root to be released in early 2020. Jesse teaches at Dine' College and lives with his wife and cats on the Navajo Nation.

Carl Marcum is a Xicanx poet and author of the collections *Cue Lazarus* and *A Camera Obscura*. Born in Nogales, Arizona and raised in Tucson, he attended the University of Arizona and was a Wallace Stegner Fellow at Stanford University. He has received grants from the NEA and the Illinois Arts Council and served as a Canto Mundo Fellow. He lives in Pittsburgh, PA.

Alexandra Martinez is a poet and baker living in Southern California. Her work has been published in *Cosmonauts Avenue, Sooth Swarm Journal,* and *No Tender Fences: An Anthology of Immigrant & First - Generation American Poetry.*

Demetria Martinez is a poet, writer, activist and creativity coach based in Albuquerque. Her books include two collections of poetry (University of Arizona Press), and the widely translated novel, *Mother Tongue* (Bantaam). She is involved with Los Jardines Institute, a community garden whose members work on food security and environmental racism issues.

Melani "Mele" Martinez is a teacher, writer, and mother. She is the recipient of Fourth Genre's First Place Editor's Prize and her work has appeared in *Bacopa Literary Review, Borderlore, Bearings,* and *Telling Tongues: A Latin Anthology on Language Experiences*. She is at work on a memoir in prose and poetry entitled *The Molino.* Mele is a Senior Lecturer in the Writing Program at the University of Arizona where she teaches foundational and food writing courses.

Pablo Miguel Martínez's collection of poems, *Brazos, Carry Me* (Kórima Press), received the 2013 PEN Southwest Book Award for Poetry. His chapbook, titled *Cuent@,* was published by Finishing Line Press in 2016. Pablo's work has received support from the Artist Foundation of San Antonio, the Alfredo Cisneros Del Moral Foundation, and the National Association of Latino Arts and Culture. He is a Co-Founder of CantoMundo, a national retreat-workshop for Latina/o poets. Currently, he is at work on a hybrid-genre memoir.

Sylvia J. Martínez is a writer and adult school ESL teacher. Her work has appeared in *Your Golden Sun Still Shines: San Francisco Stories Past, Present and Future* (Manic D Press 2017), *In Media Res: Stories from the In-Between* (WriteSpace 2016), *The East Bay Review, Cipactli, Tattoo Highway,* and *The S. F. Examiner,* among others. She is an alumna of UC Davis (B.A.), Cal State East Bay (M.A.), and San Francisco State (M.F.A.). She is currently working on her first collection of stories. She lives in the S.F. Bay Area with her husband, teenage son, and daughter (when she is home from college).

Poet, teacher, and activist **Lupe Mendez** is the author of the poetry collection *Why I Am Like Tequila* (Willow Books, 2019). He earned an MFA in creative writing (poetry) from the University of Texas at El Paso and has literary work that has appeared in *Hunger Mountain, Kenyon Review, Poetry Magazine* and *Gulf Coast,* among others. He has received fellowships from CantoMundo, Macondo, and the Crescendo Literary/Poetry Foundation's Poetry Incubator.

Matt Mendez has worked on airplanes all of his adult life and is the author of the YA novel *Barely Missing Everything* and the short story collection *Twitching Heart.* He earned his MFA from the University of Arizona where he also taught creative writing. His work has appeared in *Huizache, The Acentos Review, BorderSenses, Pank, The Literary Review,* and other places. Matt is from El Paso, Texas but now lives with his wife and two daughters in Tucson, Arizona. You can visit him at mattmendez.com or follow him on Twitter @mgmendez.

elena minor is the author of *TITULADA,* a book of bilingual poetry. Her work has been published in more than two dozen literary journals and anthologized in *Angels of the Americlypse, Best American Experimental Writing (BAX) 2015, Coiled Serpent* and *Resist Much, Obey Little.* Most recently her work has appeared in *Two Degrees Celsius, Inlandia* and *Uproot.* She is the founding editor of *PALABRA* (2006-2012) and teaches community-based creative writing to high school students.

Juan J. Morales is the son of an Ecuadorian mother and Puerto Rican father. He is the author of three poetry collections, including *The Handyman's Guide to End Times,* winner of the 2019 International Latino Book Award. He is a CantoMundo Fellow, a Macondo Fellow, the Editor/ Publisher of *Pilgrimage Press,* and Professor and Department Chair of English & World Languages at Colorado State University-Pueblo.

Cameron Moreno, a writer of fiction and poetry, holds an MFA from Western Kentucky University. He has received recognition from various journals, most recently as an Honorable Mention for the Waasnode Short Fiction Prize at *Passages North.* His work is featured or forthcoming in *Passages North, The Hunger, The Weird Reader,* and elsewhere. He was born and raised in Corpus Christi, Texas.

Gris Muñoz is a frontera poet, performer, essayist, and fiction writer. She is the author of Coatlicue Girl. Her work has been published in *The Rumpus, Bitch Media, Queen Mob's Teahouse* and will be featured in the upcoming *Third Woman Press* inaugural anthology. Gris is currently commissioned to write the biography of acclaimed LA artist Fabian Debora.

Adela Najarro is the author of three poetry collections: *Split Geography, Twice Told Over* and *My Childrens*, a chapbook that includes teaching resources. With *My Childrens* she hopes to bring Latinx poetry into the classroom so that students can explore poetry, identity, and what it means to be Latinx in US society. Every spring semester, she teaches a "Poetry for the People," workshop at Cabrillo College where students explore personal voice and social justice through poetry and spoken word. More information about Adela can be found at her website: www.adelanajarro.com

Andrew Navarro is a current MFA student at the UCR Low Residency Program. Born and raised in the Inland Empire, he teaches history in Southern California. His work explores the concepts of identity, culture, and masculinity. He lives with his wife and two daughters.

Juan Ochoa is a Mexican born in America. Juan Ochoa has been everything from a pistolero to a professor. Ochoa holds a law degree from Mexico as well as a B.A. and Masters in English along with a MFA in Creative Writing from UTPA. Ochoa has been published in English and Spanish. His works appear abroad in Beat Scene (UK) and Alecart (RO) and north and south of the U.S. Mexico border in the *Rio Grande Review* and *Analecta 37* and others. Ochoa's debut novel *Mariguano* was released by Texas Review Press in October of 2013.

Daniel García Ordaz, a.k.a. The Poet Mariachi, a writer from Mission, Texas, is the author of *Cenzontle/Mockingbird* (*YA Edition): Songs of Empowermen*t. He is a founder of the Rio Grande Valley International Poetry Festival. García is a teacher, a Navy veteran, and a former newspaper journalist. His first book is *You Know What I'm Sayin'?*. Garcia's work is being taught at colleges and universities. When he's not writing, he is a high school English teacher. García Ordaz's forthcoming book, Read Until You Bleed, is a collection of children's poetry. His work also appears in Poetry of Resistance and other anthologies.

From Eagle Pass, Texas, **Rita L. Ortiz** is a writer, songwriter, and musician based in San Antonio, Texas. An English instructor in Palo Alto College, Rita is the lead vocalist for The Velvet Hues, an independent band. Their new album, Cantares, is slated for release in November of 2019. Ortiz's work includes music, poetry, and a cinepoem (experimental short film) titled *Aldebaran* (2018) — all which explore identity and language in the context of cultural hybridity, and the surreal and symbolic nature of dreams in connection to epiphany. Aldebaran is Ortiz's film debut as a director, writer, actor, and composer.

Wendy C. Ortiz is the author of *Excavation: A Memoir, Hollywood Notebook,* and the dreamoir *Bruja*. In 2016 Bustle named her one of "9 Women Writers Who Are Breaking New Nonfiction Territory." Her work has been featured in the *Los Angeles Times, The Rumpus, the Los Angeles Review of Books,* and the *National Book Critics Circle Small Press Spotlight* blog. Her writing appears in *The New York Times, Joyland, Story Quarterly, FENCE,* and *McSweeney's,* among many others. Wendy is a psychotherapist in private practice in Los Angeles.

Jose Oseguera is an LA-based writer of poetry, short fiction and literary nonfiction. Having grown up in a primarily immigrant, urban environment, Jose has always been interested in the people and places around him, and the stories that each of these has to share. His writing has been featured in *Emrys Journal, The Hiram Poetry Review,* and *The Main Street Rag*. His work has also been nominated for the Best of the Net award (2018 and 2019) and a Pushcart Prize. He is the author of the forthcoming poetry collection *The Milk of Your Blood*.

Until his retirement, **Juan R. Palomo** worked in corporate media relations in Washington, DC. Before that he was a reporter, columnist and editorial writer for *The Houston Post*. He also covered religion/beliefs for the Austin American-Statesman and wrote a monthly column for *USA TODAY*. He lives in Houston, where he writes poetry, paints, sketches, needlepoints and photographs. His poems have been published in *The Account, Acentos, Fifth Wednesday, Sonora Review, New Mexico Review* and *Hinchas de Poesía*. He was a 2018 Houston Poetry

Fest juried poet. He writes occasionally for his blog, juanzqui.com.

Octavio Quintanilla, 2018-2020 Poet Laureate of San Antonio, TX, is the author of the poetry collection, *If I Go Missing* (Slough Press, 2014). His work appears in journals such as *Poetry Northwest, RHINO, Alaska Quarterly Review, The Texas Observer,* etc.. His Frontextos (visual poems) have been exhibited widely including at The Southwest School of Art, Presa House Gallery, and The Emma S. Barrientos Mexican American Cultural Center / Black Box Theater. He is regional editor for Texas Books in Review and poetry editor for *The Journal of Latina Critical Feminism & for Voices de la Luna: A Quarterly Literature & Arts Magazine.* Octavio teaches at Our Lady of the Lake University in San Antonio. Website: octavioquintanilla.com

Alfred Quiroz, Professor Emeritus of Art, is Tucson AZ native and Vietnam Vet who served 4 yrs. in the U.S. Navy from 1963-67. He holds a BFA Painting San Francisco Art Institute, a MAT Art Ed. R.I. School of Design, and a MFA Painting from the University of Arizona. Quiroz was Professor of Painting and Drawing in the School of Art at University of Arizona from1989-2018. His "Parade of Humanity" sculpture on the Border wall in Nogales and Agua Prieta, Sonora from 2003-2010 was a collaboration with two artists from Mexico, Alberto Morackis and Guadalupe Serrano, It was funded by an Artist Project Grant from the AZ. Commission on the Arts.

Miranda Ramirez is a writer of poetry, prose, and creative nonfiction as well as an active visual artist. In all endeavors she seeks to marry her passions for social activism, art, and literature. As a biracial American she struggles to find her place--being consistently pulled towards two cultures historically set in opposition of one another. Her works provide a jaded reflection of this experience. Her work appears in *The Bayou Review: The Women's Issue, Ripples in Space: Science Fiction Short Stories, Glass Mountain,* and within their online publication: *Shards,* and most recently within *Coffin Bell Vol. Four.* She is currently the editor for *Defunkt Magazine.*

Tisha Marie Reichle-Aguilera is a Chicana Feminist and former Rodeo Queen. She is also on the leadership team for Women Who Submit. She's a Macondista, a Bruja, an editor for *Ricochet Editions* and *VIDA Review.* She writes so the desert landscape of her childhood can be heard as loudly as the urban chaos of her adulthood. She is obsessed with food. A former high school teacher, she earned an MFA at Antioch University Los Angeles and is now in USC's Creative Writing and Literature PhD program because school is cool.

Alberto Alvaro Ríos's latest collection of poems is *Not Go Away is my Name*, preceded by *A Small Story about the Sky, The Dangerous Shirt,* and *The Theater of Night*, winner of the PEN/ Beyond Margins Award. A finalist for the National Book Award and recipient of the Western Literature Association Distinguished Achievement Award, Ríos has taught at Arizona State University since 1982. He is Arizona's inaugural poet laureate, a recent chancellor of the Academy of American Poets, and director of the Virginia G. Piper Center for Creative Writing.

Iliana Rocha is a Chicanx writer from South Texas. Her work has appeared in *The Nation, Latin American Literature Today, Virginia Quarterly Review,* and *Blackbird,* among others. Currently a MacDowell Colony fellow, my first book, *Karankawa,* won the 2014 AWP Donald Hall Prize for Poetry.

Linda Rodriguez has published three books of poetry, S*kin Hunger, Heart's Migration,* and *Dark Sister,* as well as three novels in the Skeet Bannion mystery series, *Plotting the Character-Driven Novel,* and The "I Don't Know How To Cook" Book: Mexican. Edited anthologies include *The World Is One Place: Native American Poets Visit the Middle East* and *Woven Voices: Three Generations of Puertorriqueña Poets Look at Their American Lives.* She received the Elvira Cordero Cisneros Award from the Macondo Foundation. She was a founding board member of The Writers Place and Latino Writers Collective and chair of the Indigenous Writers Caucus.

Odilia Galván Rodríguez is a poet, writer, editor, educator, and activist. She is the author of six volumes of poetry, including, *The Nature of Things*, is a collaboration with Texas photographer, Richard Loya, by Merced College Press 2016. Also, along with the late Francisco X. Alarcón, she edited the award-winning anthology, *Poetry of Resistance: Voices for Social Justice,* University of Arizona Press, 2016. Her most recent publication is *The Color of Light,* 2018

René Saldaña, Jr. is currently an associate professor of Language, Diversity, and Literacy Studies in the College of Education at Texas Tech University. He is also the author of several books, among them *The Jumping Tree, A Good Long Way,* and *Heartbeat of the Soul of the World.* His poems have appeared or are slated to appear in *The English Journal, Windward Review, Inkwell Literary Magazine, The Big Window Review,* and *Visual Verse: Anthology of Art and Words.* He is currently working on a novel in verse titled *HOME : GIRL.*

Irene Sanchez, Ph.D. is a Xicana mama, poet, and writer. She teaches high school Chicano/Latino Studies in Azusa, CA. A VONA and Pink Door Writers retreat alum, Irene is the host of the monthly open mic Poetry y Pan at Cafe con Libros in Pomona, CA where she is also Chair of Literacy Projects on their Board of Directors. Irene's work has appeared in *CNN, HuffPost, Public Radio International, Zocalo Public Square, Inside Higher Ed*, in multiple anthologies, and more. She has been featured by multiple public radio outlets including KPCC, KPFK, NPR Latino USA, and ProPublica. For more information see www.irenesanchezphd.com

Paul Sanchez graduated from Fresno State with an MFA. Previous poems can be found in *San Joaquin Review, Undercurrent,* CWAA journal 'Flies, Cockroaches, and Poets,' the *Scene and Heard Journal, Five2One,* and *PACIFIC Review.* Currently, teaching English at Fresno City College.

Raúl Sanchez is the newest City of Redmond Poet Laureate 2019-2021. A member of (WITS), Writers In The Schools through Seattle Arts and Lectures. Also a poetry mentor at Denny International Middle School through the Jack Straw Educational project. He held the Inaugural Poet in Residence position for the City of Burien 2018-2019 and volunteers for PONGO Teen Writing in the Juvenile Detention Center www.rsancheztlaltecatl.com https://moonpathpress.com

Sara Sanchez is a queer, biracial, Texan constantly in search of coffee. She lives in the space between nonfiction and poetry. Tell her your story or show her your dog on Instagram: @thatsmisssaratoyou.

Leslie Contreras Schwartz is the Houston Poet Laureate and the author of *Who Speaks For Us Here* (Skull + Wind Press, 2020), a collection of persona poems documenting the lives of people with mental illness, sex workers, women who are trafficked, and children in custody. Named among "the best work [of poetry] coming in 2020" by Library Journal, poet Diane Seuss describes Who Speaks For Us Here as "resplendent in formal range, in image-richness, in music, empathy, and wisdom (that) offer us a landscape of dissociation, of fragmentation in selfhood and in art ... (and) establishes an aesthetic of survival." Contreras Schwartz is a multigenre writer and the author of *Nightbloom & Cenote* (St. Julian Press, 2018) and *Fuego* (St. Julian Press, 2016).

Matt Sedillo is an internationally touring poet who has spoken hundreds of campuses and cultural centers across the world including The University of Cambridge and Casa De Las Americas. He has been heralded by journalists and historians as "the best political poet in America" (Greg Palast) and the "poet laureate of struggle" (Paul Ortiz). His most recent collection of poetry *Mowing Leaves of Grass* was published by FlowerSong Books in Decemeber of 2019. Sedillo is the literary director of the dA Center for the Arts in Pomona California.

Natalie Sierra is the author of "Nadine: Love Songs for Demented Housewives," "Temblors," "Strangelove: Tales of Love and Lust." Natalie also has a forthcoming poetry chapbook being published by DSTL Arts in 2020. Natalie's work has been featured in *South Broadway Ghost*

Society, Dryland: a literary journal based in South Central Los Angeles, and the *Los Angeles Times.* Natalie lives in Pomona, CA with their husband and three children. You can follow Natalie on Twitter and Instagram: @pandorademise.

ire'ne lara silva is the author of three poetry collections, *furia, Blood Sugar Canto* and *CUICA-CALLI/House of Song,* and a short story collection, *flesh to bone* which won the Premio Aztlán. She and poet Dan Vera are also the co-editors of *Imaniman: Poets Writing in the Anzaldúan Borderlands.* ire'ne is the recipient of a 2017 NALAC Fund for the Arts Grant, the final recipient of the Alfredo Cisneros del Moral Award, the Fiction Finalist for AROHO's 2013 Gift of Freedom Award, and the 2008 recipient of the Gloria Anzaldúa Milagro Award. ire'ne is currently working on her first novel, *Naci.* Website: irenelarasilva.wordpress.com

Octavio Solis is a playwright and author whose works *Mother Road, Quixote Nuevo, Lydia, Gibraltar, Dreamlandia, El Otro, Santos & Santos,* and other works have been produced in theatres such as the Oregon Shakespeare Festival, the California Shakespeare Theatre, Yale Repertory Theatre, the Denver Center for the Performing Arts, El Teatro Campesino, and the Alley Theatre in Houston. His fiction has been published in *Zyzzyva, Catamaran, Huizache,* and the *Chicago Quarterly Review.* Solis has received the United States Artists Fellowship and the Pen Center USA Award for Drama. His new book *Retablos: Stories From A Life Lived Along The Border* is published by City Lights Publishing.

Gary Soto has published more than forty books for children, young adults and adults, including *Too Many Tamales, Chato's Kitchen, Baseball in April, Buried Onions* and *The Elements of San Joaquin.* He author of *In and Out of Shadows*, a musical about undocumented youth and, most recently, *The Afterlife*, a one-act play about teen murder and teen suicide. His poem "Oranges" is the most anthologized poem in contemporary literature. His books have sold five million copies nationally and several have been translated into French, Japanese, Italian, Korean, and Spanish. He lives in Berkeley, California.

Zelene Pineda Suchilt, a Mexican born CHí-CHí (CHilanga/CHicana) award-winning multi-disciplinary artist, filmmaker and poet living in New York City. In 2005, she founded the annual poetry festival, The Word Around Town Poetry Tour, which ran for 10 years and participated in the Librotraficante Caravan in as Librotraficante Rebelené. She received the Sor Juana Ines de la Cruz Young Visionary Award from The National Museum of Mexican Art in Chicago in 2009.

Poet, author, and performance artist **Carmen Tafolla** is the author of more than thirty books, and has received the Américas Award, two Tomás Rivera Book Awards, five International Latino Book Awards, and the Art of Peace Award, among others. The first City Poet Laureate of San Antonio 2012-2014, State Poet Laureate of Texas in 2015, Professor Emerita of Bicultural Bilingual Studies at UTSA, and currently President of the Texas Institute of Letters, she was recognized by the National Association of Chicana and Chicano Studies for work which "gives voice to the peoples and cultures of this land."

Roberto Tejada is author of the poetry collections *Full Foreground* (2012), *Exposition Park* (2010), and *Mirrors for Gold* (2006), as well as *Still Nowhere in an Empty Vastness* (2019), a Latinx poetics composed of essays and manifestos on the geopolitical imagination of the Americas. Born in Los Angeles (1964) of Colombian parentage, he lived in Mexico City where he took part in the art and literary scenes of the 1980s-1990s. His art writings include *National Camera: Photography and Mexico's Image Environment* (2009) and *A Ver: Celia Alvarez Muñoz* (2009) on the pioneering Chicana conceptual artist.

Born in Mexico City, **Natalia Treviño** is the author of the poetry collection, *VirginX.* A professor of English who learned English from *Sesame Street's Bert and Ernie,* her masters in English is from UT San Antonio and her MFA is from the University of Nebraska. Her awards include the Alfredo Cisneros del Moral Award, the Dorothy Sargent Rosenburg Poetry Award, and the Me-nada Literary Award from Macedonia. Her first book, *Lavando La Dirty Laundry,* was a national and international awards finalist.

Leticia Urieta is proud Tejana writer from Austin, TX. She works as a teaching artist in the Austin community. She is a graduate of Agnes Scott College and holds an MFA in Fiction writing from Texas State University. Her work appears or is forthcoming in *Cleaver, Chicon Street Poets, Lumina, The Offing, Kweli Journal, Medium, Electric Lit* and others. Her chapbook, *The Monster* is out now from LibroMobile Press. She is currently at work completing her novel that tells the story of a Mexican soldadera caught up in the march to Texas during Texas' war with Mexico.

Luis Alberto Urrea is the author of eighteen books, among them: *The House of Broken Angels, The Hummingbird's Daughter, The Tijuana Book of the Dead, By The Lake of Sleeping Children*, and *The Devil's Highway.*

Viktoria Valenzuela is a mother to six children and a graduate student at Our Lady of the Lake University. She is also an inaugural Zoeglossia Fellow, a Macondista, the San Antonio Chapter lead for Women Who Submit, and the organizer of 100 Thousand Poets for Change: San Antonio. Her writing keeps keen focus on Chicana m(other)ing as decolonization and political action. Her work has been published in such collections as *Wordgathering, the Zoeglossia Anthology: We are not your metaphor, Poetry Bay Online Journal,* and *Mutha Magazine.*

Santiago Vaquera-Vásquez is an unrepentant border crosser, ex-dj, Xicano writer, painter, and academic. An Associate Professor of Hispanic Southwest Literatures and Cultures at University of New Mexico, he has authored four collections of short stories, *Algún día te cuento las cosas que he visto* (2012), *Luego el silencio* (2014), *One Day I'll Tell You the Things I've Seen* (2015), and *En el Lost y Found* (2016). His photographic chapbook of photos and stories from his travels in Turkey, *Yabancı [Foreigner] Extranjero* came out in 2019. Widely published in Spanish, his work appears in anthologies and journals in Spain, Italy, Latin America and the United States.

Oswaldo Vargas is a Mexican native raised in northern California. He is a former farm worker and graduate from the University of California, Davis where he studied history, human rights and Jewish studies. Publications include *IMANIMAN: Poets Writing in the Anzaldúan Borderlands* anthology, *Assaracus, Nepantla: An Anthology Dedicated to Queer Poets of Color, Huizache* and the *Green Mountains Review's* tribute issue to former U.S. Poet Laureate Juan Felipe Herrera. He lives in Sacramento, California.

Richard Vargas received his MFA from the University of New Mexico, 2010. He was recipient of the 2011 Taos Summer Writers' Conference's Hispanic Writer Award, was on the faculty of the 2012 10th National Latino Writers Conference and facilitated a workshop at the 2015 Taos Summer Writers' Conference. His three books of poetry are *McLife, American Jesus,* and *Guernica,* revisited. He edited/published *The Más Tequila Review* from 2009-2015. Currently, he resides in Madison WI.

Edward Vidaurre's writings have appeared in *The New York Times Magazine, The Texas Observer, Avalon Literary Review, The Acentos Review, Poetrybay, Voices de la Luna, Dryland Literary Journal,* as well as other journals and anthologies. Vidaurre is the author of six collections of poetry with his seventh forthcoming in March 2020. He was the 2018-2019 City of McAllen,TX Poet Laureate, a four time Pushcart Prize nominated poet and publisher of FlowerSong Books, Vidaurre is from Boyle Heights, CA and now resides in McAllen, TX with his wife and daughter.

Mar Vidaurri is an emerging writer and queer educator from the Rio Grande Valley who currently resides in Harlingen, Texas. Influences include their Chicanx roots, migrant experience, and border life. Their work is fringes on the surreal, both celebratory and painfully explorative. Mar's poems have previously been published in *Huizache, The Chachalaca Review,* and *Boundless.* They aim to unravel the truths hidden in the tucks of their grandmother's crow's feet wrinkles.

Alma Luz Villanueva is the author of four novels, most recently 'Song of The Golden Scorpion,' and eight books of poesia, most recently 'Gracias.' Her fiction and poesia are published in many anthologies, textbooks. She taught in the MFA in creative writing program Antioch University for twenty years. Mother of four grown humans, and a Mamacita tambien, Alma has lived in San Miguel de Allende, Mexico for 16 years, QUE VIVA. www.almaluzvillanueva.com

Ed Wade is one of four sons born to an Anglo-American father and Mexican immigrant mother. Presently, he lives in the quaint chaos of Hanoi, where he lectures for the Communication department at RMIT University Vietnam. Ed's first book *The Mise en Abyme Jokebook* was published in 2019 by UnCollected Press. His poems can also be found in *Rattle, The Comstock Review, The Rat's Ass Review, Sport Literate,* and *The Raw Art Review.*

Genoa Yáñez-Alaniz is an educator who promotes learning and social development through community activism. She has worked with immigrants, refugees, asylum-seekers, and survivors of human trafficking. Some of her current projects include outreach and education for homebound refugee women, Latinx Leadership collaboratives for sustainable diversity and inclusion opportunities, and organizing for sustainable access to affordable healthy foods and healthy living for underserved communities. Genoa has been writing poetry for years and frequently shares her poetry at events that bring awareness to issues related to global issues related to the refugee and immigration crisis.

Richard Yañez was born and raised on the México/U.S. Border. He is the award-winning author of *Cross Over Water: A Novel* and *El Paso del Norte: Stories on the Border.* Currently, he is working on a memoir, *Moments Between Worrying: Notebook of a Chicano Father.* A graduate of New Mexico State University and Arizona State University, he is a Professor of English at El Paso Community College, where he serves as Team Leader for the Pasos Program.

ACKNOWLEDGMENTS

Ana Castillo's *Two Men and Me* (Fifth Wednesday Journal, ed. Vern Miller; Fall, 2017Lisle, IL) "These Times" was *A Storm Upon Us, These Times, Mierda* (Fifth Wednesday Journal, ed. Vern Miller and Ana Castillo, Fall, 2018) ; *[Xicanisma Prophesies Post 2012]*   *Putin's Puppet*, <u>Chiricu Journal: Latina/o Literatures, Arts, and Cultures Vol. 3,</u> Number 2, Fall, 2019.

Rose Catacalos' poems, "From Home" and "Learning Endurance from Lupe at the J & A Ice House" appeared in her book, *Again, For The First Time,* Tooth of Time, 1984.

Diana Marie Delgado's "Last Dream" appeared in *Colorado Review*, "The Stars Are Green Tonight" appeared first in *Triquarterly*, and "Guadalajara, Mexico"appeared in *Triquarterly*

Anita Endrezze's "The Wall" appeared in Book View Cafe (via Ursula Le Guin) and her full-length poetry collection *Enigma*, Press 53, 2019.

Alma Garcia's "The Brown Invasion" is an excerpt from her novel-in-progress of the same title.

An earlier version of "We have always been weeping and searching for the dead" by Yola Gomez was published in *Entropy Magazine*'s series, *The Talking Cure* (https://entropymag.org/the-talking-cure-weve-always-been-weeping-and-searching-for-the-dead/)

Wendy C. Ortiz's "Revelations" was previously published in *Mud City*. "Pretty" was previously published in *The Nervous Breakdown.*

Alberto Rios's "We Are of a Tribe" appeared in Goodbye, Mexico Poems of Remembrance
"The Border: A Double Sonnet" and "When There Were Ghosts": A Small Story About the Sky
and "Border Boy" first appeared in Poetry Northwest

"The Last Gallantry of a Badass" by Octavio Solis originally appeared in *Catamaran Literary Reader*, Fall 2014. "Mundo Means World" by Octavio Solis originally appeared in *Catamaran Literary Reader,* Winter 2015.

"A Simple Plan" and "Summer Work" are copyrighted 1999 by Gary Soto. "At an Educational Conference Outside of Atlanta, Georgia" is copyrighted 2018 by Gary Soto. "The Heart of Justice" is from *The Elements of San Joaquin* (Chronicle Books 2018) and is copyright 2018 by Gary Soto. Used by permission of the author and Chronicle Books.

"That Smell" by Luis Alberto Urrea is n edited version that was published under a different title at time. com.)

Richard Vargas's *Tito's carnitas* was originally published in *culturalweekly.com*, 9/12/18 and his poem, *Ricardo, janitor of the U.S.S. Enterprise* was originally published in the poetry collection, *McLife,* 2005.

Edward Vidaurre's poem, "Caravan" was published first in *Poetry Bay.*

Alma Luz Villanueva's 'Voices of Our Ancestors,' is a section of her memoir-in-progress, published in the *Manifest Station 2014*, an online magazine"

"Learning Endurance...." and "From Home" first appeared in *Again for the First Time* (Tooth of Time Books, Santa Fe, 1984) and again in the book's reissue (Wings Press, San Antonio, 2013)

"Double-Fractured Sonnets," "Memory in the Making," and "Red Dirt: Atascosa County, Texas" first appeared in the handmade fine press chapbook *Begin Here* (Wings Press, San Antonio, 2013)

"From Home" appeared in the Spanish anthology, *Los Vasos Comunicantes: Antología de Poesía Chicana,* (Huerga & Fierro Editores, Valencia, 1999) Ed. Jaime B. Rosas, tr. Jaime B. Rosas and Russell Dinapoli

Matt Mendez's short story, "Girl More Still," first appeared in *Twitching Heart.*

CPSIA information can be obtained
at www.ICGtesting.com
Printed in the USA
BVHW011947110121
597562BV00012B/294